Critical Essays on
Charles Dickens's
Great Expectations

Critical Essays on
Charles Dickens's
Great Expectations

Michael Cotsell

G. K. Hall & Co. • Boston, Massachusetts

First published 1990.
10 9 8 7 6 5 4 3 2 1

Library of Congress Cataloging-in-Publication Data

Critical essays on Charles Dicken's Great expectations / [edited by]
    Michael Cotsell.
        p.   cm. — (Critical essays on British literature)
    ISBN 0-8161-8852-1 (alk. paper)
    1. Dickens, Charles, 1812–1870. Great expectations.
I. Cotsell, Michael.   II. Series.
PR4560.C68   1990
823'.8—dc20   90-4108
                                                                CIP

The paper used in this publication meets the minimum requirements of American National Standard for Information Sciences—
Permanence of Paper for Printed Library Materials, ANSI Z39.48-
1984. ∞ ™

Printed and bound in the United States of America

CRITICAL ESSAYS ON BRITISH LITERATURE

The Critical Essays on British Literature series provides a variety of approaches to both the classical writers of Britain and Ireland, and the best contemporary authors. The formats of the volumes in the series vary with the thematic designs of individual editors, and with the amount and nature of existing reviews, criticism, and scholarship. In general, the series represents the best in published criticism, augmented, where appropriate, by original essays by recognized authorities. It is hoped that each volume will be unique in developing a new overall perspective on its particular subject.

Michael Cotsell's selection of essays includes the earlier reviews and comments on the novel by some of the best-known writers and critics of the late nineteenth and early twentieth centuries (Swinburne, Gissing, Chesterton, Shaw, etc.), as well as great modern and contemporary essays that have shaped our perception of the novel. Cotsell's introduction surveys the critical canon through a brilliant analysis of the novel itself, singling out those aspects that have attracted the most critical attention.

ZACK BOWEN

University of Miami

v

CONTENTS

INTRODUCTION

Great Expectations was first published in the pages of Dickens's weekly magazine *All the Year Round* between December 1860 and August 1861. It was then issued in volume form in 1861. Dickens decided to publish *Great Expectations* in *All the Year Round* because the serialization of a dull novel by the Anglo-Irish novelist Charles Lever had adversely affected the sales of the magazine. To save the situation he would contribute a story of his own, a story that had begun as the idea for a "little paper," such as the papers in *The Uncommercial Traveller,* and had then seemed to have the potential to become a twenty-monthly number novel. Now it would be published in *All the Year Round* in weekly parts. It was, of course, reviewed in the newspapers and journals of the day, and the most interesting of those reviews have been collected in Philip Collins's *Dickens: The Critical Heritage* (New York: Barnes and Noble; London: Routledge and Kegan Paul, 1971).

The essays and extracts brought together in this volume are, with one exception, by writers from the late Victorian period through to our own time. The exception is the first extract, which consists of excerpts from Dickens's own autobiographical memoir describing his childhood experience working in a blacking factory while his father was imprisoned for debt. The passage is printed in John Forster's *The Life of Charles Dickens.* Its inclusion here is not intended to suggest that *Great Expectations* is about Dickens himself. But Dickens certainly drew on this episode for some of Pip's feelings of abandonment, for some of his anger, and for some his sense of being tainted by a connection with the criminal. A second passage from Forster, which gives an account of the composition of the novel, provides insight into Dickens's artistic organization in *Great Expectations.*

There follow a series of extracts from the critical writings on Dickens by a number of great writers of the late nineteenth and early twentieth centuries. These writers—Swinburne, Gissing, Chesterton, and Shaw—saw Dickens as one of the masters of the preceding period, the early and middle Victorian period, who had helped define modern times and modern problems. Their comments have more than a historical interest. They are closer to Dickens's age than the modern reader is; they were, in some cases, influenced in their own art by Dickens; and, at their best, they bring to their criticism the critical insight and powers of expression of genius.

Shaw's essay requires some particular comment. His interest in Dickens, though iconoclastic, was lifelong. Some of his powerful early dramas would appear to be strongly influenced by Dickens's works in general and by *Great Expectations* in particular: in his plays *Widowers' House* (1893) and *Major Barbara* (1907), for instance, he poses questions about the economic sources of culture and gentility. He believed these questions to be as powerfully present in Dickens's novels as in the ideas of Dickens's contemporary, Karl Marx. The essay included here was written as an introduction to an edition of *Great Expectations* published in 1947; it is in fact a revised version of a preface originally published in 1937. Shaw discusses the two endings of *Great Expectations*, the ending Dickens originally wrote, in which Estella and Pip are not united, and the revised ending, written after the protest of his friend, the romantic novelist Edward Bulwer-Lytton, in which they are united. Forster had published the suppressed first ending: it is given here at the end of the selection from his work, not at the end of Shaw's piece. Good modern editions provide the reader with both endings, and the question of which is preferable has, understandably, been the subject of much discussion.

Shaw insisted on the seriousness and challenge of Dickens's work at a time when much appreciation of Dickens was determinedly trivial. His essay belongs with some other substantial rereadings of Dickens's life and work made in the 1940s and 1950s that immensely deepened our understanding of Dickens. George Orwell's essay "Charles Dickens," collected in *Inside the Whale* (1940), is a reading of Dickens that, though partial and limited, is full of insight. Particularly interesting in respect of *Great Expectations* is Orwell's complaint that Dickens's heroes do not like work and that they are rewarded as soon as possible by early retirement into "radiant idleness." It has been said that Orwell was remembering the early Dickens he had read as a child and was not thinking of Dickens's mature novels. Indeed, the criticisms that Orwell makes of the underlying dreams of the early novels of young men's great expectations, are, as Bernard Shaw realized, made by Dickens himself in *Great Expectations*.

Another influential piece of this period was Edmund Wilson's essay "The Two Scrooges" in *The Wound and the Bow* (1941). Wilson sought to understand Dickens's career and writings primarily from the perspective of the shock to his childhood of being incarcerated in the blacking warehouse: the first blow, one might say, to the most normal of great expectations, those of the child. Wilson's essay has provided a model for a deeper psychological understanding of Dickens's life and works. Thus, as with

Orwell, it is curious to find that his two or three pages on *Great Expectations* are quite conventional in their appreciations.

Shaw, Orwell, and Wilson brought new depth and seriousness to the critical discussion of Dickens. Also in this period better scholarly research was beginning to reveal the complexity of Dickens's relationship to his age. Humphry House's *The Dickens World* was a leading example of the new scholarship, and the extracts from his work included here may be seen as the beginning of the serious academic study of Dickens's novel that has continued to the present day. In the rest of this introductory discussion I will suggest what have emerged as some of the major points of discussion in the tradition of criticism of *Great Expectations*.

Dickens makes some interesting remarks about the writing of *Great Expectations* in the letters Forster quotes. He writes of a "fine new, and grotesque idea," which "so opens out before *me* that I can see the whole of a serial revolving on it, in a most singular and comic manner." Then, reporting on the writing of the first number, he describes how he has introduced Pip and Joe together and adds, "Of course I have got in the pivot on which the story will turn too—and which indeed, as you remember, was the grotesque tragi-comic conception that first encouraged me." (see pp. 35). This conception, grotesque and tragicomic, the pivot on which the whole story will revolve, is the relation of Pip and Magwitch. Since 1855 Dickens had been in the habit of writing ideas for his novels in a notebook now known as his *Book of Memoranda*. For other of his later novels there are a number of entries, later marked off as "done." This is not the case for *Great Expectations*, and critics have therefore concluded that the novel came to Dickens as an unusually unified idea. In fact, one entry in the *Book of Memoranda* may have a bearing on the relationship between Pip and Magwitch. It reads like this: "The uneducated father (or uncle?) in fustian, and the educated boy in spectacles. Whom Leech and I saw at Chatham." (*Charles Dickens's Book of Memoranda*, ed. Fred Kaplan, New York: New York Public Library, 1981, 6). We understand what caught the novelist's eye when we realize that encapsulated here is much of the history of the nineteenth century (and perhaps of other centuries). Here is the gap opened up between the generations by upward social mobility and education, the gap between illiteracy and aspiring literacy (the glasses), between earning a living through labor and earning one through thinking in some way, between the poor or the working class and the middle class. Here are the possibilities of a great social drama: of ambition for others; of resentment, betrayal, forgetfulness, ingratitude, incomprehension; as well, perhaps, of self-sacrifice, gratitude, and loving memory. And here as well, of course, is the relationship between Pip and Magwitch.

That relationship is, as Dickens makes clear in those letters, what essentially structures the novel. It is what gives it the tight artistry that has led some critics to compare it to Sophocles's *Oedipus Rex*. Both works turn on a discovery that reveals a terribly implicating set of relations that have been previously unperceived, relations that reach, in their different ways, to the very essentials of culture. Pip sees that everything, the money, the girl, his very self, come from the fierce resentment and love of Magwitch. Those intense moments on the marshes with a convict are the center of his life, though he has not known it. He has lived an illusion, and he has lost his illusions. Magwitch's return has a deep inevitability, which is subtly and yet powerfully signalled by Dickens. And when Magwitch says, "I lived rough, that you should live smooth" (chapter 39), he pronounces on all inheritance, on all social "good fortune," on all comfort, ease, and culture. It is a terrible sentence. It is one of the places where morality begins. Magwitch speaks for the poor; he speaks for the ancestors; he speaks of the common debt of each generation to the past.

Great Expectations does not present the all-embracing social panorama of Dickens's twenty-monthly number novels, but it is, nevertheless, a portrait of a society. In the relationship between Pip and Magwitch it dramatically represents the class division between the "two nations" that Disraeli had described in the 1840s, "the rich and the poor" (*Sybil*, 1845). And through both Pip and Magwitch it gives with greater force than anywhere else in Dickens, except perhaps in *Oliver Twist*, the view from underneath, the child's view and the view of the underclass, the view of those who know injustice with fierce and unforgettable emotions, whose lives are forged in that injustice. It does not let us forget that society continues to rest on repression, on criminalizing, and on the coercions of law, though perhaps in the end it seeks to lay that memory to rest.

In Pip's experience of change, too, we sense the experience of a whole society. The action moves between the small towns and villages of Kent that lie along the lower Thames and the city of London. Dickens himself had spent his earliest childhood in the Kentish town of Chatham, near Rochester, and now, as a successful novelist—outwardly someone whose great expectations had been fulfilled—he was again living at Gad's Hill, near Rochester. His memories of boyhood are clear from the essay "Travelling Abroad," written around the time of *Great Expectations* and published in *The Uncommercial Traveller*:

> So smooth was the old high road, and so fresh were the horses, and so fast went I, that it was midway between Gravesend and Rochester, and the widening river was bearing the ships, white sailed or black-smoked, out to sea, when I noticed by the wayside a very queer small boy.
>
> "Holloa!" said I, to the very queer small boy, "where do you live?"
>
> "At Chatham," says he. . . .
>
> I took him up in a moment, and we went on. Presently, the very queer small boy says, "This is Gads-hill we are coming to, where Falstaff went out to rob those travellers, and ran away."
>
> "You admire that house?" said I.
>
> "Bless you, sir," said the very queer small boy, "when I was not more

than half as old as nine, it used to be a treat for me to be brought to look at it. And now I am nine, I come by myself to look at it. And ever since I can recollect, my father, seeing me so fond of it, has often said to me, 'If you were to be very persevering and were to work hard, you might some day come to live in it.' Though that's impossible!" said the very queer small boy, drawing a low breath, and now staring at the house out of the window with all his might.

I was rather amazed to be told this by the very queer small boy; for that house happens to be *my* house, and I have reason to believe that what he said was true.

In another of *The Uncommercial Traveller* essays, "Dullborough Town," the original is Rochester, which appears in *Great Expectations* as the town where Pumblechook lives:

> I call my boyhood's home . . . Dullborough. Most of us come from Dullborough who come from a country town.
> As I left Dullborough in the days when there were no railroads in the land, I left it in a stage-coach. Through all the years that have since passed, have I ever lost the smell of the damp straw in which I was packed—like game—and forwarded, carriage paid, to the Cross Keys, Wood-street, Cheapside, London? There was no other inside passenger, and I consumed my sandwiches in solitude and dreariness, and it rained hard all the way, and I thought life sloppier than I had expected to find it.

Departures and returns are the markers of the fulfillment or unfulfillment of expectations. In the novel the sense of change is communicated very much through Pip's journeyings, on foot and by carriage, as in the famous conclusion to Part One of the story: "We changed again, and yet again, and it was now too late and too far to go back, and I went on." (chapter 9).

In fact, Pip's story is enacted in locales that, together, seem to suggest the various stages of human civilization: the brutal, lawless world on the marshes; the village; the town; the city; the suburbs. Each of these locales has its representative man in the novel. The brutality of the raw marsh world would seem to be embodied in Magwitch, but in fact it really belongs to Orlick. The fire of forge and hearth is a frequent Dickensian image of the warm heart of basic community, and Joe the blacksmith is the man who stands for that rudimentary social organization. He is a figure viewed with love and sympathy, whereas the man of the town, the pompous small bourgeois tradesman, Pumblechook, is viewed satirically.

The man of the city, with its brutal realism and concealments, is Jaggers: even his home is there, and near his office Pip is startled into a perception of architectures that capture the idea of the City of the World: "So, I came into Smithfield; and the shameful place, being all asmear with filth and fat and blood and foam, seemed to stick to me. So, I rubbed it off with all possible speed by turning into a street where I saw the great black dome of Saint Paul's bulging at me from behind a grim stone building which a bystander said was Newgate Prison." (chapter 20).

Wemmick, of course, with his famous and wonderfully divided life, is the man of the suburbs, though Dickens's clever portrait of the Hammersmith world of the Pocket family should also be mentioned. The novel takes us forward and backward through each of these stages of social organization with a deepening sentiment for what is lost in change, so that it is only on Pip's last visits to the town of his childhood that Dickens mentions the religious architecture that distinguishes its original, Rochester: the point is that Pip has arrived at equivalent places in himself.

The presence of two characters runs through all of these places. One is the shadowy Compeyson, the forger, whose unmitigated villainy is linked to sexual deceit and to false gentility. The other is Magwitch, who runs as an undercurrent through the novel, rather as the Thames does through its localities, representing, it would seem, the deepest flow of things and what is not quite within society. The story of his relation to Pip is brought to a kind of conclusion in the attempted flight from England down the river. In one of the great anecdotes of literary composition, Forster tells us how Dickens, wanting to check out the course a boat would take, hired a Thames steamer and took a party of friends out for the day: "He seemed to have no care, the whole of that summer day . . . except to enjoy their enjoyment and entertain them with his own in shape of a thousand whims and fancies; but his sleepless observation was at work all the time, and nothing had escaped his keen vision on either side of the river." (see p. 37).

The journey down the river is a journey both forward to a possible future and back through English history to the settings at the novel's beginning, the ancient marshes. It ends in disappointment, at once bogged down in the ancient mud and driven down by the great steamer that epitomizes the powerful machinery of modern change. And then Magwitch is resentenced in a repetition of an old injustice. Critics differ about the element of social criticism in the novel. Shaw sees the novel's conclusion representing the defeat of Dickens's reformer's confidence: "Pip's world is therefore a very melancholy place, and his conduct, good or bad, always helpless. . . . When he [Dickens] lost his belief in bourgeois society and with it his lightness of heart he had neither an economic Utopia nor a credible religion to hitch on to. His world becomes a world of great expectations cruelly disappointed." Humphry House, on the other hand, associates the novel with the complacency of prosperous mid-nineteenth-century Britain: "The mood of the book belongs not to the imaginary date of its plot, but to the time in which it was written; for the unquestioned assumptions that Pip can be transformed by money and the minor graces it can buy, and that the loss of one fortune can be repaired on the strength of incidental gains in voice and friends, were only possible in a country secure in its internal economy, with expanding markets abroad: this could hardly be said of England in the 'twenties and 'thirties (p. 83)." Shaw's story is one of great expectations lost, House's one of great expectations modified. This range of emphasis continues in subsequent criticism.

Magwitch is resentenced, and Pip goes knocking on the midnight doors of an unjust establishment in "the weary western streets of London" (chapter 56). Magwitch then dies of the injuries sustained in the struggle with Compeyson, and so the final injustice is not enacted. But Pip, falling into the crisis of a fever, has dreams of being bricked into a wall or bound on a whirling engine. There is little action in the novel after this. It does seem that quite a lot has been lost, and it does not really have to do with Pip's having or not having money or gentility or even Estella: it has to do with the failure of a society to fulfill the suggestions of deep animal, human, and Christian fellowship (all the images are there) in the opening scenes between Pip, Magwitch, and Joe on the marshes.

A comparison may be made with a great modern novel. In Saul Bellow's *Herzog*, the main character's crisis of social faith is partly resolved when he discovers that justice is, under adverse circumstances, being done in the law courts of Chicago: that in the nether world, as it were, the rules are working. There is an order of peacefulness and acceptance at the end of *Great Expectations*, but no such consolation. G. K. Chesterton observes rather wonderfully that the story is marked by serenity, irony, and sadness, but that it is "A study in human weakness and the slow human surrender."

It is the sense of weakness and yet of great likeableness and warmth that constitutes the novel's other great interest. The character of Pip is one of the great achievements of western literature. We are close to him because we hear his voice throughout and because his voice can take us, sometimes within a phrase or a sentence, from wry and toned adult perceptions to those of a wondering, scared child. With this first-person narrator, in other words, we are brought close to an adult who can remember his child, and who therefore has access to a dimension of the self, even the spirit, that is commonly repressed or denied. And we are close, too, because Dickens's art of imagery and symbolism; his use of analogy between scene and scene, character and character; and his willingness to draw on theatrical and fairy tale traditions of writing keep him close to what we nowadays call the unconscious.

Thus we know Pip as a social actor; and as a social actor he is often condemned, sometimes humorously, and most often by himself, but certainly caught in great self-deception, foolish pomposities, worse ingratitudes. But we also know him more intimately, through the autobiographical mode as Dickens uses it, and we know him in the complexities of what is, after all, such a strange story, that it is very difficult to get our feelings clear about him. Chesterton, for instance, for all the resonances of his sympathy, began the practice of calling Pip a snob: "It is an extra chapter to the Book of Snobs," he says, referring to Thackeray's early work of 1847. House simply sees it as "a snob's progress." In addition, Chesterton, Shaw, and House all see Pip as basically (and like his author) a little vulgar: he has no religion, they say; his culture is a matter of knives and forks. The attitude of these critics may itself seem something like snobbery, as though these later writers had forgotten that Dickens belongs to a tradition, going back to Addison, Steele, Defoe, and Richardson, in which middle-class self-improvement is taken seriously.

Admitting there is some truth in the view of Pip as a snob, modern criticism has gone beyond this view, and, with John H. Hagan, observed that "Dickens is using his character to reveal some still more complex truths about society and its organization." In Hagan's account a spiritual dimension is restored to Pip's life and journey: "In his lonely struggle to work out his salvation, he is atoning for the guilt of society at large." And in G. Robert Stange's deeply suggestive essay, Pip is the bearer of all our social guilt. Pip, Stange remarks, wonders why he always experiences the taint of criminality. It is because this is "the condition of life."

Julian Moynahan takes up Stange's subtle sense of Pip's guilt. Remarking that snobbery is not a crime, he asks why Pip should feel like a criminal. He suggests that while Pip, the dreamer, is passive, other of the younger male characters in the story, particularly Orlick and Drummle, function to act out Pip's truly violent and criminal impulses, and importantly towards the women characters. Thus Orlick's attack on Mrs. Joe and Drummle's assault of Estella actually serve Pip. Whether one agrees with this or not (and it is very hard to totally disagree with it), the essay would be important for two reasons. First, it points to the fact that Pip's experience is placed in relation to a range of extremely well-drawn male characters, ranging from the sweet natured (Joe and Herbert), to the strong and brutal (Jaggers, Drummle, Orlick). Second, it shows that this is a novel marked by fierce struggles between the sexes, and strange struggles too: Mrs. Joe's satisfaction at getting Joe and Orlick to fight, Estella's at achieving the same effect between Pip and Herbert. Something about the relation between the erotic and power is at issue in *Great Expectations*. Moynahan accounts for the feeling of retreat at the novel's end by suggesting that it is a retreat from the recognition of aggressive drives:

> The brick is taken down from its giddy place, a part of the engine is hammered off. Pip cannot redeem his world. In no conceivable sense a leader, he can only lead himself into a sort of exile from his society's power centres. Living abroad as the partner of a small, unambitious firm, he is to devote his remaining life to doing the least possible harm to the smallest number of people, so earning a visitor's privileges in the lost paradise where Biddy and Joe, the genuine innocents of the novel, flourish in thoughtless content.

Moynahan's reading leads us to reconsider some of the apparent values of the novel's conclusion, or, in other words, the values that can be identified as those of the adult narrator. From this point on, critics will read *Great Expectations* in a sense "against itself," as revealing more than it knows, as though the book has an "unconscious" that contains what is not wholly known by or acceptable to its consciousness. One effect of this is that the question now arises whether the conscious voice of the adult Pip can adequately represent the child. Other questions about the novel's overt values may arise. Serenity and acceptance may be only the continuation of passivity, of the habit of expecting, just as the semiworship of Joe and Biddy towards the novel's end may be the novel's real snobbery. As in Gray's "Elegy in a Country Church Yard," a work that underscores much of the emotional range of the latter parts of the book, pity for the obscure lives of the rural poor and for oneself run easily together. Moynahan's question, is snobbery a crime, might be asked in another way: was it a crime for Pip to want more out of life than larks around the forge? Pip's problem was not that he wanted more, but the way he wanted it. He would not, or could not, say to Joe, "I am sorry; I want something more, and I am going to do everything I can to get it." But to imagine this is to realize that such a statement really would not be in Pip's character: we would have neither the rustic innocent Pip, nor the dreamy romantic Pip, nor the humbled genteel Pip.

Pip is no Balzacian hero: he cannot have the burning desire to conquer London that they have to conquer Paris. Pip will only turn to work, with its inevitable self-assertions, in his years in remote Egypt summarized toward the novel's end. Otherwise, the strong energies of social advancement are located elsewhere. Magwitch is one of their bearers, thus standing not only for proletarian resentments but also for the fierce bourgeois ambition to make ladies or gentlemen of one's children. The women also are given the taint of social ambition: Joe is content by the forge, Mrs. Joe has a parlor that bespeaks a petit bourgeois ambition for more (there is an anticipation of D. H. Lawrence's description in *The Rainbow*'s opening chapter of the women's sense of a larger world); the location of Miss Havisham's home in Pumblechook's sleepy, self-satisfied town is the very sign of fierce social discontent; and, of course, it is Estella who will conquer London.

It seems that the novel's careful separation of Pip from self-assertion is the sign of a fear or mistrust of certain energies. Perhaps in this degree it remains bound to a fairy tale feeling for the world, the fairy tale that all children are taught in some measure: if you are good you will be rewarded. It also seems that among the self-assertions magicked away in this contract is sexuality. Dickens is always very good about the embarrassed wriggling, posing stages of male puberty and adolescence with their attendant moods and rivalries. Pip's secrets and his guilt and the imagery around them can very easily and very amusingly be read in terms of a discomfort with a burgeoning sexuality. Pockets and their contents make up one amusing train of imagery; fires and fireplaces another; seeds (one meaning of "pip") and their containers a third. But despite these intimations, something seems very restrained. Good men are patient and passive in *Great Expectations*, even when this behavior annoys the women around them. The women's desire for a more assertive male appears only as a kind of self-hating perversion. It is interesting, therefore, that only one man in the novel is good-hearted *and* strong—Magwitch—and only he (other than that victim of domesticity, Mr. Pocket) fathers a child, Estella, until Joe and Biddy bring forth a shadowy little Pip.

The questions asked by Moynahan continue to resonate in the criticism that has subsequently explored Pip's character. The newer readings, which are often informed by psychoanalysis, often suggest that the novel insufficiently validates Pip's right to certain beings and energies. Robert Garis, for instance, sees Pip as bearing the weight of civilization's demand for repression of the natural instinct in a way that reminds him of Freud's great work *Civilization and Its Discontents. Great Expectations*, he says, offers "no conceivable alternative to his [Pip's] sense of horror and repulsion about the one source of power apparently available in this civilization: blood, wildness and violence. It never occurs to him that these horrors are really 'human.'"

Albert Hutter brings a trained psychoanalytic understanding to the issues of guilt and repression. In a long and thorough reading, he argues that they affect every aspect of the novel's organization. Tracing in the novel a deep desire to regress to a state of innocence, he concludes that the expression and yet fear of human energies creates both Dickens's strengths and limitations as an artist. In this, he is typical of his age: "This pronounced regressiveness does not of course make *Great Expectations* an aesthetic failure, but it does suggest inherent limits in Dickens's art and possibly in the terms of Victorian art in general. Dickens's limitations are the very basis of his ingenuity: repression demands a constant succession of bizarrely brilliant psychic improvisations."

Peter Brooks, too, analyzing the operation of plot in the novel, sees Pip as a character who begins like someone in search of a plot to live out and ends as somehow beyond plot. Victorians, he argues, associated plot with criminality and desire: the Magwitch elements. Brooks, too, thinks of Freud, this time the Freud of *Beyond the Pleasure Principle*, who saw beneath the detour of the trajectory of Eros the deeper wish for death, stasis.

Brooks's fine essay points to another emphasis in recent critical writing on *Great Expectations:* showing how Pip's possibilities for life are structured and limited by the structures of the discourse of his age. In a sense, in these readings Pip's passivity becomes an emblem of the passivity of man conceived of as driven by rather than driving large organizing structures or discourses. Such readings bring the psychological back into contact with the historical at a very deep level: they invite us to see the novel revealing what the deep structures of the nineteenth century allow and do not allow.

Brooks, as we have seen, argues that Pip's possibilities are limited by the naming of his desire as plot. Elliot Gilbert, on the other hand, sees Pip as the bearer of the large discourse of the romantic self, his story that of an isolated or secret self, beginning, as romanticism itself began, in the ultimate isolation of the graveyard; encountering the shock of Victorian materialism; and, in its end, only being confirmed in an isolation that is a symbolic death of self. In a sense what Gilbert suggests is that Pip is trapped in a certain kind of individualism, which is (already) a reaction to structuring forces, as romanticism was itself a reaction to earlier materialisms. A similar view is also taken by Jeremy Tambling in an essay that makes use of the writings of Michel Foucault. Like Gilbert, Tambling sees Dickens examining through Pip's story a self-definition that is imprisoning. "*Great Expectations* puts a simple sentimental story of coming into selfhood like *David Copperfield* into question: *Great Expectations* comes close to suggesting that in an understanding of society, the concept of the individual is unhelpful, that what is important are the total manipulations of power and language by whatever group has the power and definition and control. Autobiography provides an inadequate paradigm."

Eiichi Hara may be seen as taking the argument a stage further when he suggests that in a sense Pip as author cannot write his life story: "As Magwitch's writing of Pip's story suggests, Pip can never be the writer nor the independent hero of his own story, rather the story is structured around the central story of Pip as written by Magwitch, with other stories, also of Pip, encircling this central axis."

These recent critics suggest that *Great Expectations* is about exactly the expectation of a false and thus inevitably disappointed idea of arrival at the self, the idea of self as a deep-feeling center of a story that is one's own. Dickens shows that from the beginning such an idea of self is the product of an alienation, a compensation for loss; or, rather, it begins from the idea of such an (always) lost origin, for which it is always compensating.

Such discussions allow us to perceive Pip's whole story as a construction of self and to perceive that the idea of a self is itself at issue in the novel. After all, none of us is, in an ultimate sense, the author of our own story, or its hero. It is a common enough observation that we are all in some measure the products of our parents, of our culture, of our age, and so on. Similarly, when we think of our expectations being fulfilled, we may think of fulfillment in a common language sense, as meaning that we have some good, fairly continuous relationships, some freedoms and breaks in such relationships, some interesting projects, and so forth. We do not normally mean fulfilled in some more absolute sense, in which everything is our life turns out for us. From this commonsense perspective, when we feel unsatisfied with things, we accuse parents, society, or cultural conditions of not enabling but disabling the ordinary expectation of fulfillment. In expecting more than this, is Pip then, after all, guilty—guilty, that is, of a kind of sentimental egoism, an aggrandized claim for, or mourning for, a central self? Jack Rawlins's essay brings us back to the two strands in criticism of *Great Expectations*, the story of Pip's guilt as a personal moral failure (the story of a snob) and the story of his guilt as the experience of society's universal error, of which Hara's and Gilbert's readings are versions. Rawlins asks us to reject both guilts, to see both as the betrayal of an essential self he calls the child within. His reading recaptures, with its own emphasis, some of the radical challenging tone of Shaw's.

The concept of the child within, or divine child, is a traditional concept of radiant, generous joy in being that can be discovered in many religions and cultures, including, of course, Christianity. It has become very important in modern psychological understanding of children from dysfunctional backgrounds. There are some powerful images of the child within in the early chapters of the novel: Pip feeding Magwitch; Pip being carried on Joe's back, like the Christ child carried by St. Christopher; and, of course, it is Christmas, the time of the child. We feel Pip's power, I think, through Magwitch's love of him, as we feel Magwitch learn to feel some love for himself in that love. These images are reminiscent of the "burning babe" appearing to the traveler in the snow in the Christmas poem of the Elizabethan poet Robert Southwell, or the image of the child carried on the piper's head in the concluding plate of William Blake's *Songs of Innocence.* Child and adult are linked in such images; the child is not repressed in its joy, nor is its infant sexuality denied or distorted, and the vision of the child is a protest against abuses that, as Pip will learn, the child Magwitch experienced and that Pip himself experienced. Magwitch, though he appears as the embodiment of all that shocks Pip, is the friend of this child. There is a passage in the first chapter where Pip's terrified little squeaking voice is contrasted with Magwitch's gruff bass:

> "Tell us your name!" said the man. "Quick!"
> "Pip, sir."
> "Once more," said the man, staring at me. "Give it mouth!"
> "Pip. Pip, sir." (chapter 1)

The encouragement, which Pip but infrequently fulfills, is to speak out boldly, to affirm the self.

Poets have offered accounts of an alternative version of childhood. There is Wordsworth's passage in the "Ode: Intimations of Immortality," for instance, in which the child, departing always from its visionary beginning, becomes a "little actor," "As if his whole vocation/Were endless imitation" (lines 103,107–8). Or there is T. S. Eliot's poem of growing as loss of self, "Animula":

The heavy burden of the growing soul
Perplexes and offends more, day by day;
Week by week, offends and perplexes more
With the imperatives of "is and seems"
And may and may not, desire and control.
The pain of living and the drug of dreams
Curl up the small soul in the window seat
                                            (lines 15–21)

In such accounts, one wonders why it all seems so dreary and what has been done to the child. Behind Pip's passivity, dreaminess, feelings of guilt, sexual shame, and even shame of being, we see fear of abandonment, fear of anger. With Rawlins, we are led to believe that it might be otherwise. Many authors who discuss the child within argue that in affirming or realizing the child within us, we discover that though the story is not our own, it is in fact not anyone else's, but some higher power's.

The acceptance of one's lot does not necessarily involve the marginality of Pip's later life, or at least the marginality of Pip's life as it is presented in Dickens's original ending to the story. One of the problems created by the two endings of *Great Expectations* is that they are so radically opposed: in one, none of Pip's expectations are fulfilled, in the other, after all, they essentially are (though even in the revised ending there may be some shadow of a further parting). It is as though we are dealing not with the mixed lot of reality, but dream and undream. Either way, as Brooks suggests, again Pip originates no plot. He will either drift on with nothing of his own, or his fairy tale will prove true. Suppose he were to meet a nice woman in Egypt? The suggestion seems inappropriate; Pip has not the power to start again.

The issue of freedom to step out of the story is posed by the representation in what is a man's story of angry, restless female characters. There is surprisingly little good critical writing on the women characters of the novel, even though figures of angry, disappointed women fascinated Dickens. It is a mistake to dismiss his female characters as caricatures: they appear that way in part because they are seen through the fear, anger, or desire of the male hero. If we try to think from the women's perspective, we may ask why Mrs. Joe should be content with being "Mrs. Joe," with marriage to her husband's unaspiring cult of childishness. Is Estella a cold monster or, alternatively, a star, or is she just a girl who was brought up to be used and who is now struggling to find a self? Miss Havisham's anger against men derives from being abandoned after she has given herself to the most traditional of women's roles.

In turn, Pip is repeatedly disappointed when he ascribes to women roles in his story. Miss Havisham really is not his fairy godmother. Biddy is, in Pip's mind, the girl next door who always loved him and who is ready to marry him when he gives up on the flashy one, but when Pip comes home in that mood he discovers she has married Joe—conclusive proof that she has life and volition of her own. And Estella, in the original ending, marries a Shropshire doctor, thus both making a new start and demonstrating that her life really was not part of Pip's story at all. Even if the two endings of the novel that we have leave us with a sense of openness, Pip has apparently not arrived at the self and freedom that Estella has in at least one of them.

It is, of course, Dickens's achievement to have created a character complex enough to engage all this analysis. Pip has his faults, but he also has a fineness and sensitivity that make us wish more for him than the saddened resignation at the novel's end, even if that more is not Estella. But perhaps his resignation is the price of fineness and sensitivity, of the romantic qualities he recognizes in himself. Touched as it is by strange chances, darknesses, and beauty, who could wish Pip's story otherwise? In the depth of its portrayal of its hero, *Great Expectations* awakens our thinking about what constitutes fulfillment in life—what we desire, what we do and can expect—but our models of personal fulfillment may lead us to overlook in Pip's story the unexpected and complex beauties of lives that turn out quite otherwise than we could have planned.

MICHAEL COTSELL

University of Delaware

[From Dickens's Autobiographical Fragments]*

Charles Dickens

"—Its chief manager, James Lamert, the relative who had lived with us in Bayham-street, seeing how I was employed from day to day, and knowing what our domestic circumstances then were, proposed that I should go into the blacking warehouse, to be as useful as I could, at a salary, I think, of six shillings a week. I am not clear whether it was six or seven. I am inclined to believe, from my uncertainty on this head, that it was six at first, and seven afterwards. At any rate the offer was accepted very willingly by my father and mother, and on a Monday morning I went down to the blacking warehouse to begin my business life.

"It is wonderful to me how I could have been so easily cast away at such an age. It is wonderful to me, that, even after my descent into the poor little drudge I had been since we came to London, no one had compassion enough on me—a child of singular abilities, quick, eager, delicate, and soon hurt, bodily or mentally—to suggest that something might have been spared, as certainly it might have been, to place me at any common school. Our friends, I take it, were tired out. No one made any sign. My father and mother were quite satisfied. They could hardly have been more so, if I had been twenty years of age, distinguished at a grammar-school, and going to Cambridge.

"The blacking warehouse was the last house on the left-hand side of the way, at old Hungerford-stairs. It was a crazy, tumble-down old house, abutting of course on the river, and literally overrun with rats. Its wainscotted rooms and its rotten floors and staircase, and the old grey rats swarming down in the cellars, and the sound of their squeaking and scuffling coming up the stairs at all times, and the dirt and decay of the place, rise up visibly before me, as if I were there again. The counting-house was on the first floor, looking over the coal-barges and the river. There was a recess in it, in which I was to sit and work. My work was to cover the pots of paste-blacking; first with a piece of oil-paper, and then with a piece of blue paper; to tie them round with a string; and then to clip the paper close and neat, all round, until it looked as smart as a pot of ointment from an apothecary's shop. When a certain number of grosses of pots had attained this pitch of perfection, I was to paste on each a printed label; and then go on again with more pots. Two or three other boys were kept at similar duty downstairs on similar wages. One of them came up, in a ragged apron and a paper cap, on the first Monday morning, to show me the trick of using the string and tying the knot. His name was Bob Fagin; and I took the liberty of using his name, long afterwards, in *Oliver Twist*. . . .

*Reprinted from John Forster, *The Life of Charles Dickens*, edited by J. W. T. Ley (London: Cecil Palmer, 1928).

15

"No words can express the secret agony of my soul as I sunk into this companionship; compared these every day associates with those of my happier childhood; and felt my early hopes of growing up to be a learned and distinguished man, crushed in my breast. The deep remembrance of the sense I had of being utterly neglected and hopeless; of the shame I felt in my position; of the misery it was to my young heart to believe that, day by day, what I had learned, and thought, and delighted in, and raised my fancy and my emulation up by, was passing away from me, never to be brought back any more; cannot be written. My whole nature was so penetrated with the grief and humiliation of such considerations, that even now, famous and caressed and happy, I often forget in my dreams that I have a dear wife and children; even that I am a man; and wander desolately back to that time of my life. . . .

"I know I do not exaggerate, unconsciously and unintentionally, the scantiness of my resources and the difficulties of my life. I know that if a shilling or so were given me by any one, I spent it in a dinner or a tea. I know that I worked, from morning to night, with common men and boys, a shabby child. I know that I tried, but ineffectually, not to anticipate my money, and to make it last the week through; by putting it away in a drawer I had in the counting-house, wrapped into six little parcels, each parcel containing the same amount, and labelled with a different day. I know that I have lounged about the streets, insufficiently and unsatisfactorily fed. I know that, but for the mercy of God, I might easily have been, for any care that was taken of me, a little robber or a little vagabond. . . .

"At last, one day, my father, and the relative so often mentioned, quarrelled; quarrelled by letter, for I took the letter from my father to him which caused the explosion, but quarrelled very fiercely. It was about me. It may have had some backward reference, in part, for anything I know, to my employment at the window. All I am certain of is, that, soon after I had given him the letter, my cousin (he was a sort of cousin, by marriage) told me he was very much insulted about me; and that it was impossible to keep me, after that. I cried very much, partly because it was so sudden, and partly because in his anger he was violent about my father, though gentle to me. Thomas, the old soldier, comforted me, and said he was sure it was for the best. With a relief so strange that it was like oppression, I went home.

"My mother set herself to accommodate the quarrel, and did so next day. She brought home a request for me to return next morning, and a high character of me, which I am very sure I deserved. My father said I should go back no more, and should go to school. I do not write resentfully or angrily; for I know how all these things have worked together to make me what I am: but I never afterwards forgot, I never shall forget, I never can forget, that my mother was warm for my being sent back."

[The Composition of *Great Expectations*]*

John Forster

A *Tale of Two Cities* was published in 1859; the series of papers collected as the *Uncommercial Traveller* were occupying Dickens in 1860; and it was while engaged in these, and throwing off in the course of them capital "samples" of fun and enjoyment, he thus replied to a suggestion that he should let himself loose upon some single humorous conception, in the vein of his youthful achievements in that way. "For a little piece I have been writing—or am writing; for I hope to finish it to-day—such a very fine new, and grotesque idea has opened upon me, that I begin to doubt whether I had not better cancel the little paper, and reserve the notion for a new book. You shall judge as soon as I get it printed. But it so opens out before *me* that I can see the whole of a serial revolving on it, in a most singular and comic manner." This was the germ of Pip and Magwitch, which at first he intended to make the ground work of a tale in the old twenty-number form, but for reasons perhaps fortunate brought afterwards within the limits of a less elaborate novel. "Last week," he wrote on the 4th of October, 1860, "I got to work on the new story. I had previously very carefully considered the state and prospects of *All the Year Round*, and, the more I considered them, the less hope I saw of being able to get back, *now*, to the profit of a separate publication in the old 20 numbers." (A tale, which at the time was appearing in his serial, had disappointed expectation.)

"However, I worked on, knowing that what I was doing would run into another groove; and I called a council of war at the office on Tuesday. It was perfectly clear that the one thing to be done was, for me to strike in. I have therefore decided to begin the story as of the length of the *Tale of Two Cities* on the first of December—begin publishing, that is. I must make the most I can out of the book. You shall have the first two or three weekly parts to-morrow. The name is GREAT EXPECTATIONS. I think a good name?" Two days later he wrote: "The sacrifice of *Great Expectations* is really and truly made for myself. The property of *All the Year Round* is far too valuable, in every way, to be much endangered. Our fall is not large, but we have a considerable advance in hand of the story we are now publishing, and there is no vitality in it, and no chance whatever of stopping the fall; which on the contrary would be certain to increase. Now, if I went into a twenty-number serial, I should cut off my power of doing anything serial here for two good years—and that would be a most perilous thing. On the other hand, by dashing in now, I come in when most wanted; and if Reade and Wilkie follow me, our course,

*Reprinted from John Forster, *The Life of Charles Dickens*, edited by J. W. T. Ley (London: Cecil Palmer, 1928).

will be shaped out handsomely and hopefully for between two and three years. A thousand pounds are to be paid for early proofs of the story to America." A few more days brought the first instalment of the tale, and explanatory mention of it. "The book will be written in the first person throughout, and during these first three weekly numbers you will find the hero to be a boy-child, like David. Then he will be an apprentice. You will not have to complain of the want of humour as in the *Tale of Two Cities*. I have made the opening, I hope, in its general effect exceedingly droll. I have put a child and a good-natured foolish man, in relations that seem to me very funny. Of course I have got in the pivot on which the story will turn too—and which indeed, as you remember, was the grotesque tragi-comic conception that first encouraged me. To be quite sure I had fallen into no unconscious repetitions, I read *David Copperfield* again the other day, and was affected by it to a degree you would hardly believe."

It may be doubted if Dickens could better have established his right to the front rank among novelists claimed for him, than by the ease and mastery with which, in these two books of *Copperfield* and *Great Expectations,* he kept perfectly distinct the two stories of a boy's childhood, both told in the form of autobiography. A subtle penetration into character marks the unlikeness in the likeness; there is enough at once of resemblance and of difference in the position and surroundings of each to account for the divergences of character that arise; both children are good-hearted, and both have the advantage of association with models of tender simplicity and oddity, perfect in their truth and quite distinct from each other; but a sudden tumble into distress steadies Peggotty's little friend, and as unexpected a stroke of good fortune turns the head of the small protégé of Joe Gargery. What a deal of spoiling nevertheless, a nature that is really good at the bottom of it will stand without permanent damage, is nicely shown in Pip; and the way he reconciles his determination to act very shabbily to his early friends, with a conceited notion that he is setting them a moral example, is part of the shading of a character drawn with extraordinary skill. His greatest trial comes out of his good luck; and the foundations of both are laid at the opening of the tale, in a churchyard down by the Thames, as it winds past desolate marshes twenty miles to the sea, of which a masterly picture in half a dozen lines will give only average example of the descriptive writing that is everywhere one of the charms of the book. It is strange, as I transcribe the words, with what wonderful vividness they bring back the very spot on which we stood when he said he meant to make it the scene of the opening of his story—Cooling Castle ruins and the desolate Church, lying out among the marshes seven miles from Gadshill! "My first most vivid and broad impression . . . on a memorable raw afternoon towards evening . . . was . . . that this bleak place, overgrown with nettles, was the churchyard, and that the dark flat wilderness beyond the churchyard, intersected with dykes and mounds and gates, with scattered cattle feeding on it, was the marshes; and that the low leaden line beyond, was the river; and that the distant savage lair from which the wind was rushing, was the sea. . . . On the edge of the river. . . . only two black things in all the prospect seemed to be standing upright . . . one, the beacon by which the sailors steered, like an unhooped cask upon a pole, an ugly thing when you were near it; the other, a gibbet with some chains hanging to it which had once held a pirate." Here Magwitch, an escaped convict from Chatham, terrifies the child Pip into stealing for him food and a file; and though recaptured and transported, he carries with him to Australia such a grateful heart for the small creature's service, that on making a fortune there he resolves to make his little friend a gentleman. This requires circumspection; and is so done, through the Old-Bailey attorney who has defended Magwitch at his trial (a character of surprising novelty and truth), that Pip imagines his present gifts and "great expectations" to have come from the supposed rich lady of the story (whose eccentricities are the unattractive part of it, and have yet a weird character that somehow fits in with the kind of wrong she has suffered). When therefore the closing scenes bring back Magwitch himself, who risks his life to gratify his longing to see the gentleman he has made, it is an unspeakable horror to the youth to discover his benefactor in the convicted felon. If any one doubts Dickens's power of so drawing a character as to get to the heart of it, seeing beyond surface peculiarities into the moving springs of the human being himself, let him narrowly examine those scenes. There is not a grain of substitution of mere sentiment, or circumstance, for the inner and absolute reality of the position in which these two creatures find themselves. Pip's loathing of what had built up his fortune, and his horror of the uncouth architect, are apparent in even his most generous efforts to protect him from exposure and sentence. Magwitch's convict habits strangely blend themselves with his wild pride in, and love for, the youth whom his money has turned into a gentleman. He has a craving for his good opinion; dreads to offend him by his "heavy grubbing," or by the oaths he lets fall now and then; and pathetically hopes his Pip, his dear boy, won't think him "low"; but, upon a chum of Pip's appearing unexpectedly while they are together, he pulls out a jack-knife by way of hint he can defend himself, and produces afterwards a greasy little clasped black Testament on which the startled new-comer, being found to have no hostile intention, is sworn to secrecy. At the opening of the story there had been an exciting scene of the wretched man's chase and recapture among the marshes, and this has its parallel at the close in his chase and recapture on the river while poor Pip is helping to get him off. To make himself sure of the actual course of a boat in such circumstances, and what possible incidents the adventure might have, Dickens hired a steamer for the day from Blackwall to Southend. Eight or nine friends and three or four members of his family were on board, and he seemed to have no care, the whole of that summer day (22nd of May, 1861), except to enjoy their enjoyment and entertain them with his own in shape of a thousand whims and fancies; but his sleepless observation was at work all the time, and nothing had escaped his keen vision on either side of the river. The fifteenth chapter of the third volume is a masterpiece.

The characters generally afford the same evidence as those two that Dickens's humour, not less than his creative power, was at its best in this book. The Old-Bailey attorney Jaggers, and his clerk Wemmick (both excellent, and the last one of the oddities that live in everybody's liking for the goodheartedness of its comic surprises), are as good as his earliest efforts in that line; the Pumblechooks and Wopsles are as perfect as bits of *Nickleby* fresh from the mint; and the scene in which Pip, and Pip's chum Herbert, make up their accounts and schedule their debts and obligations, is original and delightful as Micawber himself. It is the art of living upon nothing and making the best of it, in its most pleasing form. Herbert's intentions to trade east and west, and get himself into business transactions of a magnificent extent and variety, are as perfectly warranted to us, in his way of putting them, by merely "being in a counting-house and looking about you," as Pip's means of paying his debts are lightened and made easy by his method of simply adding them up with a margin.

"The time comes," says Herbert, "when you see your opening. And you go in, and you swoop upon it, and you make your capital, and then there you are! When you have once made your capital you have nothing to do but employ it." In like manner Pip tells us, "Suppose your debts to be one hundred and sixty-four pounds four and twopence, I would say, leave a margin and put them down at two hundred." He is sufficiently candid to add, that, while he has the highest opinion of the wisdom and prudence of the margin, its dangers are that in the sense of freedom and solvency it imparts there is a tendency to run into new debt. But the satire that thus enforces the old warning against living upon vague hopes, and paying ancient debts by contracting new ones, never presented itself in more amusing or kindly shape. A word should be added of the father of the girl that Herbert marries, Bill Barley, ex-ship's purser, a gouty, bed-ridden, drunken old rascal, who lives on his back in an upper floor on Mill Pond Bank, by Chinks's Basin, where he keeps, weighs, and serves out the family stores or provisions, according to old professional practice, with one eye at a telescope which is fitted on his bed for the convenience of sweeping the river. This is one of those sketches, slight in itself but made rich with a wealth of comic observation, in which Dickens's humour took especial delight; and to all this part of the story there is a quaint river-side flavour that gives it amusing reality and relish.

Sending the chapters that contain it, which open the third division of the tale, he wrote thus: "It is a pity that the third portion cannot be read all at once, because its purpose would be much more apparent; and the pity is the greater, because the general turn and tone of the working out and winding up, will be away from all such things as they conventionally go. But what must be, must be. As to the planning out from week to week, nobody can imagine what the difficulty is, without trying. But, as in all such cases, when it is overcome the pleasure is proportionate. Two months more will see me through it, I trust. All the iron is in the fire, and I have 'only' to beat it out." One other letter throws light upon an objection taken not unfairly to the too great speed with which the heroine, after being married, reclaimed, and widowed, is in a page or two again made love to, and remarried by the hero. This summary proceeding was not originally intended. But, over and above its popular acceptance, the book had interested some whose opinions Dickens specially valued (Carlyle among them,[1] I remember), and upon Bulwer Lytton objecting to a close that should leave Pip a solitary man, Dickens substituted what now stands. "You will be surprised," he wrote, "to hear that I have changed the end of *Great Expectations* from and after Pip's return to Joe's, and finding his little likeness there. Bulwer, who has been, as I think you know, extraordinarily taken by the book, so strongly urged it upon me, after reading the proofs, and supported his view with such good reasons, that I resolved to make the change. You shall have it when you come back to town. I have put in as pretty a little piece of writing as I could, and I have no doubt the story will be more acceptable through the alteration." This turned out to be the case; but the first ending nevertheless seems to be more consistent with the drift, as well as natural working out, of the tale, and for this reason it is preserved in a note.[2]

Notes

1. A dear friend now gone would laughingly relate what outcry there used to be on the night of the week when a number was due, for "that Pip nonsense!" and what roars of laughter followed, though at first it was entirely put aside as not on any account to have time wasted over it.

2. There was no Chapter 20 as now; but the sentence which opens it ("For eleven years" in the original, altered to "eight years") followed the paragraph about his business partnership with Herbert, and led to Biddy's question whether he is sure he does not fret for Estella. ("I am sure and certain, Biddy" as originally written, altered to "O, no—I think not, Biddy"): from which point here was the close. "It was two years more, before I saw herself. I had heard of her as leading a most unhappy life, and as being separated from her husband who had used her with great cruelty, and who had become quite renowned as a compound of pride, brutality, and meanness. I had heard of the death of her husband (from an accident consequent on ill-treating a horse), and of her being married again to a Shropshire doctor, who, against his interest, had once very manfully interposed on an occasion when he was in professional attendance on Mr. Drummle, and had witnessed some outrageous treatment of her. I had heard that the Shropshire doctor was not rich, and that they lived on her own personal fortune. I was in England again—in London—and walking along

Piccadilly with little Pip—when a servant came running after me to ask would I step back to a lady in a carriage who wished to speak to me. It was a little pony carriage which the lady was driving; and the lady and I looked sadly enough on one another. 'I am greatly changed, I know; but I thought you would like to shake hands with Estella too, Pip. Lift up that pretty child and let me kiss it!' (She supposed the child, I think, to be my child). I was very glad afterwards to have had the interview; for in her face, and in her voice, and in her touch, she gave me the assurance that suffering had been stronger than Miss Havisham's teaching, and had given her a heart to understand what my heart used to be."

[*Great Expectations*]*   Algernon Swinburne

Among the highest landmarks of success ever reared for immortality by the triumphant genius of Dickens, the story of *Great Expectations* must for ever stand eminent beside that of *David Copperfield*. These are his great twin masterpieces. Great as they are, there is nothing in them greater than the very best things in some of his other books: there is certainly no person preferable and there is possibly no person comparable to Samuel Weller or to Sarah Gamp. Of the two childish and boyish autobiographers, David is the better little fellow though not the more lifelike little friend; but of all first chapters is there any comparable for impression and for fusion of humour and terror and pity and fancy and truth to that which confronts the child with the convict on the marshes in the twilight? And the story is incomparably the finer story of the two; there can be none superior, if there be any equal to it, in the whole range of English fiction. And except in *Vanity Fair* and *The Newcomes*, if even they may claim exception, there can surely be found no equal or nearly equal number of living and everliving figures. The tragedy and the comedy, the realism and the dreamery of life, are fused or mingled together with little less than Shakesperean strength and skill of hand. To have created Abel Magwitch is to be a god indeed among the creators of deathless men. Pumblechook is actually better and droller and truer to imaginative life than Pecksniff: Joe Gargery is worthy to have been praised and loved at once by Fielding and by Sterne: Mr. Jaggers and his clients, Mr. Wemmick and his parent and his bride, are such figures as Shakespeare, when dropping out of poetry, might have created, if his lot had been cast in a later century. Can as much be said for the creatures of any other man or god? The ghastly tragedy of Miss Havisham could only have been made at once credible and endurable by Dickens; he alone could have reconciled the strange and sordid horror with the noble and pathetic survival of possible emotion and repentance. And he alone could have eluded condemnation for so gross an oversight as the escape from retribution of so important a

*Reprinted from "Charles Dickens," *The Quarterly Review* 196 (1902): 31–134.

criminal as the "double murderer and monster" whose baffled or inadequate attempts are enough to make Bill Sikes seem comparatively the gentlest and Jonas Chuzzlewit the most amiable of men. I remember no such flaw in any other story I ever read. But in this story it may well have been allowed to pass unrebuked and unobserved; which yet I think it should not.

Among all the minor and momentary figures which flash into eternity across the stage of Dickens, there is one to which I have never yet seen the tribute of grateful homage adequately or even decently paid. The sonorous claims of old Bill Barley on the reader's affectionate and respectful interest have not remained without response; but the landlord's Jack has never yet, as far as I am aware, been fully recognized as great among the greatest of the gods of comic fiction. We are introduced to this lifelong friend in a waterside public-house as a "grizzled male creature, the 'Jack' of the little causeway, who was as slimy and smeary as if he had been low watermark too." It is but for a moment that we meet him: but eternity is in that moment.

> While we were comforting ourselves by the fire after our meal, the Jack—who was sitting in a corner, and who had a bloated pair of shoes on, which he had exhibited, while we were eating our eggs and bacon, as interesting relics that he had taken a few days ago from the feet of a drowned seaman washed ashore—asked me if we had seen a four-oared galley going up with the tide? When I told him No, he said she must have gone down then, and yet she "took up two," when she left there.
>
> "They must ha' thought better on't for some reason or another," said the Jack, "and gone down."
>
> "A four-oared galley, did you say?" said I.
>
> "A four," said the Jack, "and two sitters."
>
> "Did they come ashore here?"
>
> "They put in with a stone two-gallon jar for some beer, I'd ha' been glad to pison the beer myself," said the Jack, "or put some rattling physic in it."
>
> "Why?"
>
> "*I* know why," said the Jack. He spoke in a slushy voice, as if much mud had washed into his throat.
>
> "He thinks," said the landlord, a weakly meditative man with a pale eye, who seemed to rely greatly on his Jack, "he thinks they was, what they wasn't."
>
> "*I* knows what I thinks," observed the Jack.
>
> "You thinks Custum 'Us, Jack?" said the landlord.
>
> "I do," said the Jack."
>
> "Then you're wrong, Jack."
>
> "AM I!"
>
> In the infinite meaning of his reply and his boundless confidence in his views, the Jack took one of his bloated shoes off, looked into it, knocked a few stones out of it on the kitchen floor, and put it on again.

He did this with the air of a Jack who was so right that he could afford to do anything.

"Why, what do you make out that they done with their buttons then, Jack?" said the landlord, vacillating weakly.

"Done with their buttons?" returned the Jack. "Chucked 'em overboard. Swallered 'em. Sowed 'em, to come up small salad. Done with their buttons!"

"Don't be cheeky, Jack," remonstrated the landlord, in a melancholy and pathetic way.

"A Custum 'Us officer knows what to do with his Buttons," said the Jack, repeating the obnoxious word with the greatest contempt, "when they comes betwixt him and his own light. A Four and two sitters don't go hanging and hovering, up with one tide and down with another, and both with and against another, without there being Custum 'Us at the bottom of it." Saying which, he went out in disdain.

To join Francis the drawer and Cob the water-bearer in an ever-blessed immortality.

This was the author's last great work: the defects in it are as nearly imperceptible as spots on the sun or shadows on a sunlit sea.

[Passages on *Great Expectations*]*   George Gissing

It may be noted, however, with what frankness Dickens accepts the conventionality of a story told in the first person. David relates in detail conversations which take place before he is born, and makes no apology for doing so. Why should he? The point never occurs to the engrossed reader. In *Bleak House*, where the same expedient is used (in part), such boldness is not shown, though the convention still demands abundant sacrifice of probability in another way. Finally, in *Great Expectations* we have a narrative in the first person, which, granting to the narrator nothing less than Dickens's own equipment of genius, preserves verisimilitude with remarkable care, nothing being related, as seen or heard, which could not have been seen or heard by the writer. This instance serves to show that Dickens did become conscious of artistic faults, and set himself to correct them. . . .

Great Expectations (1861), would be nearly perfect in its mechanism but for the unhappy deference to Lord Lytton's judgment, which caused the end to be altered. Dickens meant to have left Pip a lonely man, and of course rightly so; by the irony of fate he was induced to spoil his work

*Reprinted from George Gissing, *Charles Dickens: A Critical Study* (London: Gresham Publishing Company, 1903).

through a brother novelist's desire for a happy ending—a strange thing, indeed, to befall Dickens. Observe how finely the narrative is kept in one key. It begins with a mournful impression—the foggy marshes spreading drearily by the seaward Thames—and throughout recurs this effect of cold and damp and dreariness; in that kind Dickens never did anything so good. Despite the subject, we have no stage fire—except around the person of Mr. Wopsle, a charming bit of satire, recalling and contrasting with the far-off days of *Nickleby*. The one unsatisfactory feature is the part concerned with Miss Havisham and Estella. Here the old Dickens survives in unhappy fashion; unable to resist the lure of eccentricity, but no longer presenting it with the gusto which was wont to be more than an excuse. Passing this, one can hardly overpraise the workmanship. No story in the first person was ever better told. . . .

Dickens's best bit of work is Pip, in *Great Expectations:* Pip, the narrator of his own story, who exhibits very well indeed the growth of a personality, the interaction of character and event. One is not permitted to lose sight of the actual author; though so much more living than Esther Summerson, Pip is yet embarrassed, like her, with the gift of humour. We know very well whose voice comes from behind the scenes when Pip is describing Mr. Wopsle's dramatic venture. Save for this, we acknowledge a true self-revelation. What could be better than a lad's picture of his state of mind, when, after learning that he has "great expectations," he quits the country home of his childhood and goes to London? "I formed a plan in outline for bestowing a dinner of roast beef and plum-pudding, a pint of ale, and a gallon of condescension upon everybody in the village" (chapter 19). It is one of many touches which give high value to this book. . . .

Of an average middle-class family in Dickens's earlier time—decent, kindly, not unintelligent folk—we have the best example in the Meagles group, from *Little Dorrit*. This household may be contrasted with, say, that of the Maylies in *Oliver Twist*, which is merely immature work, and with the more familiar family circles on which Dickens lavishes his mirth and his benevolence. The Meagles do not much interest us, which is quite right; they are thoroughly realized, and take their place in social history. Well done, too, is the Pocket family in *Great Expectations*, an interesting pendant to that of the Jellybys in *Bleak House;* showing how well, when he chose, Dickens could satirize without extravagance. Mrs. Pocket is decidedly more credible than Mrs. Jellyby; it might be urged, perhaps, that she belongs to the Sixties instead of to the Fifties, a point of some importance. The likeness in dissimilitude between these ladies' husbands is very instructive. As for the son, Herbert Pocket, he is a capital specimen of the healthy, right-minded, and fairly-educated middle-class youth. Very skillfully indeed is he placed side by side with Pip; each throwing into relief the other's natural and acquired characteristics. We see how long it will take the blacksmith's foster-child (he telling the tale himself) to reach the point of mental and moral refinement to which Herbert Pocket has been bred. . . .

That rich little book, *Great Expectations*, contains a humbug less offensive than Casby, and on the surface greatly amusing, but illustrative of a contemptible quality closely allied with the commercial spirit. Seen at a distance Mr. Pumblechook is a source of inextinguishable laughter; near at hand he is seen to be a very sordid creature. A time-server to his marrow, he adds the preposterous self-esteem which always gave Dickens so congenial an opportunity. Here we have a form of moral dishonesty peculiar to no one people. Mr. Pumblechook's barefaced pretence that he is the maker of Pip's fortune, his heavy patronage whilst that fortune endures, and his sour desertion of the young man when circumstances alter, is mere overfed humanity discoverable all the world over. He has English traits, and we are constrained to own the man as a relative; we meet him as often as we do the tailor who grovels before the customer unexpectedly become rich. Compare him with the other embodiments of dishonesty, and it is seen, not only what inexhaustible material of this kind lay at Dickens's command, but with what excellent art he differentiates his characters. . . .

It certainly is a troublesome fact for sensitive female readers that this, a great English novelist of the Victorian age, so abounds in women who are the curse of their husbands' lives. A complete list of them would, I imagine, occupy nearly a page of this book. Mrs. Jellyby I have already discussed. I have spoken of the much more lifelike Mrs. Pocket, a capital portrait. I have alluded to the uncommon realism of Dr. Marigold's wife. A mention must at least be made of Mr. Macstinger, who, as Mrs. Bunsby, enters upon such a promising field of fresh activity. But there remains one full-length picture which we may by no means neglect, its name Mrs. Joe Gargery.

Mrs. Gargery belongs to Dickens's later manner. In such work as this, his hand was still inimitably true, and his artistic conscience no longer allowed him to play with circumstance as in the days of Mrs. Varden. The blacksmith's wife is a shrew of the most highly developed order. If ever she is good-tempered in the common sense of the word, she never lets it be suspected; without any assignable cause, she is invariably acrid, and ready at a moment's notice to break into fury of abuse. It gratifies her immensely to have married the softest-hearted man that ever lived, and also that he happens to be physically one of the strongest; the joy of trampling upon him, knowing that he who could kill her with a backhand blow will never even answer the bitterest insult with an unkind word! It delights her, too, that she has a little brother, a mere baby still, whom she can ill-use at her leisure, remembering always that every harshness to the child is felt still worse by the big good fellow, her husband. Do you urge that Dickens should give a cause for this evil temper? Cause there is none— save of that scientific kind which has no place in English novels. It is the peculiarity of these women that no one can conjecture why they behave so ill. The nature of the animals—nothing more can be said.

Notice, now, that in Mrs. Gargery, though he still disguises the worst of the situation with his unfailing humour, Dickens gives us more of the harsh truth than in any previous book. That is a fine scene where the woman, by a malicious lie, causes a fight between Joe and Orlick; a true illustration of character, and well brought out. Again, Mrs. Joe's punishment. Here we are very far from the early novels. Mrs. Gargery shall be brought to quietness; but how? By a half-murderous blow on the back of her head, from which she will never recover. Dickens understood by this time that there is no other efficacious way with these ornaments of their sex. A felling and stunning and all but killing blow, followed by paralysis and slow death. A sharp remedy, but no whit sharper than the evil it cures. Mrs. Gargery, under such treatment, learns patience and the rights of other people. We are half sorry she cannot rise and put her learning into practice, but there is always a doubt. As likely as not she would take to drinking, and enter on a new phase of ferocity. . . .

Pathos of this graver and subtler kind is the distinguishing note of *Great Expectations*, a book which Dickens meant, and rightly meant, to end in the minor key. The old convict, Magwitch, if he cannot be called a tragical personality, has feeling enough to move the reader's deeper interest, and in the very end acquires through suffering a dignity which makes him very impressive. Rightly seen, is there not much pathos in the story of Pip's foolishness? It would be more manifest if we could forget Lytton's imbecile suggestion, and restore the original close of the story.

[Writings on *Great Expectations*]*   G. K. Chesterton

[FROM *CHARLES DICKENS*]

I repeat that this graver note is varied, but it remains a graver note. We see it struck, I think, with particular and remarkable success in *Great Expectations* (1860–61). This fine story is told with a consistency and quietude of individuality which is rare in Dickens. But so far had he travelled along the road of a heavier reality, that he even intended to give the tale an unhappy ending, making Pip lose Estella for ever; and he was only dissuaded from it by the robust romanticism of Bulwer-Lytton.

*Reprinted from G. K. Chesterton, *Charles Dickens* (London: Methuen, 1906) and G. K. Chesterton, *Appreciations and Criticisms of the Works of Charles Dickens* (London: Dent, 1911).

But the best part of the tale—the account of the vacillations of the hero between the humble life to which he owes everything, and the gorgeous life from which he expects something, touch a very true and somewhat tragic part of morals; for the great paradox of morality (the paradox to which only the religions have given an adequate expression) is that the very vilest kind of fault is exactly the most easy kind. We read in books and ballads about the wild fellow who might kill a man or smoke opium, but who would never stoop to lying or cowardice or to "anything mean." But for actual human beings opium and slaughter have only occasional charm; the permanent human temptation is the temptation to be mean. The one standing probability is the probability of becoming a cowardly hypocrite. The circle of the traitors is the lowest of the abyss, and it is also the easiest to fall into. That is one of the ringing realities of the Bible, that it does not make its great men commit grand sins; it makes its great men (such as David and St. Peter) commit small sins and behave like sneaks.

Dickens has dealt with this easy descent of desertion, this silent treason, with remarkable accuracy in the account of the indecisions of Pip. It contains a good suggestion of that weak romance which is the root of all snobbishness: that the mystery which belongs to patrician life excites us more than the open, even the indecent virtues of the humble. Pip is keener about Miss Havisham, who may mean well by him, than about Joe Gargery, who evidently does.

[FROM *APPRECIATIONS AND CRITICISMS OF THE WORKS OF CHARLES DICKENS*]

Great Expectations, which was written in the afternoon of Dickens's life and fame, has a quality of serene irony and even sadness, which puts it quite alone among his other works. At no time could Dickens possibly be called cynical, he had too much vitality; but relatively to the other books this book is cynical; but it has the soft and gentle cynicism of old age, not the hard cynicism of youth. To be a young cynic is to be a young brute; but Dickens, who had been so perfectly romantic and sentimental in his youth, could afford to admit this touch of doubt into the mixed experience of his middle age. At no time could any books by Dickens have been called Thackerayan. Both of the two men were too great for that. But relatively to the other Dickensian productions this book may be called Thackerayan. It is a study in human weakness and the slow human surrender. It describes how easily a free lad of fresh and decent instincts can be made to care more for rank and pride and the degrees of our stratified society than for old affection and for honour. It is an extra chapter to *The Book of Snobs*.

The best way of stating the change which this book marks in Dickens can be put in one phrase. In this book for the first time the hero disappears. The hero had descended to Dickens by a long line which begins with the gods, nay, perhaps if one may say so, which begins with God. First comes Deity and then the image of Deity; first comes the god and then the demi-god, the Hercules who labours and conquers before he receives his heavenly crown. That idea, with continual mystery and modification, has continued behind all romantic tales; the demi-god became the hero of paganism; the hero of paganism became the knight-errant of Christianity; the knight-errant who wandered and was foiled before he triumphed became the hero of the later prose romance, the romance in which the hero had to fight a duel with the villain but always survived, in which the hero drove desperate horses through the night in order to rescue the heroine, but always rescued her.

This heroic modern hero, this demi-god in a top-hat, may be said to reach his supreme moment and typical example about the time when Dickens was writing that thundering and thrilling and highly unlikely scene in *Nicholas Nickleby*, the scene where Nicholas hopelessly denounces the atrocious Gride in his hour of grinning triumph, and a thud upon the floor above tells them that the heroine's tyrannical father has died just in time to set her free. That is the apotheosis of the pure heroic as Dickens found it, and as Dickens in some sense continued it. It may be that it does not appear with quite so much unmistakable youth, beauty, valour, and virtue as it does in Nicholas Nickleby. Walter Gay is a simpler and more careless hero, but when he is doing any of the business of the story he is purely heroic. Kit Nubbles is a humbler hero, but he is a hero; when he is good he is very good. Even David Copperfield, who confesses to boyish tremors and boyish evasions in his account of his boyhood, acts the strict stiff part of the chivalrous gentleman in all the active and determining scenes of the tale. But *Great Expectations* may be called, like *Vanity Fair*, a novel without a hero. Almost all Thackeray's novels except *Esmond* are novels without a hero, but only one of Dickens's novels can be so described. I do not mean that it is a novel without a *jeune premier*, a young man to make love; *Pickwick* is that and *Oliver Twist*, and, perhaps, *The Old Curiosity Shop*. I mean that it is a novel without a hero in the same far deeper and more deadly sense in which *Pendennis* is also a novel without a hero. I mean that it is a novel which aims chiefly at showing that the hero is unheroic.

All such phrases as these must appear of course to overstate the case. Pip is a much more delightful person than Nicholas Nickleby. Or to take a stronger case for the purpose of our argument, Pip is a much more delightful person than Sydney Carton. Still the fact remains. Most of Nicholas Nickleby's personal actions are meant to show that he is heroic. Most of Pip's actions are meant to show that he is not heroic. The study of Sydney Carton is meant to indicate that with all his vices

Sydney Carton was a hero. The study of Pip is meant to indicate that with all his virtues Pip was a snob. The motive of the literary explanation is different. Pip and Pendennis are meant to show how circumstances can corrupt men. Sam Weller and Hercules are meant to show how heroes can subdue circumstances.

This is the preliminary view of the book which is necessary if we are to regard it as a real and separate fact in the life of Dickens. Dickens had many moods because he was an artist; but he had one great mood, because he was a great artist. Any real difference therefore from the general drift, or rather (I apologize to Dickens) the general drive of his creation is very important. This is the one place in his work in which he does, I will not say feel like Thackeray, far less think like Thackeray, less still write like Thackeray, but this is the one of his works in which he understands Thackeray. He puts himself in some sense in the same place; he considers mankind at somewhat the same angle as mankind is considered in one of the sociable and sarcastic novels of Thackeray. When he deals with Pip he sets out not to show his strength like the strength of Hercules, but to show his weakness like the weakness of Pendennis. When he sets out to describe Pip's great expectation he does not set out, as in a fairy tale, with the idea that these great expectations will be fulfilled; he sets out from the first with the idea that these great expectations will be disappointing. We might very well, as I have remarked elsewhere, apply to all Dickens's books the title *Great Expectations*. All his books are full of an airy and yet ardent expectation of everything; of the next person who shall happen to speak, of the next chimney that shall happen to smoke, of the next event, of the next ecstasy; of the next fulfillment of any eager human fancy. All his books might be called *Great Expectations*. But the only book to which he gave the name of *Great Expectations* was the only book in which the expectation was never realized. It was so with the whole of that splendid and unconscious generation to which he belonged. The whole glory of that old English middle class was that it was unconscious; its excellence was entirely in that, that it was the culture of the nation, and that it did not know it. If Dickens had ever known that he was optimistic, he would have ceased to be happy.

It is necessary to make this first point clear: that in *Great Expectations* Dickens was really trying to be a quiet, a detached, and even a cynical observer of human life. Dickens was trying to be Thackeray. And the final and startling triumph of Dickens is this: that even to this moderate and modern story, he gives an incomparable energy which is not moderate and which is not modern. He is trying to be reasonable; but in spite of himself he is inspired. He is trying to be detailed, but in spite of himself he is gigantic. Compared to the rest of Dickens this is Thackeray; but compared to the whole of Thackeray we can only say in supreme praise of it that it is Dickens.

Take, for example, the one question of snobbishness. Dickens has achieved admirably the description of the doubts and vanities of the wretched Pip as he walks down the street in his new gentlemanly clothes, the clothes of which he is so proud and so ashamed. Nothing could be so exquisitely human, nothing especially could be so exquisitely masculine as that combination of self-love and self-assertion and even insolence with a naked and helpless sensibility to the slightest breath of ridicule. Pip thinks himself better than every one else, and yet anybody can snub him; that is the everlasting male, and perhaps the everlasting gentleman. Dickens has described perfectly this quivering and defenceless dignity. Dickens has described perfectly how ill-armed it is against the coarse humour of real humanity—the real humanity which Dickens loved, but which idealists and philanthropists do not love, the humanity of cabmen and costermongers and men singing in a third-class carriage; the humanity of Trabb's boy. In describing Pip's weakness Dickens is as true and as delicate as Thackeray. But Thackeray might have been easily as true and as delicate as Dickens. This quick and quiet eye for the tremors of mankind is a thing which Dickens possessed, but which others possessed also. George Eliot or Thackeray could have described the weakness of Pip. Exactly what George Eliot and Thackeray could not have described was the vigour of Trabb's boy. There would have been admirable humour and observation in their accounts of that intolerable urchin. Thackeray would have given us little light touches of Trabb's boy, absolutely true to the quality and colour of the humour, just as in his novels of the eighteenth century, the glimpses of Steele or Bolingbroke or Doctor Johnson are exactly and perfectly true to the colour and quality of their humour. George Eliot in her earlier books would have given us shrewd authentic scraps of the real dialect of Trabb's boy, just as she gave us shrewd and authentic scraps of the real talk in a Midland country town. In her later books she would have given us highly rationalistic explanations of Trabb's boy; which we should not have read. But exactly what they could never have given, and exactly what Dickens does give, is the *bounce* of Trabb's boy. It is the real unconquerable rush and energy in a character which was the supreme and quite indescribable greatness of Dickens. He conquered by rushes; he attacked in masses; he carried things at the spear point in a charge of spears; he was the Rupert of Fiction. The thing about any figure of Dickens, about Sam Weller or Dick Swiveller, or Micawber, or Bagstock, or Trabb's boy,—the thing about each one of these persons is that he cannot be exhausted. A Dickens character hits you first on the nose and then in the waistcoat, and then in the eye and then in the waistcoat again, with the blinding rapidity of some battering engine. The scene in which Trabb's boy continually overtakes Pip in order to reel and stagger as at a first encounter is a thing quite within the real competence of such a character; it might have been suggested by Thackeray, or George Eliot, or any realist. But the point with Dickens is that there is a rush in the boy's rushings; the writer and the reader rush with him. They start with him, they stare with him, they stagger with him, they share an inexpressible vitality in the air which emanates from this violent and capering satirist. Trabb's boy is among other things a boy; he has a physical rapture in hurling himself like a boomerang and in bouncing to the sky like a ball. It is just exactly in describing this quality that Dickens is Dickens and that no one else comes near him. No one feels in his bones that Felix Holt was strong as he feels in his bones that little Quilp was strong. No one can feel that even Rawdon Crawley's splendid smack across the face of Lord Steyne is quite so living and life-giving as the "kick after kick" which old Mr. Weller dealt the dancing and quivering Stiggins as he drove him towards the trough. This quality, whether expressed intellectually or physically, is the profoundly popular and eternal quality in Dickens; it is the thing that no one else could do. This quality is the quality which has always given its continuous power and poetry to the common people everywhere. It is life; it is the joy of life felt by those who have nothing else but life. It is the thing that all aristocrats have always hated and dreaded in the people. And it is the thing which poor Pip really hates and dreads in Trabb's boy.

A great man of letters or any great artist is symbolic without knowing it. The things he describes are types because they are truths. Shakespeare may, or may not, have ever put it to himself that Richard the Second was a philosophical symbol; but all good criticism must necessarily see him so. It may be a reasonable question whether the artist should be allegorical. There can be no doubt among sane men that the critic should be allegorical. Spenser may have lost by being less realistic than Fielding. But any good criticism of *Tom Jones* must be as mystical as the *Faery Queen*. Hence it is unavoidable in speaking of a fine book like *Great Expectations* that we should give even to its unpretentious and realistic figures a certain massive mysticism. Pip is Pip, but he is also the well-meaning snob. And this is even more true of those two great figures in the tale which stand for the English democracy. For, indeed, the first and last word upon the English democracy is said in Joe Gargery and Trabb's boy. The actual English populace, as distinct from the French populace or the Scotch or Irish populace, may be said to lie between those two types. The first is the poor man who does not assert himself at all, and the second is the poor man who asserts himself entirely with the weapon of sarcasm. The only way in which the English now ever rise in revolution is under the symbol and leadership of Trabb's boy. What pikes and shillelahs were to the Irish populace, what guns and barricades were to the French populace, that chaff is to the English populace. It is their weapon, the use of which they really understand. It is the one way in which they can make a rich man feel uncomfortable, and they use it very justifiably for all it is worth. If they do not cut off the heads of tyrants at least they sometimes do their best to make the tyrants lose their heads. The gutter boys of the great towns carry the art of personal criticism to so rich and delicate a degree that some well-dressed persons when they walk past a file of them feel as if they were walking past a row of omniscient critics or judges with a power of life and death. Here and there only is some ordinary human custom, some natural human pleasure suppressed in deference to the fastidiousness of the rich. But all the rich tremble before the fastidiousness of the poor.

Of the other type of democracy it is far more difficult to speak. It is always hard to speak of good things or good people, for in satisfying the soul they take away a certain spur to speech. Dickens was often called a sentimentalist. In one sense he sometimes was a sentimentalist. But if sentimentalism be held to mean something artificial or theatrical, then in the core and reality of his character Dickens was the very reverse of a sentimentalist. He seriously and definitely loved goodness. To see sincerity and charity satisfied him like a meal. What some critics call his love of sweet stuff is really his love of plain beef and bread. Sometimes one is tempted to wish that in the long Dickens dinner the sweet courses could be left out; but this does not make the whole banquet other than a banquet singularly solid and simple. The critics complain of the sweet things, but not because they are so strong as to like simple things. They complain of the sweet things because they are so sophisticated as to like sour things; their tongues are tainted with the bitterness of absinthe. Yet because of the very simplicity of Dickens's moral tastes it is impossible to speak adequately of them; and Joe Gargery must stand as he stands in the book, a thing too obvious to be understood. But this may be said of him in one of his minor aspects, that he stands for a certain long-suffering in the English poor, a certain weary patience and politeness which almost breaks the heart. One cannot help wondering whether that great mass of silent virtue will ever achieve anything on this earth.

[Foreword to *Great Expectations*][*]   [George] Bernard Shaw

Great Expectations is the last of the three full-length stories written by Dickens in the form of an autobiography. Of the three, *Bleak House*, as the autobiography of Miss Esther Summerson, is naturally the least personal, as Esther is not only a woman but a maddening prig, though we are forced to admit that such paragons exist and are perhaps worthy of the reverent admiration with which Dickens regarded them. Ruling her out,

*Reprinted from the 1947 Hamish Hamilton/Novel Library edition of *Great Expectations*, by permission of the Society of Authors on behalf of the Bernard Shaw Estate.

we have *David Copperfield* and *Great Expectations*. David was, for a time at least, Dickens's favourite child, perhaps because he had used him to express the bitterness of that episode in his own experience which had wounded his boyish self-respect most deeply. For Dickens, in spite of his exuberance, was a deeply reserved man: the exuberance was imagination and acting (his imagination was ceaseless, and his outward life a feat of acting from beginning to end); and we shall never know whether in that immensely broadened outlook and knowledge of the world which began with *Hard Times* and *Little Dorrit*, and left all his earlier works behind, he may not have come to see that making his living by sticking labels on blacking bottles and rubbing shoulders with boys who were not gentlemen, was as little shameful as being the genteel apprentice in the office of Mr. Spenlow, or the shorthand writer recording the unending twaddle of the House of Commons and electioneering bunk on the hustings of all the Eatanswills in the country.

That there was a tragic change in his valuations can be shown by contrasting Micawber with William Dorrit, in which light Micawber suddenly becomes a mere marionette pantaloon with a funny bag of tricks which he repeats until we can bear no more of him, and Dorrit a portrait of the deadliest and deepest truth to nature. Now contrast David with Pip; and believe, if you can, that there was no revision of his estimate of the favorite child David as a work of art and even as a vehicle of experience. The adult David fades into what stage managers call a walking gentleman. The reappearance of Mr. Dickens in the character of a blacksmith's boy may be regarded as an apology to Mealy Potatoes.

Dickens did in fact know that *Great Expectations* was his most compactly perfect book. In all the other books, there are episodes of wild extravagance, extraordinarily funny if they catch you at the right age, but recklessly grotesque as nature studies. Even in *Little Dorrit*, Dickens's masterpiece among many masterpieces, it is impossible to believe that the perfectly authentic Mr. Pancks really stopped the equally authentic Mr. Casby in a crowded street in London and cut his hair; and though Mr. F.'s aunt is a first-rate clinical study of senile deficiency in a shrewd old woman, her collisions with Arthur Clennam are too funny to be taken seriously. We cannot say of Casby, Pancks, and the aunt, as we can say of Sam Weller, that such people never existed; for most of us have met their counterparts in real life; but we can say that Dickens's sense of fun ran away with him over them. If we have absolutely no fun in us we may even state gravely that there has been a lapse from the artistic integrity of the tragic picture of English society which is the subject of the book.

In *Great Expectations* we have Wopsle and Trabb's boy; but they have their part and purpose in the story and do not overstep the immodesty of nature. It is hardly decent to compare Mr. F.'s aunt with Miss Havisham; but as contrasted studies of madwomen they make you shudder at the thought of what Dickens might have made of Miss Havisham if he had seen her as a comic personage. For life is no laughing matter in *Great Expectations;* the book is all-of-one piece and consistently truthful as none of the other books are, not even the compact *Tale of Two Cities,* which is pure sentimental melodrama from beginning to end, and shockingly wanting in any philosophy of history in its view of the French Revolution.

Dickens never regarded himself as a revolutionist, though he certainly was one. His implacable contempt for the House of Commons, founded on his experience as a parliamentary reporter, never wavered from the account of the Eatanswill election and of Nicholas Nickleby's interview with Pugstyles to the Veneering election in *Our Mutual Friend,* his last book (*Edwin Drood* is only a gesture by a man three-quarters dead). And this was not mere satire, of which there had been plenty. Dickens was the first writer to perceive and state definitely that the House of Commons, working on the Party system, is an extraordinarily efficient device for dissipating all our reforming energy and ability in Party debate and when anything urgently needs to be done, finding out "how not to do it." It took very little time to get an ineffective Factory Act. It took fifty years to make it effective, though the labour conditions in the factories and mines were horrible. After Dickens's death, it took thirty years to pass an Irish Home Rule Bill, which was promptly repudiated by the military plutocracy, leaving the question to be settled by a competition in slaughter and house burning, just as it would have been between two tribes of savages. Liberty under the British parliamentary system means slavery for nine-tenths of the people, and slave exploitation or parasitic idolatry and snobbery for the rest. Parliament men—one cannot call them statesmen—and even historians, keep declaring that the British parliamentary system is one of the greatest blessings British political genius has given to the world; and the world has taken it at its self-valuation and set up imitations of it all over Europe and America, always with the same result: political students outside Parliament exposing the most frightful social evils and prescribing their remedies, and Parliament ignoring them as long as possible and then engulfing their disciples and changing them from reformers into partisans with time for nothing but keeping their party in power or opposing the Government, rightly or wrongly ("it is the duty of the Opposition to oppose"), as the case might be. In the middle of the nineteenth century Dickens saw this and said it. He had to be ignored, as he would not stand for Parliament and be paralyzed.

Europe has had to learn from hard experience what it would not learn from Dickens. The Fascist and Communist revolutions which swept the great parliamentary sham into the dustbin after it had produced a colossal Anarchist war, made no mention of Dickens; but on the parliamentary point he was as much their prophet as Marx was the economic prophet of the Soviets. Yet a recent reactionist against Dickens worship declares that he "never went ahead of his public."

Marx and Dickens were contemporaries living in the same city and pursuing the same profession of literature; yet they seem to us like creatures of a different species living in different worlds. Dickens, if he had ever become conscious of Karl Marx, would have been classed with him as a revolutionist. The difference between a revolutionist and what Marx called a bourgeois is that the bourgeois regards the existing social order as the permanent and natural order of human society, needing reforms now and then and here and there, but essentially good and sane and right and respectable and proper and everlasting. To the revolutionist it is transitory, mistaken, objectionable, and pathological: a social disease to be cured, not to be endured. We have only to compare Thackeray and Trollope with Dickens to perceive this contrast. Thackeray reviled the dominant classes with a savagery which would have been unchivalrous in Dickens: he denied to his governing class characters even the common good qualities and accomplishments of ladies and gentleman, making them mean, illiterate, dishonest, ignorant, sycophantic to an inhuman degree, whilst Dickens, even when making his aristocrats ridiculous and futile, at least made gentlemen of them. Trollope, who regarded Thackeray as his master and exemplar, had none of his venom, and has left us a far better balanced and more truthful picture of Victorian well-off society, never consciously whitewashing it, though allowing it its full complement of black sheep of both sexes. But Trollope's politics were those of the country house and the hunting field just as were Thackeray's. Accordingly, Thackeray and Trollope were received and approved by fashionable society with complete confidence. Dickens, though able to fascinate all classes, was never so received or approved except by quite goodnatured or stupid ladies and gentlemen who were incapable of criticizing anyone who could make them laugh and cry. He was told that he could not describe a gentleman and that *Little Dorrit* is twaddle. And the reason was that in his books the west-end heaven appears as a fool's paradise that must pass away instead of being an indispensable preparatory school for the New Jerusalem of Revelation. A leading encyclopedia tells us that Dickens has "no knowledge of country gentlemen." It would have been nearer the mark to say that Dickens knew all that really mattered about Sir Leicester Dedlock and that Trollope knew nothing that really mattered about him. Trollope and Thackeray could see Chesney Wold; but Dickens could see through it. And this was no joke to Dickens. He was deeply concerned about it, and understood how revolutions begin with burning the chateaux.

The difference between Marx and Dickens was that Marx knew that he was a revolutionist whilst Dickens had not the faintest suspicion of that part of his calling. Compare the young Dickens looking for a job in a lawyer's office and teaching himself shorthand to escape from his office stool to the reporters' gallery, with the young Trotsky, the young Lenin, quite deliberately facing disreputable poverty and adopting revolution as their profession with every alternative of bourgeois security and respectability much more fully open to them than to Dickens.

And this brings us to Dickens's position as a member of the educated and cultured classes who had neither education nor culture. This was fortunate for him and for the world in one way, as he escaped the school and university routine which complicates cultural Philistinism with the mentality of a Red Indian brave. Better no schooling at all than the schooling of Rudyard Kipling and Winston Churchill. But there are homes in which a mentally acquisitive boy can make contact with the fine arts. I myself learnt nothing at school, but gained in my home an extensive and highly educational knowledge of music. I had access to illustrated books on painting which sent me to the National Gallery; so that I was able to support myself as a critic of music and painting as Dickens supported himself by shorthand. I devoured books on science and on the religious controversies of the day. It is in this way, and not in our public schools and universities that such culture as there is in England is kept alive.

Now the Dickenses seem to have been complete barbarians. Dickens mentions the delight with which he discovered in an attic a heap of eighteenth-century novels. But Smollett was a grosser barbarian than Dickens himself; and *Don Quixote* and *The Arabian Nights*, though they gave the cue to his eager imagination, left him quite in the dark as to the philosophy and art of his day. To him a philosopher, an intellectual, was a figure of fun. Count Smorltork is the creation by a street Arab: Dickens did not even know that the Count's method of studying Chinese metaphysics by studying metaphysics and China and "combining the information" was not only sensible and correct, but the only possible method. To Dickens as to most Victorian Englishmen metaphysics were ridiculous, useless, unpractical, and the mark of a fool. He was musical enough to have a repertory of popular ballads which he sang all over the house to keep his voice in order; and he made Tom Pinch play the organ in church as an amiable accomplishment; but I cannot remember hearing that he ever went to a classical concert, or even knew of the existence of such entertainments. The articles on the National Gallery in *All the Year Round*, though extremely funny in their descriptions of "The Apotheosis" of "William the Silent" (the title alone would make a cat laugh), and on some profane points sensible enough, are those of a complete Philistine. One cannot say that he disliked all painters in the face of his friendship with Maclise and Clarkson Stanfield; but it was not a cultural friendship: Stanfield was a scene painter who appealed to that English love of landscape which is so often confused with a love of art; and Maclise was a pictorial anecdotist who presented scenes from Shakespear's plays exactly as they were presented on the stage. When Dickens introduced in his stories a character whom he intensely disliked he chose an artistic profession for him. Henry Gowan in *Little Dorrit* is a painter. Pecksniff is an architect. Harold Skimpole is a musician. There is real hatred in his treatment of them.

Now far be it from me to imply that they are false to nature. Artists are often detestable human beings; and the famous Anti-Scrape, officially The Society for the Protection of Ancient Buildings, was founded by William Morris and his friends to protect ancient buildings from architects. What is more, the ultra-artistic sets, the Pre-Raphaelites and the aesthetes grouped round Rossetti and Morris and Ruskin, were all Dickens worshippers who made a sort of cult of Trabb's boy and would have regarded me as a traitor if they had read what I am now writing. They knew better than anyone else that Leigh Hunt deserved all he got as Harold Skimpole, that Gowan's shallow sort of painting was a nuisance, and that architecture was just the right profession for a parasite on Salisbury Cathedral like Pecksniff. But all their Dickensian enthusiasm, and all the truth to life of Dickens's portraiture cannot extenuate the fact that the cultural side of art was as little known to Dickens as it is possible for a thing so public to remain to a man so apprehensive. You may read the stories of Dickens from beginning to end without ever learning that he lived through a period of fierce revivals and revolutionary movements in art, in philosophy, in sociology, in religion: in short, in culture. Dean Inge's remark that "the number of great subjects in which Dickens took no interest whatever is amazing" hits the nail exactly on the head. As to finding such a person as Karl Marx among his characters, one would as soon look for a nautilus in a nursery.

Yet *Little Dorrit* is a more seditious book than *Das Kapital*. All over Europe men and women are in prison for pamphlets and speeches which are to *Little Dorrit* as red pepper to dynamite. Fortunately for social evolution Governments never know where to strike. Barnacle and Stiltstalking were far too conceited to recognize their own portraits. Parliament, wearying its leaders out in a few years in the ceaseless drudgery of finding out how not to do it, and smothering it in talk, could not conceive that its heartbreaking industry could have any relation to the ridiculous fiction of the Coodle-Doodle discussions in Sir Leicester Dedlock's drawingroom. As to the Circumlocution Office, well, perhaps the staffs, owing their posts to patronage and regarding them as sinecures, were a bit too insolent to the public, and would be none the worse for a little chaff from a funny fellow like Dickens; but their inefficiency as a public service was actually a good thing, as it provided a standing object lesson in the superiority of private enterprise. Mr. Sparkler was not offended: he stuck to his job and never read anything. *Little Dorrit* and *Das Kapital* were all the same to him: they never entered his world; and to him that world was the whole world.

The mass of Dickens readers, finding all these people too funny to be credible, continued to idolize Coodle and Doodle as great statesmen, and made no distinction between John Stuart Mill at the India Office and Mr.

Sparkler. In fact the picture was not only too funny to be credible: it was too truthful to be credible. But the fun was no fun to Dickens: the truth was too bitter. When you laugh at Jack Bunsby, or at The Orfling when the handle of her corkscrew came off and smote her on the chin, you have no doubt that Dickens is laughing with you like a street boy, despite Bunsby's tragic end. But whilst you laugh at Sparkler or young Barnacle, Dickens is in deadly earnest: he means that both of them must go into the dustbin if England is to survive.

And yet Dickens never saw himself as a revolutionist. It never occurred to him to found a Red International, as Marx did, not even to join one out of the dozens of political reform societies that were about him. He was an English gentleman of the professional class, who would not allow his daughter to go on the stage because it was not respectable. He knew so little about revolutionists that when Mazzini called on him and sent in his card, Dickens, much puzzled, concluded that the unknown foreign gentleman wanted money, and very kindly sent him down a sovereign to get rid of him. He discovered for himself all the grievances he exposed, and had no sense of belonging to a movement, nor any desire to combine with others who shared his subversive views. To educate his children religiously and historically he wrote *A Child's History of England* which had not even the excuse of being childish, and a paraphrase of the gospel biography which is only a belittling of it for little children. He had much better have left the history to Little Arthur and Mrs. Markham and Goldsmith, and taken into account the extraordinary educational value of the Authorized Version as a work of literary art. He probably thought as seldom of himself as a literary artist as of himself as a revolutionist; and he had his share in the revolt against the supernatural pretensions of the Bible which was to end in the vogue of Agnosticism and the pontificate of Darwin. It blinded that generation to the artistic importance of the fact that at a moment when all the literary energy in England was in full eruption, when Shakespear was just dead and Milton just born, a picked body of scholars undertook the task of translating into English what they believed to be the words of God himself. Under the strain of that conviction they surpassed all their normal powers, transfiguring the original texts into literary masterpieces of a splendor that no merely mortal writers can ever again hope to achieve. But the nineteenth century either did not dare think of the Bible in that way, it being fetish, or else it was in such furious reaction against the fetishism that it would not allow the so-called Holy Scriptures even an artistic merit. At all events Dickens thought his Little Nell style better for his children than the English of King James's inspired scribes. He took them (for a time at least) to churches of the Unitarian persuasion, where they could be both skeptical and respectable; but it is hard to say what Dickens believed or did not believe metaphysically or metapolitically, though he left us in no doubt as to his opinion of the Lords, the Commons, and the ante-Crimean Civil Service.

On the positive side he had nothing to say. Marxism and Darwinism came too late for him. He might have been a Comtist—perhaps ought to have been a Comtist, but was not. He was an independent Dickensian, a sort of unphilosophic Radical, with a complete disbelief in government by the people and an equally complete hostility to government in any other interest than theirs. He exposed many abuses and called passionately on the rulers of the people to remedy them; but he never called on the people themselves. He would as soon have thought of calling on them to write their own novels.

Meanwhile he overloaded himself and his unfortunate wife with such a host of children that he was forced to work himself to death prematurely to provide for them and for the well-to-do life he led. The reading public cannot bear to think of its pet authors as struggling with the economic pressures that often conflict so cruelly with the urge of genius. This pressure was harder on Dickens than on many poorer men. He had a solid bourgeois conscience which made it impossible for him to let wife and children starve whilst he followed the path of destiny. Marx let his wife go crazy with prolonged poverty whilst he wrote a book which changed the mind of the world. But then Marx had been comfortably brought up and thoroughly educated in the German manner. Dickens knew far too much of the horrors of impecuniosity to put his wife through what his mother had gone through, or have his children pasting labels on blacking bottles. He had to please his public or lapse into that sort of poverty. Under such circumstances the domestic conscience inevitably pushes the artistic conscience into the second place. We shall never know how much of Dickens's cheery optimism belied his real outlook on life. He went his own way far enough to make it clear that when he was not infectiously laughing he was a melancholy fellow. Arthur Clennam is one of the Dismal Jemmies of literature. For any gaiety of heart we have to turn to the impossible Dick Swiveller, who by the way, was designed as a revoltingly coarse fortune hunter, and still appears in that character in the single scene which precedes his sudden appeal to Dickens's sense of fun, and consequent transformation into a highly entertaining and entirely fantastic clown. This was a genuine conversion and not a concession to public taste; but the case of Walter Gay in *Dombey and Son,* whose high spirits were planned as a prelude to his degeneration and ruin, is a flagrant case of a manufactured happy ending to save a painful one. Martin Chuzzlewit begins as a study in selfishness and ends nowhere. Mr. Boffin, corrupted by riches, gets discharged without a stain on his character by explaining that he was only pretending for benevolent purposes, but leaves us with a feeling that some of his pretences were highly suspicious. Jarndyce, a violently good man, keeps on doing generous things, yet ends by practicing a heartlessly cruel and indelicate deception on Esther

Summerson for the sake of giving her a pleasant melodramatic surprise. I will not go so far as to say that Dickens's novels are full of melancholy intentions which he dares not carry through to their unhappy conclusions; but he gave us no vitally happy heroes and heroines after Pickwick (begun, like Don Quixote, as a contemptible butt). Their happy endings are manufactured to make the books pleasant. Nobody who has endured the novels of our twentieth-century emancipated women, enormously cleverer and better informed than the novels of Dickens, and ruthlessly calculated to leave their readers hopelessly discouraged and miserable, will feel anything but gratitude to Dickens for his humanity in speeding his parting guests with happy faces by turning from the world of destiny to the world of accidental good luck; but as our minds grow stronger some of his consolations become unnecessary and even irritating. And it happens that it is with just such a consolation that *Great Expectations* ends.

It did not always end so. Dickens wrote two endings, and made a mess of both. In the first ending, which Bulwer Lytton persuaded him to discard, Pip takes little Pip for a walk in Piccadilly and is stopped by Estella, who is passing in her carriage. She is comfortably married to a Shropshire doctor, and just says how d'y'do to Pip and kisses the little boy before they both pass on out of one another's lives. This, though it is marred by Pip's pious hope that her husband may have thrashed into her some understanding of how much she has made him suffer, is true to nature. But it is much too matter-of-fact to be the right ending to a tragedy. Piccadilly was impossible in such a context; and the passing carriage was unconsciously borrowed from *A Day's Ride: A Life's Romance*, the novel by Lever which was so unpopular that *Great Expectations* had to be written to replace it in *All The Year Round*. But in Lever's story it is the man who stops the carriage, only to be cut dead by the lady. Dickens must have felt that there was something wrong with this ending; and Bulwer's objection confirmed his doubt. Accordingly, he wrote a new ending, in which he got rid of Piccadilly and substituted a perfectly congruous and beautifully touching scene and hour and atmosphere for the meeting. He abolished the Shropshire doctor and left out the little boy. So far the new ending was in every way better than the first one.

Unfortunately, what Bulwer wanted was what is called a happy ending, presenting Pip and Estella as reunited lovers who were going to marry and live happily ever after; and Dickens, though he could not bring himself to be quite so explicit in sentimental falsehood, did, at the end of the very last line, allow himself to say that there was "no shadow of parting" between them. If Pip had said "Since that parting I have been able to think of her without the old unhappiness; but I have never tried to see her again, and I know I never shall" he would have been left with at least the prospect of a bearable life. But the notion that he could ever have been happy with Estella: indeed that anyone could ever have been happy with Estella, is positively unpleasant. I can remember when the Cowden

Clarks ventured to hint a doubt whether Benedick and Beatrice had a very delightful union to look forward to; but that did not greatly matter, as Benedick and Beatrice have none of the reality of Pip and Estella. Shakespear could afford to trifle with *Much Ado About Nothing*, which is avowedly a potboiler; but *Great Expectations* is a different matter. Dickens put nearly all his thought into it. It is too serious a book to be a trivially happy one. Its beginning is unhappy; its middle is unhappy; and the conventional happy ending is an outrage on it.

Estella is a curious addition to the gallery of unamiable women painted by Dickens. In my youth it was commonly said that Dickens could not draw women. The people who said this were thinking of Agnes Wickfield and Esther Summerson, of Little Dorrit and Florence Dombey, and thinking of them as ridiculous idealizations of their sex. Gissing put a stop to that by asking whether shrews like Mrs. Raddle, Mrs. Macstinger, Mrs. Gargery, fools like Mrs. Nickleby and Flora Finching, warped spinsters like Rosa Dartle and Miss Wade, were not masterpieces of woman drawing. And they are all unamiable. But for Betsy Trotwood, who is a very lovable fairy godmother and yet a genuine nature study, and an old dear like Mrs. Boffin, one would be tempted to ask whether Dickens had ever in his life met an amiable female. The transformation of Dora into Flora is diabolical, but frightfully true to nature. Of course Dickens with his imagination could invent amiable women by the dozen; but somehow he could not or would not bring them to life as he brought the others. We doubt whether he ever knew a little Dorrit; but Fanny Dorrit is from the life unmistakably. So is Estella. She is a much more elaborate study than Fanny, and, I should guess, a recent one.

Dickens, when he let himself go in *Great Expectations*, was separated from his wife and free to make more intimate acquaintances with women than a domesticated man can. I know nothing of his adventures in this phase of his career, though I daresay a good deal of it will be dug out by the little sect of anti-Dickensites whose fanaticism has been provoked by the Dickens Fellowships. It is not necessary to suggest a love affair; for Dickens could get from a passing glance a hint which he could expand into a full-grown character. The point concerns us here only because it is the point on which the ending of *Great Expectations* turns: namely, that Estella is a born tormentor. She deliberately torments Pip all through for the fun of it; and in the little we hear of her intercourse with others there is no suggestion of a moment of kindness: in fact her tormenting of Pip is almost affectionate in contrast to the cold disdain of her attitude towards the people who were not worth tormenting. It is not surprising that the unfortunate Bentley Drummle, whom she marries in the stupidity of sheer perversity, is obliged to defend himself from her clever malice with his fists: a consolation to us for Pip's broken heart, but not altogether a credible one; for the real Estellas can usually intimidate the real Bentley Drummles. At all events the final sugary suggestion of Estella redeemed by Bentley's thrashings and waste of her money, and living happily with Pip for ever after, provoked even Dickens's eldest son to rebel against it, most justly.

Apart from this the story is the most perfect of Dickens's works. In it he does not muddle himself with the ridiculous plots that appear like vestiges of the stone age in many of his books, from *Oliver Twist* to the end. The story is built round a single and simple catastrophe: the revelation to Pip of the source of his great expectations. There is, it is true, a trace of the old plot superstition in Estella turning out to be Magwitch's daughter; but it provides a touchingly happy ending for that heroic Warmint. Who could have the heart to grudge it to him?

As our social conscience expands and makes the intense class snobbery of the nineteenth century seem less natural to us, the tragedy of *Great Expectations* will lose some of its appeal. I have already wondered whether Dickens himself ever came to see that his agonizing sensitiveness about the blacking bottles and his resentment of his mother's opposition to his escape from them was not too snobbish to deserve all the sympathy he claimed for it. Compare the case of H. G. Wells, our nearest to a twentieth-century Dickens. Wells hated being a draper's boy; but he was not in the least ashamed of it, and did not blame his mother for regarding it as the summit of her ambition for him. Fate having imposed on that engaging cricketer Mr. Wells's father an incongruous means of livelihood in the shape of a small shop, shopkeeping did not present itself to the young Wells as beneath him, whereas to the genteel Dickens being a warehouse boy was an unbearable comedown. Still, I cannot help speculating on whether if Dickens had not killed himself prematurely to pile up money for that excessive family of his, he might not have reached a stage at which he could have got as much fun out of the blacking bottles as Mr. Wells got out of his abhorred draper's counter.

Dickens never reached that stage; and there is no prevision of it in *Great Expectations;* for in it he never raises the question why Pip should refuse Magwitch's endowment and shrink from him with such inhuman loathing. Magwitch no doubt was a Warmint from the point of view of the genteel Dickens family and even from his own; but Victor Hugo would have made him a magnificent hero, another Valjean. Inspired by an altogether noble fixed idea, he had lifted himself out of his rut of crime and honestly made a fortune for the child who had fed him when he was starving. If Pip had no objection to be a parasite instead of an honest blacksmith, at least he had a better claim to be a parasite on Magwitch's earnings than, as he imagined, on Miss Havisham's property. It is curious that this should not have occurred to Dickens; for nothing could exceed the bitterness of his exposure of the futility of Pip's parasitism. If all that came of sponging on Miss Havisham (as he thought) was the privilege of being one of the Finches of the Grove, he need not have felt his dependence on Magwitch to be incompatible with his entirely baseless self-respect. But Pip—and I am afraid Pip must be to this extent identified with Dickens—could not see Magwitch as an animal of the same species as himself or Miss Havisham. His feeling is true to the nature of snobbery; but his creator says no word in criticism of that ephemeral limitation.

The basic truth of the situation is that Pip, like his creator, has no culture and no religion. Joe Gargery, when Pip tells a monstrous string of lies about Miss Havisham, advises him to say a repentant word about it in his prayers; but Pip never prays; and church means nothing to him but Mr. Wopsle's orotundity. In this he resembles David Copperfield, who has gentility but neither culture nor religion. Pip's world is therefore a very melancholy place, and his conduct, good or bad, always helpless. This is why Dickens worked against so black a background after he was roused from his ignorant middle-class cheery optimism by Carlyle. When he lost his belief in bourgeois society and with it his lightness of heart he had neither an economic Utopia nor a credible religion to hitch on to. His world becomes a world of great expectations cruelly disappointed. The Wells world is a world of greater and greater expectations continually being fulfilled. This is a huge improvement. Dickens never had time to form a philosophy or define a faith; and his later and greater books are saddened by the evil that is done under the sun; but at least he preserved his intellectual innocence sufficiently to escape the dismal pseudo-scientific fatalism that was descending on the world in his latter days, founded on the preposterous error as to causation in which the future is determined by the present, which has been determined by the past. The true causation, of course, is always the incessant irresistible activity of the evolutionary appetite.

[Writings on *Great Expectations* and George Bernard Shaw]*   Humphry House

[FROM *THE DICKENS WORLD*]

Dickens was attempting to define within the middle classes some such boundary as he had already accepted in the lower between the respectable and the low. In the last resort he shared Magwitch's belief that money and education can make a "gentleman," that birth and tradition count for little or nothing in the formation of style. The final wonder of *Great Expectations* is that in spite of all Pip's neglect of Joe and coldness

*Reprinted from *The Dickens World* (London: Oxford University Press, 2d ed., 1942) and "G. B. S. on *Great Expectations*," *Dickensian* 44 (Spring 1948): 63–70, by permission of Oxford University Press and Rachel Thurley.

towards Biddy and all the remorse and self-recrimination that they caused him, he is made to appear at the end of it all a really better person than he was at the beginning. It is a remarkable achievement to have kept the reader's sympathy throughout a snob's progress. The book is the clearest artistic triumph of the Victorian bourgeoisie on its own special ground. The expectations lose their greatness, and Pip is saved from the grosser dangers of wealth; but by the end he has gained a wider and deeper knowledge of life, he is less rough, better spoken, better read, better mannered; he has friends as various as Herbert Pocket, Jaggers, and Wemmick; he has earned in his business abroad enough to pay his debts, he has become third partner in a firm that "had a good name, and worked for its profits, and did very well." Who is to say that these are not advantages? Certainly not Dickens. But he shirks the implications of the reconciliation with Joe and Biddy: there is one emotional scene with friendliness all round, which shows that in spite of his new accent and new manners Pip is the same decent little fellow after all: but what if he had had no Herbert to fall back on, and had been forced to build his fortunes again from scratch in the old village with Gargerys and Wopsles? Dickens does not face this: he takes Pip's new class position as established, and whisks him off to the East, where gentlemen grow like mushrooms. Yet we do not feel that this is artistically wrong, as the final marriage to Estella is wrong:[1] for the book is the sincere, uncritical expression of a time when the whole class-drift was upwards and there was no reason to suppose that it would ever stop being so. The social ideals of Pip and Magwitch differ only in taste. Though Pip has shuddered at the convict for being coarse and low, he consoles him on his death-bed with the very thought that first fired and then kept alive his own love for Estella: "You had a child. . . . She is a lady and very beautiful."

Here is the story allegorized by Mr. Jackson, writing as a Marxist:

> Self-satisfied, mid-Victorian, British society buoyed itself up with as great "expectations" of future wealth and glory as did poor, deluded Pip. If it had but known, its means of ostentation came from a source (the labour of the depressed and exploited masses) to which it would have been as shocked to acknowledge indebtedness as Pip was to find he owed all his acquired gentility to the patronage of a transported felon. Magwitch differed little from the uncouth monster which respectable society envisaged to itself as the typical "labouring man." And in literal truth, good, respectable society owed as much to these working men, and was as little aware of it, as was Pip of the source of his advantages. And respectable society is as little grateful as Pip, whenever the truth is revealed.

This would be very plausible if only the rest of the class distinctions in the novel were what Mr. Jackson makes them out to be: "Such class-antagonism as there is in *Great Expectations* is not that between aristocrats (as such) and common people, but that between, on the one side, the 'gentlemen' (who are for one reason or another either crazily vengeful or callously cold-hearted and corrupt) and with them their sycophants and attendant slum-hooligans and on the other, the honest, working section of the population." Applied in detail this means Bentley Drummle, Compeyson, and Pumblechook on one side, with Joe, Biddy, Matthew and Herbert Pocket, Jaggers, and Wemmick all lumped together on the other. This is virtually to say that in the end class distinctions are identical with moral distinctions, without even being particularly nice about morals; it is to ignore all the facts of class difference that Dickens was so subtly analyzing. It is in things like Estella's early treatment of Pip, Pip's first weeks with Herbert, Jaggers's treatment of Estella's mother, and the behaviour of Trabb's boy, that these real differences are to be found.

Chesterton professed to find in Trabb's boy the last word upon the triumphant revolutionary sarcasm of the English democracy; you might almost as well find the ultimate English democrat in old Orlick, the soured "hand" turning to crime because of his inferior status, whom Mr. Jackson just leaves as a "blackguard"—a man who in another novel might well have been the leader of a no-Popery mob or of physical-force Chartists. The assault of Trabb's boy, which brings Pip's class-consciousness to a head, is more personal than political: Dickens doesn't mean that good clothes are worse than bad or that they are intrinsically funny and that the class that wears them is doomed to die of jeers. Trabb's boy was not among those who pointed at Stephen Spender (*Poems*, 1937, 22):

> I feared the salt coarse pointing of those boys
> Who copied my lisp behind me on the road.
>
> They were lithe, they sprang out behind hedges
> Like dogs to bark at our world. They threw mud
> And I looked another way, pretending to smile.
> I longed to forgive them, yet they never smiled.

As things were he was a good pin to prick Pip's conceit; but if he himself had come into a fortune, he would have been just as nasty about it as Pip in his own way; and his way might have been worse.

Great Expectations is the perfect expression of a phase of English society: it is a statement, to be taken as it stands, of what money can do, good and bad; of how it can change and make distinctions of class; how it can pervert virtue, sweeten manners, open up new fields of enjoyment and suspicion. The mood of the book belongs not to the imaginary date of its plot, but to the time in which it was written; for the unquestioned assumptions that Pip can be transformed by money and the minor graces it can buy, and that the loss of one fortune can be repaired on the strength of incidental gains in voice and friends, were only possible in a country secure in its internal economy, with expanding markets abroad: this could hardly be said of England in the 'twenties and 'thirties.

Pip's acquired "culture" was an entirely bourgeois thing: it came to little more than accent, table manners, and clothes. In these respects a country gentleman with an estate in a remoter part of England would probably have been, even at Queen Victoria's accession, more like the neighbouring farmers than like Mr. Dombey. The process of diffusing standard "educated," London and Home Counties, speech as the norm expected of a gentleman was by no means complete: its rapid continuance through the Dickens period was an essential part of the increasing social uniformity between the middle and upper classes, helped on by the development of the "public" schools.[2]

We are told that Pip "read" a great deal, and that he enjoyed it; but we do not know what he read, or how it affected his mind, or what kind of pleasures he got from it. He knew enough about Shakespeare and acting to realize that Mr. Wopsle turned Waldengarver was ridiculous; but what other delights he found in theatre-going in his prosperous days we are left to judge for ourselves; painting and music certainly had no large part in his life. People like Pip, Herbert Pocket, and Traddles have no culture but domestic comfort and moral decency. They are sensitive, lovable, and intelligent, but their normal activities are entirely limited to a profession and a fireside. When one of their kind extends his activities beyond this range it is in the direction of "social work," and even that is likely to be governed by his profession, as Allan Woodcourt is a good doctor, and Mr. Milvey a good parson. David Copperfield's other activity is to write novels like *Great Expectations* and *David Copperfield:* so we come full circle.

G. B. S. ON *GREAT EXPECTATIONS*

The publication for the first time in England of an essay by Mr. Shaw on Dickens is not an event to let slip with just a casual notice. His Introduction to *Great Expectations* was first printed in the U.S.A. in 1937, preceding an elaborate edition of the novel illustrated by Gordon Ross, published by the Limited Editions Club of New York; it is thus almost unknown in the United States and scarcely heard of here. It is not mentioned by William Miller in *The Dickens Student and Collector,* for which much of the work was done at Harvard: yet its sixteen pages are worth more than many groups of sixteen volumes that could be arranged from the portentous mass of Dickensiana listed by Mr. Miller. It has, of course, a clear, vigorous text with some punch in every sentence: and this lifts it at once above the drivelling and trivial verbosity that passes so often for criticism of Dickens; and I am told from two sources that the English text is the same as the American but for a few very small changes.

First, it is a delight to find Mr. Shaw expressing the opinion that *Great Expectations* is Dickens's "most compactly perfect book." He justifies this by stressing its freedom from "episodes of wild extravagance" and the fact that it is "all-of-one-piece and consistently truthful as none of the other books are": "the story is built round a single and simple catastrophe." Dickens knew and cared to know little about "The Art of the Novel." Readers and critics even in his later days were reaching with difficulty the admission of such an art; and Dickens would have been almost the last novelist to qualify as an artist. Nor would he have wanted to qualify. Mr. Shaw is excellent on "Dickens's position as a member of the educated and cultured classes who had neither education nor culture." "When Dickens," he says, "introduced in his stories a character whom he intensely disliked he chose an artistic profession for him. . . . There is real hatred in his treatment of them." Many of his comments on the visual arts were "those of a complete Philistine." All this is very well borne out by the careers of the two Dickens heroes who are closest to Dickens—David and Pip. David actually ends as a novelist, and we have no description whatever of the kind of novels he wrote or the problems he tackled in writing them; we are left to assume that he took them in his stride, as Dickens took his. Pip the blacksmith's apprentice becomes a "gentleman," and "reading" is often mentioned as one of his great accomplishments in gentility; but nothing is revealed about what he read or his taste, or what good he thought he got out of it. Music and painting have no part in his life. He acquired a liking for the theatre (again, one assumes, like Dickens); but the only detailed account of his theatre-going is that of the visit to see Mr. Wopsle as Hamlet; and at the end the reader is left with more awareness of the problems of the dresser in fitting the heroic actor's stockings than of the tragic dilemmas of the hero.

"The cultural side of art," says Mr. Shaw with complete justice, "was as little known to Dickens as it is possible for a thing so public to remain to a man so apprehensive"; yet *Great Expectations*, for all the failure of its ending, is a great work of art, fine in form and style; it is quite unique among Dickens's books: it is, paradoxically, the artistic expression of that otherwise artless and cultureless society which it describes and exposes. It has a unity of tone and purpose, a reality and seriousness found in none other of the novels.

Mr. Shaw says that in *Great Expectations* Dickens "let himself go." The critical importance of these words varies with the emphasis: they are more important if the emphasis is on "himself" than if it is on "go." For in countless other parts of his work he "let go" his other self, the impersonator, the actor who grimaced and spoke the words of his characters aloud as he wrote about them, forgetting all the details of ordinary life. His great grotesques are all "lettings-go" in this sense. And his great criminal, distorted, evil characters are "lettings-go" of a secret inner strain of his. But in *Great Expectations* it was his more open, social autobiographical self he let go; it is the pendant to the first part of *David Copperfield*, the more mature revision of the progress of a young man in the world.

2

It is, of course, a snob's progress; and the novel's greatest achievement is to make it sympathetic. When Pip plays Beggar-my-Neighbour and, later on, sophisticated French games of cards with Estella; when he has just heard of his fortune, and the cattle on the marshes seem "in their dull manner, to wear a more respectful air now"; when he first dines with Herbert Pocket; when he visits the town in the Havisham-Pocket context without calling on Joe at the forge, and then, on getting back to London, sends him some fish and a barrel of oysters to salve his conscience; above all, when Magwitch comes to his rooms in the Temple—on these and countless other such occasions Dickens is touching the very quick of that delicate, insinuating, pervasive class-consciousness which achieved in England a subtle variegation and force to which other countries, with fewer gradations between the feudal and the "low," have scarcely aspired. Many of our novels have played on class themes, but none with such lingering, succulent tenderness. Mr. Shaw says that "as our social conscience expands and makes the intense class snobbery of the nineteenth century seem less natural to us, the tragedy of *Great Expectations* will lose some of its appeal." It may need a little more effort to understand—and the novel is indeed already a historical document of the first importance; but its permanent appeal derives from its adaptation of an age-old theme to a particular complex modern society.

Many critics have seen in it an allegory or at least a symbolism. The disappointment of Pip's expectations, following upon the discovery of their source, is taken to be an expression of disgust at the groundless optimism and "progressive" hope of mid-Victorian society. What Mr. Shaw calls the bitterness of Dickens's "exposure of the futility of Pip's parasitism" is often taken to be a bitterness in the knowledge that all the material wealth and boasted progress of that age were parasitic on the drudgery of an exploited working-class, a hideous underworld of labour. Mr. Shaw does not push his social interpretation quite so far. But he does take the novel to be a "tragedy," and he says: "Its beginning is unhappy; its middle is unhappy; and the conventional happy ending is an outrage on it." "Pip's world is a very melancholy place, and his conduct, good or bad, always helpless." And he says of all Dickens's later work: "When he lost his belief in bourgeois society and with it his lightness of heart he had neither an economic Utopia nor a credible religion to hitch on to. His world becomes a world of great expectations cruelly disappointed."

All this is very important. It is plain that in the later novels—*Little Dorrit, Great Expectations* and *Our Mutual Friend* above all—Dickens's attitude to money and to the power of money in life has undergone a drastic revision, and that this reflects the development of capitalism in mid-century: the joint-stock company and investment have taken the place of the old-fashioned honest "counting-house" businessmen of the

Fezziwig-Cherryble-Garland type, who plainly worked for their living and often lived over the office. The new power of money is vaster, anonymous and secret; and those who make the big fortunes do not work for them, but juggle with paper. Merdle, Veneering and Lammle are the new businessmen. The clearest expression of Dickens's opinion about the effect of this upon society is in the rhythmical satiric exhortation to "Have Shares" and be mighty, in *Our Mutual Friend.* The plots of all these three novels turn on Big Money; and in each a main point is that the money bears no intelligible relation to the amount and quality of the work put into earning it. Pip's is an extreme case: he doesn't even know where the money comes from. When he learns he is appalled: his fortune turns to dust and ashes.

3

But is the melancholy contemplation of dust and ashes the final scene and mood of the novel? Is utter despair and unrelieved disgust at the whole scheme of society into which he has "risen" Pip's final state? Even leaving out the botched-up ending with Estella, it is not; and it is clear from trains of action laid earlier in the story that Dickens never meant it to be. Pip is not utterly corrupted and brought low either in feeling or in fortune. He does two actions which bring benefit to his middle-class friends; both concern money. He secretly arranges the funds to set up Herbert in a partnership, and he praises Matthew Pocket to Miss Havisham, so that she leaves him "a cool four thousand." Furthermore, it is his provision for Herbert which saves his own fortune after the Magwitch bubble bursts. Dickens must have planned this reward for good-heartedness early on; it was not part of the tacked-on happy ending. Pip is enabled to keep his acquired class character; he goes off to the East as a member of a firm of which he says: "We were not in a grand way of business, but we had a good name, and worked for our profits and did very well." Are we to conclude, as the tragic interpreters conclude, that this part of the ending, though not tacked on, was yet planned as a concession by Dickens to his readers, because he had set himself, as Mr. Shaw insists, to earn enough to bring up a large family in high style (?) because he could not financially afford to leave Pip to what in his inner heart he believed to be his proper fate? I don't believe it. If that was the motive, why be so explicit? When Dickens wrote so clearly that Pip's firm worked for their profits, he went out of his way to restate what he still believed to be the proper basis of the wealth of a "respectable" middle class. Even in the later fifties and the sixties he was still clinging, though rather desperately, to his ideal of the businessman in the small private firm. His hatred for the gross and illegitimate wealth of such as Merdle did not extend to all middle-class standards and values.

It is important to the understanding of the novel that Pip has aspirations before he has expectations; these are developed in the scene with Biddy in Ch. 17.

> "Biddy," said I, after binding her to secrecy, "I want to be a gentleman."
>
> "Oh, I wouldn't, if I was you!" she returned. "I don't think it would answer."
>
> "Biddy," said I with some severity, "I have particular reasons for wanting to be a gentleman."

The particular reasons are, of course, to do with his passion for Estella: and when his fortune comes the wretched Pip sees his expectations through Estella-coloured glasses; he thinks of his fortune as a means of realizing the longing hopes and day-dreams which concentrate on her. The emotional tension of the book up to the time of Magwitch's return derives from this sexual situation, not from the money situation alone: in fact Pip takes his money very calmly for granted; he doesn't take Estella calmly at all. Mr. Shaw says that she "is a curious addition to the gallery of unamiable women painted by Dickens," and that the notion "that anyone could ever have been happy with Estella is positively unpleasant." He suggests that the portrait of her is an elaborate and recent study from life: the clue to understanding her is that "Estella is a born tormentor." This is not quite the whole story; for the interest of Estella as an individual is to see the impact of Miss Havisham's reiterated bitter teaching on a ditch-born orphan. Dickens was rarely quite clear in his expressions of the relation between heredity and environment, though the themes preoccupied him. Oliver Twist is one notable anomaly; Estella is another, rather more complex. He hints rather than states that with her parentage you could hardly expect the girl to turn out otherwise. But the explicit emphasis is all on Miss Havisham's upbringing: "with my praises, and with my jewels, and with my teachings, and with this figure of myself always before her, a warning to back and point my lessons, I stole her heart away and put ice in its place." She has been trained to be a tormentor and has learned the lesson gladly.

4

The critique of snobbery is so full, so convincing and so sympathetic because Dickens has woven the snobbery so skillfully and even unobtrusively with the sexual passion. Estella does not appear often in the book, but she is always there in the back of Pip's mind. The collapse of Pip's expectations about Estella should have been every bit as much the matter of the title as the collapse of his expectations about money. His snobbery had its root in his desire; and all the irony of the book turns on the fact that both the money and the girl derive from Magwitch; this is very bitter indeed. There is a significance in it far beyond the particular case, a far deeper and more universal significance, I think, than in any supposed political allegory. The sexual element in snobbery is one which social critics and historians have not always emphasized enough. The daydreams of a genteel life include daydreams of a woman who is a "lady," a creature of great beauty, brilliance, delicacy, fineness, able in idleness to keep her beauty fresh, to be unsullied by work either in the house or as an earner; the desire to possess, maintain and cherish such a creature, with all the fascinating attributes of a mistress that a fervid adolescent imagination can invent, is one of the impulses that make men want to "better themselves." Pip's dreams of Estella are sharpened by the other women in the book. His sister, Joe's first wife, is the soured working-class woman, old before her time, always in her apron, always self-pitying about her chores, always scolding, a woman in whom all the fascinations of femininity either never flowered or withered soon. Contrasted with her is the fatuous, pure "lady," Mrs. Pocket, who spends all her time reading the *Peerage*, helpless to look after even herself, letting her husband, household and children fecklessly slide: she too is a complainer. At one end of the scale is Mrs. Joe, the extreme from which Pip hopes to "rise"; at the other is Mrs. Pocket, the *reductio ad absurdum* of being "up in the world." Between them is Biddy, who is of the world of Agnes, though her class is different. Wise, generous, loving, attractive, mild but strong—she is the good, living woman who waits in reserve in many Dickens books; but they never have very much personality, and that's the trouble. Pip knows Biddy's worth all right, but, with his big ideas, he can't take her quite seriously; he slights her when he merely tries to be nice. Estella has all the vigour and obvious vividness and glamour—something to aspire to— that Biddy lacks. Biddy is something to accept; Estella is something to build on. And building is Pip's special weakness. A distinguished French critic has here recently touched the spot: Ce qui caractérise le parvenu, c'est qu'il espére trop, c'est qu'il a de la chance dans ses espérances, et c'est ainsi qu'il aime. Il sait bien qu'il n'est pas aimé; mais il garde son espérance et revient avec un courage obstiné.

5

The special unity of the book, which Mr. Shaw and all its admirers particularly stress, is brought out by the ingenuity of plot through which both the amorous and social expectations are ultimately seen to derive from the same source. When Pip has made that discovery he reveals to Magwitch on his deathbed a secret of his own heart. It was partly Estella's being a "lady" that had fed his passion for her from boyhood, when he believed she was the real article by birth. The aim of all Magwitch's transport life had been to make Pip a "gentleman." At the deathbed, for all the horror that he feels for Magwitch, Pip reveals to him the story of Estella:

"Dear Magwitch, I must tell you, now at last. You understand what
I say?"

A gentle pressure on my hand.

"You had a child once, whom you loved and lost."

A stronger pressure on my hand.

"She lived and found powerful friends. She is living now. She is a
lady and very beautiful. And I love her!"

Having just heard and understood, Magwitch then immediately dies. In
that scene everything has come full circle; every word of it tells. It had
been his own coarseness as a blacksmith's apprentice that had made
Estella seem so remotely far above him, and he had been ashamed; it had
been Magwitch who gave him the means to lose the coarseness and almost overcome the shame; he had scarcely assimilated the knowledge
that this was the low and terrifying convict's doing than he discovered
that this man was indeed the father of the very girl whom in her beauty
and ladyhood had seemed so wildly and desperately remote. That deathbed scene is the confession from Pip that ultimately he and Magwitch had
been actuated by the same sort of motive. Mr. Shaw does not quite give
full weight to this scene: "But Pip, he says,—I am afraid Pip must be to
this extent identified with Dickens—could not see Magwitch as an animal of the same species as himself or Miss Havisham. His feeling is true to
the nature of snobbery; but his creator says no word in criticism of that
ephemeral limitation." Surely this last scene is criticism enough without
any labouring of the point. "Dear Magwitch . . . . ." says Pip; at the moment of death he can use the word of love, can recognize the kinship, can
even admit community of ultimate thought. This is indeed too terribly
true to the nature of snobbery; Pip could never have maintained such a
mood with Magwitch alive, and if he had thought he would recover he
would never have told him about Estella. It was a sort of viaticum. And
surely Dickens knew what he was doing.

Mr. Shaw rather complains that Dickens "never raises the question
why Pip should refuse Magwitch's endowment and shrink from him with
such inhuman loathing. . . . Inspired by an altogether noble fixed idea, he
had lifted himself out of his rut of crime and honestly made a fortune for
the child who had fed him when he was starving. If Pip had no objection
to be a parasite instead of an honest blacksmith, at least he had a better
claim to be a parasite on Magwitch's earnings than, as he imagined, on
Miss Havisham's property. It is curious that this should not have occurred
to Dickens. . . ." The novel is not an essay in ethics; this may have occurred
to Dickens, but the important point is that it did not occur to Pip; and that
is in general keeping with the truth to life which Mr. Shaw praises. The
horror of Magwitch which Pip had as a child in the churchyard and during
the fight with Compeyson in the ditch on the marshes would have stayed
with him for life; he had indelible memories of terror linked to Magwitch;
the beginning of the book is so fine, so well in keeping with all that fol-

lows, because it gives the full weight and proportion to those childish fears; and those very fears are caught up again into the mood of apparently crude snobbery in the Temple. This is one of Dickens's greatest novels just because the moral problems are not seen too simply. Pip is not a young philosopher acting and feeling on argued moral principle. The childish fears hitched on to social snobbery by a complex, unconscious process in which the sexual love for Estella had the strongest play. It is just because Pip could not have rationally defended his loathing of the Warmint that it is so strong and awful. And indeed it does seem to be going a little far to say that Magwitch's fixed idea is "altogether noble"; for he was not concerned so much about Pip's true well-being as about his own capacity to make a "gentleman" of him; Pip was to be Magwitch's means of self-expression, just as Estella was to be Miss Havisham's; they each wanted to use a child to redress the balance of a world gone wrong, to do vicariously what they had failed to do direct. In the Temple Magwitch is not really concerned much about the grateful return for Pip's help on the marshes; he is concerned to view, assess, appraise the "dear boy" as his own creation. For Magwitch is a snob too. It is curious that this should not have occurred to Mr. Shaw. A main theme of the book, running in two parallel strands of the plot, is that the attempt through money and power to exploit a child will lead to ingratitude and even more bitterness. Pip's presence both at the death of Magwitch and at the awful scene of Miss Havisham's repentance is meant to show him as the channel through which they purge themselves of their errors too.

Thus, emotionally as well as socially and financially, Pip appears as "helpless." He directs nothing; things happen to him; everybody except Joe and Biddy uses him for purposes of their own. They let him go his own way and help him out of scrapes. But there is never any question of his return to the village for good, with an effective, working reconciliation with them. His new class character—amounting to very little more than voice and table manners and range of friends—is firmly established and he is left to continue in it. Dickens was not going to say that all his gains were negligible. Of the two children used for experiment Estella suffers in the long run worse than Pip; she is not of the receptive kind.

Dickens did not himself anywhere, I think, call the book a "tragedy"; but he did say from the very beginning when he was planning it that a "grotesque tragi-comic conception" first encouraged him. And in view of later criticism it is almost harsh to find him saying of Joe and Pip: "I have put a child and a good-natured foolish man, in relations that seem to me very funny." And Pumblechook is there all along to prick Pip's tragic element; it is as if Polonius were allowed all through to gloss Hamlet's soliloquies; but it is significant that not even Pumblechook twits Pip about Estella. The fact is that all Dickens's stories published in parts or in serial—and *Great Expectations* was a serial in *All the Year Round*—grew in the writing beyond their first conception. But the growth of this novel never became rank; it never got out of hand. Though Pumblechook and Wopsle are grotesque characters, and belong to the histrionic method of "letting-go," they never get out of hand and spoil the proportion of things. A great feature of the book is the way in which minor characters, like Orlick and Wemmick, grow as it proceeds; each of them has, in his own way, a dream, and each is a comment on Pip. Wemmick's castle is not a castle in the air, but a castle at Walworth with a deaf old man inside. The acknowledgment of the lasting difference between Walworth and Little Britain is just the acknowledgment that in his life Pip could not yet make. Orlick's mad resentment against Mrs. Gargery is a release of what Pip bottled up.

6

The book is every bit as rich as any other Dickens novel; but not with a squandered and disordered richness. The grotesques are under control and all fit directly into the external narrative and also into the main psychological theme. This applies even to Miss Havisham. She is not in the ordinary realistic sense of the word an utterly impossible person. It has to be remembered too that in this, as in most of Dickens's novels, the imaginary date of the action is considerably earlier than the date of writing. I have not worked out an exact internal chronology from the hints given up and down *Great Expectations*—and indeed it might not be possible to do so; but it is clear at any rate from the mere span of Pip's life that the beginning of the book cannot have been later than the 1830's. In other words Miss Havisham belongs to an age in which great eccentrics were a more normal part of the English social scene; the greater uniformity of manners, the muting and levelling of style, the suppression of feeling by what was called taste had not yet clouded our life. But though these things had not made Miss Havisham "impossible," they have coloured Dickens's treatment of her, writing as he was in the early sixties. She is a private, secret grotesque, unknown to the world: she does not storm outrageously through the action of the book like a Mrs. Gamp or a Quilp. As usual, various suggestions have been made about "originals" for Miss Havisham and for items in her life. Some such old recluse was burned to death in her house near Hyde Park; a wedding-breakfast room, with cake and all, had been sealed up in the tavern called "Dirty Dick's" in Bishopsgate Street Without. On 29th January, 1850, an inquest was held on Martha Joachim, who had died at the age of 62 at York Buildings, Marylebone: "In 1825 a suitor of the deceased, whom her mother rejected, shot himself while sitting on the sofa with her, and she was covered with his brains. From that instant she lost her reason. Since her mother's death, eighteen years ago, she had led the life of a recluse, dressed in white, and never going out. A char-woman occasionally brought her what supplied her wants. Her only companions were the bull-dog, which she nursed like a child, and two cats." This report Dickens certainly read, as it is taken from *The Household Narrative* (1850, p. 10) of which he was the editor. It seems clear that Miss Havisham is another example of Dickens's regular habit of fusing together items from a number of different sources, remembered over a considerable time. In the details of the spiders and so on he let his imagination run, just as he did over such things as the workhouse diet at the beginning of *Oliver Twist*. But Miss Havisham's peculiar greatness is that she is built so convincingly into the main structure of the book, linked to Compeyson, Magwitch, Pip, Jaggers and the Pockets with such a clever combination of converging possibilities that she presides over the plot like a convincing Fate. "In *Great Expectations*," writes Mr. Shaw; "we have Wopsle and Trabb's boy; but they have their part and purpose in the story and do not overstep the immodesty of nature. It is hardly decent to compare Mr. F.'s aunt with Miss Havisham; but as contrasted studies of madwomen they make you shudder at the thought of what Dickens might have made of Miss Havisham if he had seen her as a comic personage. For life is no laughing matter in *Great Expectations*. . . ."

Notes

1. The ending was altered to suit Bulwer Lytton, but only "from and after Pip's return to Joe's, and finding his little likeness there." Pip's success abroad was thus in the original scheme (Forster, *Life of Charles Dickens*, Bk. 9, Chapter 3.)

2. It is interesting that there is no description of such a school anywhere in Dickens, though he described so many different kinds of private school, and sent his own sons to Eton. The extension of the term "public school" to an increasing number of boarding schools was a process of the 'forties. (See, for instance, McCulloch's *Account of the British Empire*, 3rd. ed., 1847, Vol. 2, p. 329.) It was, of course, the most influential expression of the "gentleman" idea.

The Poor Labyrinth:
The Theme of Social Injustice in Dickens's
*Great Expectations**   John H. Hagan, Jr.

On the surface *Great Expectations* is simply another very good example of that perennial *genre*, the education novel. In particular, it is the story of a restless young boy from the lower classes who comes into possession of a fortune he has done nothing to earn, founds a host of romantic aspirations upon it at the cost of becoming a snob, comes to be disap-

*Reprinted from *Nineteenth-Century Fiction* 9 (November 1954): 169–78, by permission.
© 1954 by the Regents of the University of California.

pointed both romantically and socially, and, finally, with a more mature knowledge of himself and the world, works out his regeneration. As such, the novel is what G. K. Chesterton once called it, "an extra chapter to *The Book of Snobs.*" But while admitting that Pip is a fairly good specimen of a certain type of mentality so dear to Dickens's satirical spirit, we cannot overlook the fact that Dickens is using his character to reveal some still more complex truths about society and its organization.

Though its shorter length and more compact organization have prevented it from being classed with *Bleak House, Little Dorrit,* and *Our Mutual Friend, Great Expectations* is really of a piece with that great social "trilogy" of Dickens's later years. In the briefer novel Dickens is attempting only a slightly less comprehensive anatomization of social evil; thematically, the implications of Pip's story are almost as large. Consider, for instance, how many different strata of society are gotten into the comparatively small number of pages that story takes up. In the first six chapters alone we meet members of the criminal, the military, and the artisan classes, together with a parish clerk and two well-to-do entrepreneurs. The principal difference between *Great Expectations* and the more massive panoramic novels lies more in the artistic means employed than in the intellectual content. In *Great Expectations* Dickens strips the larger novels to their intellectual essentials. The point of one line of action in *Bleak House,* we remember, was to show how Lady Dedlock had been victimized by social injustice operating in the form of conventional morality and its hypocrisies. But into that novel Dickens also packed a great deal else; the Lady Dedlock action was but part of a gigantic network. In *Great Expectations* all such additional ramifications are discarded. Dickens concentrates with great intensity upon a single line of development, and, to our surprise, this line turns out to be remarkably similar in its theme to that of Lady Dedlock's story. For Pip's career shows not only a hapless young man duped by his poor illusions, but a late victim in a long chain of widespread social injustice.

The story's essential features make this fact plain. We learn in chapter 42 that the prime mover, so to speak, of the entire course of events which the novel treats immediately or in retrospect is a man by the name of Compeyson, a cad who adopts the airs of a "gentleman." Significantly, he remains throughout the book shrouded in mist (literal and figurative), vague, remote, and terrifying, like some vast impersonal force. Through his actions two people once came to grief. First, after stripping her of a great deal of her fortune, he jilted the spoiled and naïve Miss Havisham, and thereby turned her wits against the whole male sex. Secondly, he further corrupted a man named Magwitch who had already been injured by poverty, and revealed to him how easily the law may be twisted into an instrument of class. The trial of Magwitch and Compeyson is so important a key to the novel's larger meanings that the former's description of it in the later pages of the book should be read in entirety. What the passage reveals is that impartiality in the courts is often a myth. Judges and jury alike may be swayed by class prejudice. The whole judicial system may tend to perpetuate class antagonism and hostility. In short, an important element at the root of Magwitch's career is great social evil: the evil of poverty, and the evil of a corruptible judicial system. Though not entirely so, Magwitch is certainly, in part, a victim. The conventional words Pip speaks over his corpse at the end—"O Lord, be merciful to him a sinner"—remain merely conventional, for the man was more sinned against than sinning. From his very first appearance in the novel, when we see him shivering on the icy marshes, he is depicted with sympathy, and by the time we get to the end, he has risen to an almost heroic dignity.

The connection of all this with Pip is plain. The young boy becomes for both Magwitch and Miss Havisham a means by which, in their different ways, they can retaliate against the society that injured them. One of Miss Havisham's objects is, through Pip, to frustrate her greedy relatives who, like Compeyson himself, are interested in her for her money alone, and who, again like Compeyson, typify the rapacious and predatory elements of society at large. Magwitch, on the other hand, retaliates against society by striving to meet it on the ground of its own special prejudices. Though deprived from childhood of the opportunity to become a "gentleman" himself, he does not vow destruction to the "gentleman" class. Having seen in Compeyson the power of that class, the deference it receives from society, he fashions a gentleman of his own to take his place in it. He is satisfied to live vicariously through Pip, to show society that he can come up to its standards, and, by raising his pawn into the inner circle, to prove that it is no longer impregnable.

Thus Pip, in becoming the focal point for Miss Havisham's and Magwitch's retaliation—the one who is caught in the midst of the cross fire directed against society by two of the parties it injured, who, in turn, display in their desire for proprietorship some of the very tyranny and selfishness against which they are rebelling—becomes society's scapegoat. It is he who must pay the price for original outrages against justice, who must suffer for the wider injustices of the whole society of which he is but a humble part. The result is that he too takes on society's vices, its selfishness, ingratitude, extravagance, and pride. He, too, becomes something of an impostor like Compeyson himself, and thereby follows in the fatal footsteps of the very man who is indirectly the cause of his future misery. Thus the worst qualities of society seem inevitably to propagate themselves in a kind of vicious circle. Paralleling the case of Pip is that of Estella. As Pip is the creation of Magwitch, she is the creation of Miss Havisham. Her perversion has started earlier; as the novel opens, it is Pip's turn next. He is to be the latest heir of original injustice, the next to fall victim to the distortions that have already been forced upon Magwitch, Miss Havisham, and Estella. He is to be the latest product of Compeyson's evil as it continues to infect life.

But injustice does not come to bear upon Pip through Magwitch and Miss Havisham alone. There is injustice under the roof of his own house. Throughout the first stage of Pip's career, Dickens presents dramatically in scene after scene the petty tyranny exercised over the boy by his shrewish sister, Mrs. Gargery, and some of her friends, particularly Mr. Pumblechook, the blustering corn merchant, and Wopsle, the theatrically-minded parish clerk. It is the constant goading Pip receives from these people that makes him peculiarly susceptible to the lure of his "great expectations" with their promise of escape and freedom. But more important is the fact that it is Pumblechook and Mrs. Gargery who first put the treacherous idea into Pip's head that Miss Havisham is his secret patroness. One of the very reasons they insist upon his waiting on the old woman in the first place is their belief that she will liberally reward him, and thereafter they never let the idea out of the boy's mind. In short, Mrs. Gargery, Pumblechook, and Wopsle do as much as Magwitch and Miss Havisham to turn Pip into his erring ways. To be sure, the novel is not an essay in determinism. But despite the legitimacy of the reproaches of Pip's conscience, we cannot forget how early his impressionable mind was stamped with the images of greed and injustice—images that present a small-scale version of the greedy and unjust world of "respectability" as a whole. The tyranny exercised over Pip by his sister, Pumblechook, and their like is a type of the tyranny exercised by the conventionally "superior" elements of society over the suffering and dispossessed. Theirs is a version in miniature of the society that tolerates the existence of the dunghills in which Magwitch and his kind are spawned, and then throws such men into chains when they violate the law. When Pumblechook boasts of himself as the instrument of Pip's wealth, he is truthful in a way he never suspects or would care to suspect. For the obsequious attitude toward money he exemplifies is, indirectly, at the root of Pip's new fortune. It was just such an attitude that resulted in the debasing of Magwitch below Compeyson at their trial, and thus resulted in the former's fatal determination to transform Pip into a "gentleman."

Injustice is thus at the heart of the matter—injustice working upon and through the elders of Pip and Estella, and continuing its reign in the children themselves. With these children, therefore, we have a theme analogous to one deeply pondered by another great Victorian novelist: the idea of "consequences" as developed by George Eliot. Both she and Dickens are moved by a terrifying vision of the wide extent to which pollution can penetrate the different, apparently separate and unrelated, members of society. Once an act of injustice has been committed, there is no predicting to what extent it will affect the lives of generations yet unborn and of people far removed in the social scale from the victims of the original oppression. Though on a smaller scale, Dickens succeeds no less in *Great Expectations* than in his larger panoramic novels in suggesting a comprehensive social situation. No less than in *Bleak House, Little Dorrit,* and *Our Mutual Friend*— and in *A Tale of Two Cities* as well—the different levels of society are brought together in a web of sin, injustice, crime, and destruction. The scheme bears an analogy to the hereditary diseases running throughout several generations in Zola's *Les Rougons-Macquarts* series. Dickens compresses his material more than Zola by starting *in medias res*, and showing Pip as the focal point for the past, present, and future at once. In him are concentrated the effects of previous injustice, and he holds in himself the injustice yet to come. The interest of the novel is never restricted merely to the present. Dickens opens a great vista, a "poor labyrinth," through which we may see the present as but the culmination of a long history of social evil. Society is never able to smother wholly the facts of its injustice. As Dickens shows in novel after novel, somehow these facts will come to light again: Bounderby's mother in *Hard Times* rises to reveal her son's hypocrisy to the crowd he has bullied for so many years; the facts of Mrs. Clennam's relationship to the Dorrit family, and of society's injury to Lady Dedlock, her lover, and her child, are all unearthed in the end. Immediate victims may be skillfully suppressed, as Magwitch, returning from exile, is finally caught and imprisoned again. But the baleful effects of social evil go on in a kind of incalculable chain reaction. It is the old theme of tragic drama read into the bleak world of Mid-Victorian England: the sins of the fathers will be visited upon the heads of their children; the curse on the house will have to be expiated by future generations of sufferers.

Thus it is fair to say that Pip's story is more than a study of personal development. In his lonely struggle to work out his salvation, he is atoning for the guilt of society at large. In learning to rise above selfishness, to attain to a selfless love for Magwitch, he brings to an end the chain of evil that was first forged by the selfish Compeyson. His regeneration has something of the same force as Krook's "spontaneous combustion" in *Bleak House*, or the collapse of the Clennam mansion in *Little Dorrit*, or even the renunciation of his family heritage by Charles Darnay in *A Tale of Two Cities*. Just as Darnay must atone for the guilt of his family by renouncing his property, so Pip must atone for the evils of the society that has corrupted him by relinquishing his unearned wealth. And as Darnay marries the girl whose father was one of the victims of his family's oppression, so Pip desires to marry the girl whose father, Magwitch, is the victim of the very society whose values Pip himself has embraced.

In giving his theme imaginative embodiment Dickens used what are perhaps some of the most ingenious and successful devices of his entire career. With disarming suddenness, for example, *Great Expectations* opens with the presentation of a physical phenomenon almost as memorable as that of the fog in *Bleak House:* the marshes. More than a Gothic detail casually introduced to give the story an eerie beginning, the marshes reappear again and again, not only in the first six chapters, where indeed they figure most prominently, but throughout the book.

They haunt the novel from start to finish, becoming finally one of its great informing symbols. The variety of ways in which Dickens manages unobtrusively to weave them, almost like a musical motif, into the texture of his tale is remarkable. At one time they may flicker briefly across the foreground of one of Pip's casual reveries; at another they may provide the material of a simile; or Pip may return to them in fact when he is summoned there late in the story by Orlick; or, again, he may see them from a distance when he is helping Magwitch make his getaway down the Thames. "It was like my own marsh country," Pip says of the landscape along the part of the river he and Magwitch traverse: ". . . some ballast-lighters, shaped like a child's first rude imitation of a boat, lay low in the mud; and a little squat shoal-lighthouse on open piles, stood crippled in the mud on stilts and crutches; and slimy stakes stuck out of the mud, and slimy stones stuck out of the mud, and red landmarks and tidemarks stuck out of the mud, and an old landing-stage and an old roofless building slipped into the mud, and all about us was stagnation and mud.

Mud is a peculiarly appropriate symbol for the class of society that Magwitch represents—the downtrodden and oppressed of life, all those victims of injustice whom society has tried to submerge. It is a natural image of the social dunghill in which violence and rebellion are fomented, the breeding place of death. Likewise, it is the condition of death itself upon which certain forms of life must feed. It is no accident on Dickens's part that when Pip and his companions stop at a public house on their journey down the river, they meet a "slimy and smeary" dock attendant whose clothes have all been taken from the bodies of drowned men. In fact, the motif of life thriving upon death is underlined more than once throughout the novel in a number of small but brilliant ways. On his first trip to Newgate, Pip meets a man wearing "mildewed clothes, which had evidently not belonged to him originally, and which, I took it into my head, he had bought cheap of the executioner." Trabb, the haberdasher and funeral director of Pip's village, is still another kind of scavenger. He, too, like the many undertakers in Dickens's other novels and Mrs. Gamp in *Martin Chuzzlewit*, profits hideously by the misfortunes of others. It is this condition that Dickens sums up most effectively in the repulsive image of mud.

But together with the marshes, he uses still another symbol to keep the idea of social injustice and its consequences before us. Chapter 1 opens with a description of the graveyard in which Pip's parents and several infant brothers are buried. Though less prominent as an image than the marshes, that of the grave presents much more explicitly the idea of the death-in-life state to which Magwitch and others in his predicament are condemned. We remember that it is from among the tombstones that Magwitch first leaps forth into the story; and when, at the end of the chapter, he is going away, Pip has been so impressed by his likeness to a risen corpse that he imagines the occupants of the graveyard reaching forth to reclaim him. This is not a merely facetious or lurid detail. The grave imagery suggests in a highly imaginative way the novel's basic situation. Magwitch, in relation to the "respectable" orders of society, is dead; immured in the Hulks or transported to the fringes of civilization, he is temporarily removed from active life. But when in the opening scene of the book he rises from behind the tombstone, he is figuratively coming back to life again, and we are witnessing the recurrence of an idea Dickens made a central motif of *A Tale of Two Cities,* the idea of resurrection and revolution. When Magwitch looms up from the darkened stairwell of Pip's London lodging house at the end of the second stage of the boy's career, we are witnessing, as in the case of Dr. Manette's being "recalled to life" from the Bastille, an event of revolutionary implications. For what this means is that one whom society has tried to repress, to shut out of life, has refused to submit to the edict. He has come back to take his place once more in the affairs of men, and to influence them openly in a decisive way. The injuries society perpetrates on certain of its members will be thrust back upon it. Society, like an individual, cannot escape the consequences of its injustice; an evil or an injury once done continues to infect and poison life, to pollute the society responsible for it.

This is suggested by the very way in which the material of the novel is laid out. Within the first six chapters, Dickens regularly alternates outdoor and indoor scenes, each one of which is coincident with a chapter division. There is a steady movement back and forth between the shelter and warmth of the Gargery's house and the cold misery and danger of the marshes. Thus, while getting his plot under way, Dickens is at the same time vividly impressing upon us his fundamental idea of two worlds: the world of "respectability" and the world of ignominy; of oppressors and of oppressed; of the living and of the dead. In the first six chapters these worlds are separate; it is necessary to come in or to go out in order to get from either one to the other. But in his excursions from the house to the marshes and back again, Pip is already forging the link that is to bring them together at the end of the second stage of his adventures when Magwitch, refusing to be left out in the cold any longer, actually becomes an inhabitant of Pip's private rooms. The clearest hint of this coming revolution is given when the soldiers burst from the marshes into Joe's house, and disrupt the solemn Christmas dinner. The breaking in upon it of the forces of another world shows on what a sandy foundation the complacency of Pumblechook and his kind is based. Beneath the self-assured crust of society, the elements of discontent and rebellion are continually seething, continually threatening to erupt. Thus the alternation between worlds that gives the novel's first six chapters their order supplies the reader at once with the basic moral of the book as a whole: the victims of injustice cannot be shut out of life forever; sooner or later they will come into violent contact with their oppressors.

Moving from the early pages of the book to the larger pattern, we discover that alternation between two different locales is basic to the whole. Pip tries to make his home in London, but he is forced a number of times to return to the site of his former life, and each return brings him a new insight into the truth of his position, one progressively more severe than another. The alternation between London and the old village becomes for Dickens a means of suggesting what the alternation between outdoor and indoor scenes in the first six chapters suggested: pretend as one will, reality will eventually shatter the veil of self-deception. Like the individual who has come to sacrifice his integrity for society's false values only to find it impossible to deny indefinitely his origins and the reality upon which his condition rests, society cannot effectively stifle all the victims of its injustice and oppression. There will always be men like Jaggers—men to connect the dead with the living, to act as the link between the underground man and the rest of society. As a defender of criminals, Jaggers is the great flaw in society's repression of its victims; he is their hope of salvation and resurrection. Like Tulkinghorn, the attorney in *Bleak House*, he knows everybody's secrets; he is the man to whom the lines between the high and the low, the men of property and the dispossessed, are no barrier. A wise and disillusioned Olympian, Jaggers comments like a tragic chorus on the two great worlds that are the product and expression of social injustice, for the existence of which Pip and others must suffer the terrible consequences.

Expectations Well Lost:
Dickens's Fable for His Time*   G. Robert Stange

Great Expectations is a peculiarly satisfying and impressive novel. It is unusual to find in Dickens's work so rigorous a control of detail, so simple and organic a pattern. In this very late novel the usual features of his art—proliferating sub-plots, legions of minor grotesques—are almost entirely absent. The simplicity is that of an art form that belongs to an ancient type and concentrates on permanently significant issues. *Great Expectations* is conceived as a moral fable; it is the story of a young man's development from the moment of his first self-awareness, to that of his mature acceptance of the human condition.

So natural a theme imposes an elemental form on the novel: the overall pattern is defined by the process of growth, and Dickens employs many of the motifs of folklore. The story of Pip falls into three phases which clearly display a dialectic progression. We see the boy first in his natural condition in the country, responding and acting instinctively and

*Reprinted from *College English* 16 (October 1954): 9–17. Copyright 1954 by the National Council of Teachers of English. Reprinted with permission.

therefore virtuously. The second stage of his career involves a negation of child-like simplicity; Pip acquires his "expectations," renounces his origins, and moves to the city. He rises in society, but since he acts through calculation rather than through instinctive charity, his moral values deteriorate as his social graces improve. This middle phase of his career culminates in a sudden fall, the beginning of a redemptive suffering which is dramatically concluded by an attack of brain fever leading to a long coma. It is not too fanciful to regard this illness as a symbolic death; Pip rises from it regenerate and percipient. In the final stage of growth he returns to his birthplace, abandons his false expectations, accepts the limitations of his condition, and achieves a partial synthesis of the virtue of his innocent youth and the melancholy insight of his later experience.

Variants of such a narrative are found in the myths of many heroes. In Dickens's novel the legend has the advantage of providing an action which appeals to the great primary human affections and serves as unifying center for the richly conceived minor themes and images which form the body of the novel. It is a signal virtue of this simple structure that it saves *Great Expectations* from some of the startling weaknesses of such excellent but inconsistently developed novels as *Martin Chuzzlewit* or *Our Mutual Friend*.

The particular fable that Dickens elaborates is as interesting for its historical as for its timeless aspects. In its particulars the story of Pip is the classic legend of the nineteenth century: *Great Expectations* belongs to that class of education or development-novels which describe the young man of talents who progresses from the country to the city, ascends in the social hierarchy, and moves from innocence to experience. Stendhal in *Le Rouge et le Noir*, Balzac in *Le Père Goriot* and *Les Illusions perdues*, use the plot as a means of dissecting the post-Napoleonic world and exposing its moral poverty. This novelistic form reflects the lives of the successful children of the century, and usually expresses the mixed attitudes of its artists. Dickens, Stendhal, Balzac communicate their horror of a materialist society, but they are not without admiration for the possibilities of the new social mobility; *la carrière ouverte aux talents* had a personal meaning for all three of these energetic men.

Pip, then, must be considered in the highly competitive company of Julien Sorel, Rubempré, and Eugène de Rastignac. Dickens's tale of lost illusions, however, is very different from the French novelists'; *Great Expectations* is not more profound than other development-novels, but it is more mysterious. The recurrent themes of the genre are all there: city is posed against country, experience against innocence; there is a search for the true father; there is the exposure to crime and the acceptance of guilt and expiation. What Dickens's novel lacks is the clarity and, one is tempted to say, the essential tolerance of the French. He could not command either the saving ironic vision of Stendhal or the disenchanted practicality and secure Catholicism of Balzac. For Dickens, always the

Victorian protestant, the issues of a young man's rise or fall are conceived as a drama of the individual conscience; enlightenment (partial at best) is to be found only in the agony of personal guilt.

With these considerations and possible comparisons in mind I should like to comment on some of the conspicuous features of *Great Expectations*. The novel is interesting for many reasons: it demonstrates the subtlety of Dickens's art; it displays a consistent control of narrative, imagery, and theme which gives meaning to the stark outline of the fable, and symbolic weight to every character and detail. It proves Dickens's ability (which has frequently been denied) to combine his genius for comedy with his fictional presentation of some of the most serious and permanently interesting of human concerns.

The principal themes are announced and the mood of the whole novel established in the opening pages of *Great Expectations*. The first scene with the boy Pip in the graveyard is one of the best of the superbly energetic beginnings found in almost all Dickens's mature novels. In less than a page we are given a character, his background, and his setting; within a few paragraphs more we are immersed in a decisive action. Young Pip is first seen against the background of his parents' gravestones—monuments which communicate to him no clear knowledge either of his parentage or of his position in the world. He is an orphan who must search for a father and define his own condition. The moment of this opening scene, we learn, is that at which the hero has first realized his individuality and gained his "first most vivid and broad impression of the identity of things." This information given the reader, the violent meeting between Pip and the escaped convict abruptly takes place.

The impression of the identity of things that Pip is supposed to have received is highly equivocal. The convict rises up like a ghost from among the graves, seizes the boy suddenly, threatens to kill him, holds him upside down through most of their conversation, and ends by forcing the boy to steal food for him. The children of Dickens's novels always receive rather strange impressions of things, but Pip's epiphany is the oddest of all, and in some ways the most ingenious. This encounter in the graveyard is the germinal scene of the novel. While he is held by the convict, Pip sees his world upside down; in the course of Dickens's fable the reader is invited to try the same view. This particular change of viewpoint is an ancient device of irony, but an excellent one: Dickens's satire asks us to try reversing the accepted senses of innocence and guilt, success and failure, to think of the world's goods as the world's evils.

A number of ironic reversals and ambiguous situations develop out of the first scene. The convict, Magwitch, is permanently grateful to Pip for having brought him food and a file with which to take off his leg-iron. Years later he expresses his gratitude by assuming in secrecy an economic parenthood; with the money he has made in Australia he will, unbeknownst to Pip, make "his boy" a gentleman. But the money the convict furnishes him makes Pip not a true gentleman, but a cad. He lives as a *flâneur* in London, and when he later discovers the disreputable source of his income is snobbishly horrified.

Pip's career is a parable which illustrates several religious paradoxes: he can gain only by losing all he has; only by being defiled can he be cleansed. Magwitch returns to claim his gentleman, and finally the convict's devotion and suffering arouse Pip's charity; by the time Magwitch has been captured and is dying Pip has accepted him and come to love him as a true father. The relationship is the most important one in the novel: in sympathizing with Magwitch Pip assumes the criminal's guilt; in suffering with and finally loving the despised and rejected man he finds his own real self.

Magwitch did not have to learn to love Pip. He was naturally devoted to "the small bundle of shivers," the outcast boy who brought him the stolen food and the file in the misty graveyard. There is a natural bond, Dickens suggests, between the child and the criminal; they are alike in their helplessness; both are repressed and tortured by established society, and both rebel against its incomprehensible authority. In the first scene Magwitch forces Pip to commit his first "criminal" act, to steal the file and food from his sister's house. Though this theft produces agonies of guilt in Pip, we are led to see it not as a sin but as an instinctive act of mercy. Magwitch, much later, tells Pip: "I first become aware of myself, down in Essex, a thieving turnips for my living." Dickens would have us, in some obscure way, conceive the illicit act as the means of self-realization.

In the opening section of the novel the view moves back and forth between the escaped criminal on the marshes and the harsh life in the house of Pip's sister, Mrs. Joe Gargery. The "criminality" of Pip and the convict is contrasted with the socially approved cruelty and injustice of Mrs. Joe and her respectable friends. The elders who come to the Christmas feast at the Gargerys' are pleased to describe Pip as a criminal: the young are, according to Mr. Hubble, "naterally wicious." During this most bleak of Christmas dinners the child is treated not only as outlaw, but as animal. In Mrs. Joe's first speech Pip is called a "young monkey"; then, as the spirits of the revellers rise, more and more comparisons are made between boys and animals. Uncle Pumblechook, devouring his pork, toys with the notion of Pip's having been born a "Squeaker":

> "If you had been born such, would you have been here now? Not you. . . ."
> "Unless in that form," said Mr. Wopsle, nodding towards the dish.
> "But I don't mean in that form, sir," returned Mr. Pumblechook, who had an objection to being interrupted; "I mean, enjoying himself with his elders and betters, and improving himself with their conversa-

tion, and rolling in the lap of luxury. Would he have been doing that? No, he wouldn't. And what would have been your destination?" turning on me again. "You would have been disposed of for so many shillings according to the market price of the article, and Dunstable the butcher would have come up to you as you lay in your straw, and he would have whipped you under his left arm, and with his right he would have tucked up his frock to get a penknife from out of his waistcoat-pocket, and he would have shed your blood and had your life. No bringing up by hand then. Not a bit of it!"

This identification of animal and human is continually repeated in the opening chapters of the novel, and we catch its resonance throughout the book. When the two convicts—Pip's "friend" and the other fugitive, Magwitch's ancient enemy—are captured, we experience the horror of official justice, which treats the prisoners as if they were less than human: "No one seemed surprised to see him, or interested in seeing him, or glad to see him, or sorry to see him, or spoke a word, except that somebody in the boat growled as if to dogs, 'Give way, you!'" And the prison ship, lying beyond the mud of the shore, looked to Pip "like a wicked Noah's ark."

The theme of this first section of the novel—which concludes with the capture of Magwitch and his return to the prison ship—might be called "the several meanings of humanity." Only the three characters who are in some way social outcasts—Pip, Magwitch, and Joe Gargery the child-like blacksmith—act in charity and respect the humanity of others. To Magwitch Pip is distinctly not an animal, and not capable of adult wickedness: "You'd be but a fierce young hound indeed, if at your time of life you could help to hunt a wretched warmint." And when, after he is taken, the convict shields Pip by confessing to have stolen the Gargerys' pork pie, Joe's absolution affirms the dignity of man: "'God knows you're welcome to it—so far as it was ever mine,' returned Joe, with a saving remembrance of Mrs. Joe. 'We don't know what you have done, but we wouldn't have you starved to death for it, poor miserable fellow-creatur.—Would us, Pip?'"

The next section of the narrative is less tightly conceived than the introductory action. Time is handled loosely; Pip goes to school, and becomes acquainted with Miss Havisham of Satis House and the beautiful Estella. The section concludes when Pip has reached early manhood, been told of his expectations, and has prepared to leave for London. These episodes develop, with variations, the theme of childhood betrayed. Pip himself renounces his childhood by coming to accept the false social values of middle-class society. His perverse development is expressed by persistent images of the opposition between the human and the non-human, the living and the dead.

On his way to visit Miss Havisham for the first time, Pip spends the night with Mr. Pumblechook, the corn-chandler, in his lodgings behind his shop. The contrast between the aridity of this old hypocrite's spirit and the viability of his wares is a type of the conflict between natural growth and social form. Pip looks at all the shop-keeper's little drawers filled with bulbs and seed packets and wonders "whether the flower-seeds and bulbs ever wanted of a fine day to break out of those jails and bloom." The imagery of life repressed is developed further in the descriptions of Miss Havisham and Satis House. The first detail Pip notices is the abandoned brewery where the once active ferment has ceased; no germ of life is to be found in Satis House or in its occupants: ". . . there were no pigeons in the dove-cot, no horses in the stable, no pigs in the sty, no malt in the storehouse, no smells of grains and beer in the copper or the vat. All the uses and scents of the brewery might have evaporated with its last reek of smoke. In a by-yard, there was a wilderness of empty casks. . . ."

On top of these casks Estella dances with solitary concentration, and behind her, in a dark corner of the building, Pip fancies that he sees a figure hanging by the neck from a wooden beam, "a figure all in yellow white, with but one shoe to the feet; and it hung so, that I could see that the faded trimmings of the dress were like earthy paper, and that the face was Miss Havisham's."

Miss Havisham *is* death. From his visits to Satis House Pip acquires his false admiration for the genteel; he falls in love with Estella and fails to see that she is the cold instrument of Miss Havisham's revenge on human passion and on life itself. When Pip learns he may expect a large inheritance from an unknown source he immediately assumes (incorrectly) that Miss Havisham is his benefactor; she does not undeceive him. Money, which is also death, is appropriately connected with the old lady rotting away in her darkened room.

Conflicting values in Pip's life are also expressed by the opposed imagery of stars and fire. Estella is by name a star, and throughout the novel stars are conceived as pitiless: "And then I looked at the stars, and considered how awful it would be for a man to turn his face up to them as he froze to death, and see no help or pity in all the glittering multitude." Estella and her light are described as coming down the dark passage of Satis House "like a star," and when she has become a woman she is constantly surrounded by the bright glitter of jewelry.

Joe Gargery, on the other hand, is associated with the warm fire of the hearth or forge. It was his habit to sit and rake the fire between the lower bars of the kitchen grate, and his workday was spent at the forge. The extent to which Dickens intended the contrast between the warm and the cold lights—the vitality of Joe and the frigid glitter of Estella—is indicated in a passage that describes the beginnings of Pip's disillusionment with his expectations:

> When I woke up in the night . . . I used to think, with a weariness on
> my spirits, that I should have been happier and better if I had never seen
> Miss Havisham's face, and had risen to manhood content to be partners
> with Joe in the honest old forge. Many a time of an evening, when I sat
> alone looking at the fire, I thought, after all, there was no fire like the
> forge fire and the kitchen fire at home.
>
> Yet Estella was so inseparable from all my restlessness and disquiet
> of mind, that I really fell into confusion as to the limits of my own part in
> its production.

At the end of the novel Pip finds the true light on the homely hearth,
and in a last twist of the father-son theme, Joe emerges as a true parent—
the only kind of parent that Dickens could ever fully approve, one that remains a child. The moral of this return to Joe sharply contradicts the
accepted picture of Dickens as a radical critic of society: Joe is a humble
countryman who is content with the place in the social order he has been
appointed to fulfill. He fills it "well and with respect"; Pip learns that he
can do no better than to emulate him.

The second stage of Pip's three-phased story is set in London, and
the moral issues of the fiction are modulated accordingly. Instead of the
opposition between custom and the instinctive life, the novelist treats the
conflict between man and his social institutions. The topics and themes
are specific, and the satire, some of it wonderfully deft, is more social
than moral. Not all Dickens's social message is presented by means that
seem adequate. By satirizing Pip and his leisure class friends (The
Finches of the Grove, they call themselves) the novelist would have us realize that idle young men will come to a bad end. Dickens is here expressing the Victorian Doctrine of Work—a pervasive notion that both
inspired and reassured his industrious contemporaries.

The difficulty for the modern reader, who is unmoved by the objects
of Victorian piety, is that the doctrine appears to be the result, not of
moral insight, but of didactic intent; it is presented as statement, rather
than as experience or dramatized perception, and consequently it never
modifies the course of fictional action or the formation of character. The
distinction is crucial: it is between the Dickens who *sees* and the Dickens
who *professes;* often between the good and the bad sides of his art.

The novelist is on surer ground when he comes to define the nature
of wealth in a mercantile society. Instead of moralistic condemnation we
have a technique that resembles parable. Pip eventually learns that his
ornamental life is supported, not by Miss Havisham, but by the labor and
suffering of the convict Magwitch: "I swore arterwards, sure as ever I
spec'lated and got rich, you should get rich. I lived rough, that you should
live smooth; I worked hard that you should be above work. What odds,
dear boy? Do I tell it fur you to feel a obligation? Not a bit. I tell it, fur you
to know as that there dung-hill dog wot you kep like in, got his head so

high that he could make a gentleman—and, Pip, you're him!" The convict would not only make a gentleman but own him. The blood horses of the colonists might fling up the dust over him as he was walking, but, "I says to myself, 'If I ain't a gentleman, nor yet ain't got no learning, I'm the owner of such. All on you owns stock and land; which on you owns a brought-up London gentleman?'"

In this action Dickens has subtly led us to speculate on the connections between a gentleman and his money, on the dark origins of even the most respectable fortunes. We find Magwitch guilty of trying to own another human being, but we ask whether his actions are any more sinful than those of the wealthy *bourgeois*. There is a deeper moral in the fact that Magwitch's fortune at first destroyed the natural gentleman in Pip, but that after it was lost (it had to be forfeited to the state when Magwitch was finally captured) the "dung-hill dog" did actually make Pip a gentleman by evoking his finer feelings. This ironic distinction between "gentility" and what the father of English poetry meant by "gentilesse" is traditional in our literature and our mythology. In *Great Expectations* it arises out of the action and language of the fiction; consequently it moves and persuades us as literal statement never can.

The middle sections of the novel are dominated by the solid yet mysterious figure of Mr. Jaggers, Pip's legal guardian. Though Jaggers is not one of Dickens's greatest characters he is heavy with implication; he is so much at the center of this fable that we are challenged to interpret him— only to find that his meaning is ambiguous. On his first appearance Jaggers strikes a characteristic note of sinister authority:

> He was a burly man of an exceedingly dark complexion, with an exceedingly large head and a correspondingly large hand. He took my chin in his large hand and turned up my face to have a look at me by the light of the candle. . . . His eyes were set very deep in his head, and were disagreeably sharp and suspicious. . . .
> "How do *you* come here?"
> "Miss Havisham sent for me, sir," I explained.
> "Well! Behave yourself. I have a pretty large experience of boys, and you're a bad set of fellows. Now mind!" said he, biting the side of his great forefinger, as he frowned at me, "you behave yourself."

Pip wonders at first if Jaggers is a doctor. It is soon explained that he is a lawyer—what we now ambiguously call a *criminal* lawyer—but he is like a physician who treats moral malignancy, with the doctor's necessary detachment from individual suffering. Jaggers is interested not in the social operations of the law, but in the varieties of criminality. He exudes an antiseptic smell of soap and is described as washing his clients off as if he were a surgeon or a dentist.

Pip finds that Jaggers has "an air of authority not to be disputed . . . with a manner expressive of knowing something secret about every one of us that would effectually do for each individual if he chose to disclose it." When Pip and his friends go to dinner at Jaggers's house Pip observes that he "wrenched the weakest parts of our dispositions out of us." After the party his guardian tells Pip that he particularly liked the sullen young man they called Spider: "'Keep as clear of him as you can. But I like the fellow, Pip; he is one of the true sort. Why if I was a fortune-teller. . . . But I am not a fortune-teller,' he said. . . . 'You know what I am don't you?'" This question is repeated when Pip is being shown through Newgate Prison by Jaggers's assistant, Wemmick. The turnkey says of Pip: "Why then . . . he knows what Mr. Jaggers is."

But neither Pip nor the reader ever fully knows what Mr. Jaggers is. We learn, along with Pip, that Jaggers has manipulated the events which have shaped the lives of most of the characters in the novel; he has, in the case of Estella and her mother, dispensed a merciful but entirely personal justice; he is the only character who knows the web of secret relationships that are finally revealed to Pip. He dominates by the strength of his knowledge the world of guilt and sin—called *Little Britain*—of which his office is the center. He has, in brief, the powers that an artist exerts over the creatures of his fictional world, and that a god exerts over his creation.

As surrogate of the artist, Jaggers displays qualities of mind—complete impassibility, all-seeing unfeelingness—which are the opposite of Dickens's, but of a sort that Dickens may at times have desired. Jaggers can be considered a fantasy figure created by a novelist who is forced by his intense sensibility to re-live the sufferings of his fellow men and who feels their agonies too deeply.

In both the poetry and fiction of the nineteenth century there are examples of a persistent desire of the artist *not to care*. The mood, which is perhaps an inevitable concomitant of Romanticism, is expressed in Balzac's ambivalence toward his great character Vautrin. As arch-criminal and Rousseauistic man, Vautrin represents all the attitudes that Balzac the churchman and monarchist ostensibly rejects, yet is presented as a kind of artist-hero, above the law, who sees through the social system with an almost noble cynicism.

Related attitudes are expressed in the theories of art developed by such different writers as Flaubert and Yeats. While—perhaps because—Flaubert himself suffered from hyperaesthesia, he conceived the ideal novelist as coldly detached, performing his examination with the deft impassivity of the surgeon. Yeats, the "last Romantic," found the construction of a mask or anti-self necessary to poetic creation, and insisted that the anti-self be cold and hard—all that he as poet and feeling man was not.

Dickens's evocation of this complex of attitudes is less political than Balzac's, less philosophical than Flaubert's or Yeats's. Jaggers has a complete understanding of human evil but, unlike the living artist, can wash his hands of it. He is above ordinary institutions; like a god he dispenses justice, and like a god displays infinite mercy through unrelenting severity:

> "Mind you, Mr. Pip," said Wemmick, gravely in my ear, as he took my arm to be more confidential: "I don't know that Mr. Jaggers does a better thing than the way in which he keeps himself so high. He's always so high. His constant height is of a piece with his immense abilities. That Colonel durst no more take leave of *him*, than that turnkey durst ask him his intentions respecting a case. Then between his height and them, he slips in his subordinate—don't you see?—and so he has 'em soul and body."

Pip merely wishes that he had "some other guardian of minor abilities."

The final moral vision of *Great Expectations* has to do with the nature of sin and guilt. After visiting Newgate Pip, still complacent and self-deceived, thinks how strange it was that he should be encompassed by the taint of prison and crime. He tries to beat the prison dust off his feet and to exhale its air from his lungs; he is going to meet Estella, who must not be contaminated by the smell of crime. Later it is revealed that Estella, the pure, is the bastard child of Magwitch and a murderess. Newgate is figuratively described as a greenhouse, and the prisoners as plants carefully tended by Wemmick, assistant to Mr. Jaggers. These disturbing metaphors suggest that criminality is the condition of life. Dickens would distinguish between the native, inherent sinfulness from which men can be redeemed, and that evil which destroys life: the sin of the hypocrite or oppressor, the smothering wickedness of corrupt institutions. The last stage of Pip's progression is reached when he learns to love the criminal and to accept his own implication in the common guilt.

Though Dickens's interpretation is theologically heterodox, he deals conventionally with the ancient question of free will and predestination. In one dramatic paragraph Pip's "fall" is compared with the descent of the rock slab on the sleeping victim in the Arabian Nights tale: Slowly, slowly, "all the work, near and afar, that tended to the end, had been accomplished; and in an instant the blow was struck, and the roof of my stronghold dropped upon me." Pip's fall was the result of a chain of predetermined events but he was, nevertheless, responsible for his own actions; toward the end of the novel Miss Havisham gravely informs him: "You have made your own snares. *I* never made them."

The patterns of culpability in *Great Expectations* are so intricate that the whole world of the novel is eventually caught in a single web of awful responsibility. The leg-iron, for example, which the convict removed with the file Pip stole for him is found by Orlick and used as a weapon to brain Mrs. Joe. By this fearsome chain of circumstance Pip shares the guilt for his sister's death.

Profound and suggestive as is Dickens's treatment of guilt and expiation in this novel, to trace its remoter implications is to find something excessive and idiosyncratic. A few years after he wrote *Great Expectations* Dickens remarked to a friend that he felt always as if he were wanted by the police—"irretrievably tainted." Compared to most of the writers of his time the Dickens of the later novels seems to be obsessed with guilt. The way in which his development-novel differs from those of his French compeers emphasizes an important quality of Dickens's art. The young heroes of *Le Rouge et le Noir* and *Le Père Goriot* proceed from innocence, through suffering to learning. They are surrounded by evil, and they can be destroyed by it. But Stendhal, writing in a rationalist tradition, and Balzac displaying the worldliness that only a Catholic novelist can command, seem astonishingly cool, even callous, beside Dickens. *Great Expectations* is outside either Cartesian or Catholic rationalism; profound as only an elementally simple book can be, it finds its analogues not in the novels of Dickens's English or French contemporaries, but in the writings of that other irretrievably tainted artist, Fyodor Dostoevski.

The Hero's Guilt: The Case of
Great Expectations°   Julian Moynahan

Two recent essays on *Great Expectations* have stressed guilt as the dominant theme. They are Dorothy Van Ghent's "On Great Expectations" (*The English Novel: Form and Function*, New York, 1953) and G. R. Stange's "Dickens's Fable for his Time" (*College English*, 16, October 1954). Mr. Stange remarks *inter alia* that 'profound and suggestive as is Dickens's treatment of guilt and expiation in this novel, to trace its remoter implications is to find something excessive and idiosyncratic'; and he has concluded that "compared to most of the writers of his time the Dickens of the later novels seems to be obsessed with guilt." He does not develop this criticism, if it is a criticism, but one might guess he is disturbed by a certain discrepancy appearing in the narrative between the hero's sense of guilt and the actual amount of wrong-doing for which he may be said to be responsible. Pip has certainly one of the guiltiest consciences in literature. He not only suffers *agenbite of inwit* for his sin of snobbish ingratitude toward Joe and Biddy, but also suffers through much of the novel from what can only be called a conviction of criminal guilt. Whereas he expiates his sins of snobbery and ingratitude by ultimately accepting the convict Magwitch's unspoken claim for his protection and help, by willingly renouncing his great expectations, and by returning in

°Reprinted with permission from *Essays in Criticism* 10 (1960):60–79.

a chastened mood to Joe and Biddy, he cannot expiate—or exorcise—his conviction of criminality, because it does not seem to correspond with any real criminal acts or intentions.

Snobbery is not a crime. Why should Pip feel like a criminal? Perhaps the novel is saying that snobbery of the sort practiced by Pip in the second stage of his career is not very different from certain types of criminal behaviour. For instance, a severe moralist might point out that snobbery and murder are alike in that they are both offences against persons rather than property, and both involve the culpable wish to repudiate or deny the existence of other human beings. On this view, Pip reaches the height of moral insight at the start of the trip down the river, when he looks at Magwitch and sees in him only "a much better man than I had been to Joe." By changing places with the convict here, he apparently defines his neglectful behaviour toward Joe as criminal. Does this moment of vision objectify Pip's sense of criminality and prepare the way for expiation? Perhaps, but if so, then Pip's pharisaic rewording of the publican's speech, which occurs a few pages later while he is describing Magwitch's death in the prison, must somehow be explained away: "Mindful, then, of what we had read together, I thought of the two men who went up into the Temple to pray, and I thought I knew there were no better words that I could say beside his bed, than 'O Lord, be merciful to him, a sinner!'" Even Homer nods, and Dickens is not, morally speaking, at his keenest in deathbed scenes, where his love of the swelling organ tone is apt to make him forget where he is going. Still, we ought not to explain anything away before the entire problem of Pip's guilt has been explored at further length.

Other answers to the question I have raised are possible. Consider the following passage, wherein Pip most fully expresses his sense of a criminal "taint." He has just strolled through Newgate prison with Wemmick and is waiting near a London coach office for the arrival of Estella from Miss Havisham's:

> I consumed the whole time in thinking how strange it was that I should be encompassed by all this taint of prison and crime; that, in my childhood out on our lonely marshes on a winter evening I should have first encountered it; that, it should have reappeared on two occasions, starting out like a stain that was faded but not gone; that, it should in this new way pervade my fortune and advancement. While my mind was thus engaged, I thought of the beautiful young Estella, proud and refined, coming toward me, and I thought with absolute abhorrence of the contrast between the jail and her. I wished that Wemmick had not met me, or that I had not yielded to him and gone with him, so that, of all days in the year, on this day I might not have had Newgate in my breath and on my clothes. I beat the prison dust off my clothes as I sauntered to and fro, and I shook it out of my dress, and I exhaled its air from my lungs. So contaminated did I feel, remembering who was coming, that the coach came

quickly after all, and I was not yet free from the soiling consciousness of Mr. Wemmick's conservatory, when I saw her face at the coach window and her hand waving at me.

Without question, Pip here interprets the frequent manifestations in his experience of criminal elements—the runaway prisoner on the marshes, the man with the two pound notes, the reappearance of the same man in chains on the coach going down into the marsh country, the reappearance of Magwitch's leg iron as the weapon which fells Mrs. Joe, the accident making the criminal lawyer Jaggers, whose office is beside Newgate prison, the financial agent of his unknown patron—as signs that indicate some deep affinity between him and a world of criminal violence. But a question that the reader must face here and elsewhere in the novel is whether to accept Pip's interpretation. If we conclude that Pip is in fact tainted with criminality, we must rest our conclusion on a kind of symbolic reading of the coincidences of the plot. Through these coincidences and recurrences, which violate all ordinary notions of probability, Dickens, so this argument must go, weaves together a net in whose meshes his hero is entrapped. Regardless of the fact that Pip's association with crimes and criminals is purely adventitious and that he evidently bears no responsibility for any act or intention of criminal violence, he must be condemned on the principle of guilt by association.

Nevertheless, if the reader is himself not to appear a bit of a pharisee, he must be able to show good reason for accepting the principle of guilt by association in settling the question of the hero's criminality. Both Mr. Stange and Miss Van Ghent present readings of the guilt theme which are an attempt to validate this principle. Mr. Stange decides that "the last stage of Pip's progression is reached when he learns to love the criminal and to accept his own implication in the common guilt." He believes that one of Dickens's major points is that "criminality is the condition of life." Pip, therefore, feels criminal guilt because he is criminal as we are all criminal. Along similar lines, Miss Van Ghent remarks, "Pip . . . carries the convict inside him, as the negative potential of his 'great expectations'—Magwitch is the concretion of his potential guilt." The appearance of Magwitch at Pip's apartment in the Temple is "from a metaphysical point of view . . . that of Pip's own unwrought deeds." Finally, she maintains that Pip bows down before Magwitch, who has been guilty towards him, instead of bowing down before Joe, toward whom Pip has been guilty. In so doing Pip reveals by a symbolic act that he takes his guilt of the world on his shoulders—rather in the style of Father Zossima in *The Brothers Karamazov*. This is shown particularly by the fact that Pip assumes culpability in a relationship where he is, in fact, the innocent party.

Objections to these metaphysical readings can be raised. If criminality is the condition of life, and if guilt is universal in the world of the novel, what world may Joe Gargery, Biddy, and Herbert Pocket be said to inhabit? Miss Van Ghent's theory of Pip's guilt as the negative potential of his great expectations is more promising, because it seems to exempt humble people from the guilt attaching itself to a society of wealth and power which thrives on the expropriation of the fruits of labour of its weaker members. But in her description of Pip's redemptory act, Miss Van Ghent insists upon the pervasiveness of guilt throughout the Dickens world. Less disturbing than this contradiction but still questionable is her assumption that Magwitch has been guilty of great wrong-doing towards Pip. Metaphysics aside, how badly has he treated Pip? Does his wrong-doing stand comparison with the vicious practices of an Orlick or even a Miss Havisham? Who, in the light of the virtues of faithfulness and love, virtues which the novel surely holds up for admiration, is the better, Magwitch or his daughter Estella?

My final objection to these interpretations is Pip's language at Magwitch's deathbed. Pip, after all, tells his own story. Evidence that he has attained an unflawed moral grasp of experience in which the distinction between criminal and non-criminal forms of evil is transcended through the confession *mea culpa* must come, at least partly, from Pip himself. On the strength—on the weakness rather—of his biblical flight, this reader is not convinced that the evidence is clear.

Miss Van Ghent's and Mr. Stange's efforts to demonstrate Pip's metaphysical involvement in the criminal milieu of *Great Expectations* are dictated, rightly enough, by their concern for the unifying and inclusive significance of the guilt theme. Their readings provide a means of bridging the gulf between Pip's social sins and the more drastic phenomena of criminality presented in the novel—attempts to moralise the melodrama, as it were, attempts to make the complete narrative presentation revolve around the crucial question of Pip's moral nature. Sensitive readers of the novel will sympathise with this effort, but I do not believe they will agree that the gulf *is* bridged by making criminal guilt a universal condition and by insisting that this is what Pip comes to understand by the time his story is told.

2

In my opinion, Pip's relation to the criminal milieu of *Great Expectations* is not that of an Everyman to a universal condition. It is rather a more concrete and particularised relation than the metaphysical approach would indicate, although the novel defines that relation obliquely and associatively, not through discursive analysis. Miss Van Ghent has suggested a metaphoric connection between Magwitch and Pip. Her proposal of such implicit relations between character and character, even though they do not become rationalised anywhere, is an illuminating insight into the artistic method of the mature Dickens. But her principle can be applied differently and yield rather different results.

I would suggest that Orlick rather than Magwitch is the figure from the criminal milieu of the novel whose relations to him come to define Pip's implicit participation in the acts of violence with which the novel abounds. Considered by himself, Orlick is a figure of melodrama. He is unmotivated, his origins are shrouded in mystery, his violence is unqualified by regret. In this last respect he is the exact opposite of Pip, who is, of course, filled with regret whenever he remembers how he has neglected his old friends at the forge.

On the other hand, if we consider Orlick in his connections with Pip, some rather different observations can be made. In the first place, there is a peculiar parallel between the careers of the two characters. We first encounter Orlick as he works side by side with Pip at the forge. Circumstances also cause them to be associated in the assault on Mrs. Joe. Orlick strikes the blow, but Pip feels, with some justification, that he supplied the assault weapon. Pip begins to develop his sense of alienation from the village after he has been employed by Miss Havisham to entertain her in her house. But Orlick too turns up later on working for Miss Havisham as gatekeeper. Finally, after Pip has become a partisan of the convict, it turns out that Orlick also has become a partisan of an ex-convict, Compeyson, who is Magwitch's bitter enemy.

Up to a point, Orlick seems not only to dog Pip's footsteps, but also to present a parody of Pip's upward progress through the novel, as though he were in competitive pursuit of some obscene great expectations of his own. Just as Pip centres his hopes successively on the forge, Satis House, and London, so Orlick moves his base of operations successively from the forge, to Satis House, and to London. From Pip's point of view, Orlick has no right to interest himself in any of the people with whom Pip has developed close times. For instance, he is appalled when he discovers that his tender feeling for Biddy is given a distorted echo by Orlick's obviously lecherous interest in the same girl. And when he discovers that Orlick has the right of entry into Satis House he warns Jaggers to advise Miss Havisham to get rid of him. But somehow he cannot keep Orlick out of his affairs. When Magwitch appears at Pip's London lodging half-way through the novel, Orlick is crouching in darkness on the landing below Pip's apartment. And when Pip is about to launch the escape attempt down the Thames, his plans are frustrated by the trick which brings him down to the marshes to face Orlick in the hut by the limekiln. Its lurid melodrama and the awkwardness of its integration with the surrounding narrative has made many readers dismiss this scene as a piece of popular writing aimed at the less intelligent members of Dickens's audience. But the confrontation of Orlick and Pip on the marshes is crucial for an understanding of the problem I am discussing, because it is the scene in which

Dickens comes closest to making explicit the analogy between the hero and the novel's principal villain and criminal.

Orlick inveigles Pip to the limepit not only to kill him but to overwhelm him with accusations. Addressing Pip over and over again as "Wolf," an epithet he might more readily apply to himself, he complains that Pip has cost him his place, come between him and a young woman in whom he was interested, tried to drive him out of the country, and been a perpetual obstacle in the path of his own uncouth ambitions. But the charge he makes with the greatest force and conviction is that Pip bears the final responsibility for the assault on Mrs. Joe:

> "I tell you it was your doing—I tell you it was done through you," he retorted, catching up the gun and making a blow with the stock at the vacant air between us. "I come upon her from behind, as I come upon you to-night. I giv' it to her! I left her for dead, and if there had been a lime-kiln as nigh her as there is now nigh you, she shouldn't have come to life again. But it warn't old Orlick as did it; it was you. You was favoured, and he was bullied and beat. Old Orlick bullied and beat, eh? Now you pays for it. You done it; now you pays for it."

The entire scene was a nightmare quality. This is at least partly due to the weird reversal of roles, by which the innocent figure is made the accused and the guilty one the accuser. As in a dream the situation is absurd, yet like a dream it may contain hidden truth. On the one hand Orlick, in interpreting Pip's character, seems only to succeed in describing himself—ambitious, treacherous, murderous, and without compunction. On the other hand, several of Orlick's charges are justified, and it is only in the assumption that Pip's motives are as black as his own that he goes wrong. We know, after all, that Pip is ambitious, and that he has repudiated his early associates as obstacles to the fulfilment of his genteel aspirations. Another interesting observation can be made about Orlick's charge that "it was you as did for your shrew sister." Here Orlick presents Pip as the responsible agent, himself merely as the weapon. But this is an exact reversal of Pip's former assumptions about the affair. All in all, Orlick confronts the hero in this scene, not merely as would-be murderer, but also as a distorted and darkened mirror-image. In fact, he presents himself as a monstrous caricature of the tender-minded hero, insisting that they are two of a kind with the same ends, pursued through similarly predatory and criminal means. This is what his wild accusations come down to.

3

Is Orlick mistaken in representing himself in this scene as a sort of double, *alter ego*, or shadow of Pip? Is he merely projecting his own qualities upon him, or do Orlick's accusations, in any sense, constitute a partially or wholly valid comment on Pip's actions? In order to answer these questions we shall have to begin by analysing the fantasy of great expectations which gives the book so much of its universal appeal. This fantasy, so the psychologists tell us, is a well-nigh universal imaginative flight of childhood. By creating for himself a fiction wherein the world is made to conform to his desire and will, the child succeeds in compensating himself for the fact that his real position is without power and that the quantity of love and nurture to which he believes himself entitled is greatly in excess of the amount he actually receives. Out of this unbalance between an unbounded demand and a limited supply of love and power proceed the fairy godmothers as well as the vicious step-parents and bad giants in which world legend abounds. The fantasy element *Great Expectations* shares with such stories as *Cinderella* and *Jack and the Beanstalk* contains, then, two implicit motives: the drive for power and the drive for more mother-love. However, of the two, the power motive, since it involves the aggressive wish to push beyond the authoritarian figures who hold the child powerless, is apt to be more productive of guilt and, consequently, is likely to be expressed with a certain amount of concealment. Thus, Jack in the folk tale conquers authority in the fictional guise of killing the wicked giant. But there is no attempt to disguise that fact that he steals from the giant in order to live in affluence with his widowed mother, enjoying her undivided love and admiration. We might add that the type of love sought in this fantasy is a childish version of mature love. It is largely passive. It is associated with a super-abundance of the good things of life, often with the enjoyment of great wealth.

In *Great Expectations*, the second motive is clearly represented in the early stages of Pip's career. His early experiences follow the fairy-tale pattern. Circumstances magically conspire to rescue him from the spartan rigours of Mrs. Joe. In taking him up, Miss Havisham plays the role of fairy godmother, and later permits him to continue in his belief that she is also the sponsor of his luxury in London—until he is brought up short by the rough figure of Magwitch. Until the real world breaks in on him, Pip allows himself to be pushed along, never challenging the requirement that he must not look too closely into the sources of his good fortune. Likewise, he is passive in his longing for Estella, who, in her metaphoric associations with precious jewels and lofty stars, comes to symbolise to him the final goal of his dreams of love, luxury, and high position. Instead of trying to capture her through an aggressive courtship he simply pines, assuming on very little evidence that one day she will be bestowed upon him by Miss Havisham as everything else has been.

Upon the return of Magwitch, Pip is forced to wake up and recognise that life is not, after all, a fairy tale. He learns that his own wealth comes from a criminal, that even the magical figures of Satis House, Miss Havisham and Estella have criminal connections, and, as we have seen, that his callous treatment of Joe Gargery was essentially criminal. This linking up of the criminal milieu and the milieu of wealth and high position is a way of drawing the strongest possible contrast between Pip's regressive fantasy-world, where wealth and good luck have seemed unremitting and uncompromised, and a real world where the dominant moral colouring is at best a dirty grey.

In terms of what we have called the love-motive, then, Dickens has shown fantasy in collision with reality. Pip learns that the world is not a vast mammary gland from which he can draw rich nourishment with moral impunity. He finds that he must hunger and struggle like all the rest. Furthermore, he must accept the unhappy fact that his participation in the old dream of great expectations has hurt real people. With his awakening to reality he develops a capacity for active, self-bestowing love. But the mature tough-minded perspective from which the hero's development is viewed does not permit him to move on into happiness and fulfilment. In the final chapters of *Great Expectations* Pip wants to give himself, but there is no longer anyone in a position to accept his gift. Magwitch's fate is upon him; the circumstance of marriage has carried both Biddy and Estella beyond his reach. In bestowing himself upon the family of Herbert Pocket, Pip comes to rest in a kind of limbo. The book seems to imply that Pip is doomed to a lifetime of vicarious experience, because he lingered too long in his condition of alienation from the real.

This is not a complete account of Dickens's critique of the great expectations fantasy, that dream of huge and easy success which has always haunted the imagination of children and also haunted the imaginations of adults in the increasingly commercial and industrial society of nineteenth-century England. In *Great Expectations,* as in its legendary prototypes, the theme of ambition is treated under the two aspects of desire and will, the search for a superabundance of love and the drive for power. And it is in his presentation of the theme in the latter aspect that Dickens makes the more profound analysis of the immoral and criminal elements in his hero's (and the century's) favourite dream.

But Pip's ambition is passive. He only becomes active and aggressive after he has ceased to be ambitious. How then does *Great Expectations* treat the theme of ambition in terms that are relevant to the total action of which Pip is the centre? I have already begun to suggest an answer to the question. Ambition as the instinct of aggression, as the pitiless drive for power directed against what we have called authority-figures is both coalesced and disguised in the figure of Orlick. And Orlick is bound to be the hero by ties of analogy as double, *alter ego* and dark mirror-image. We are dealing here with an art which simultaneously disguises and reveals its deepest implications of meaning, with a method which apparently dissociates its thematic materials and its subject matter into moral fable-*cum*-melodramatic accompaniment, yet simultaneously presents through patterns of analogy a dramatic perspective in which the apparent opposites are unified. In *Great Expectations* criminality is displaced from the hero on to a melodramatic villain. But on closer inspection that villain becomes part of a complex unity—we might call it Pip-Orlick—in which all aspects of the problem of guilt become interpenetrant and co-operative. The only clue to this unity which is given at the surface level of the narrative is Pip's obsession of criminal guilt. Pip tells us over and over again that he feels contaminated by crime. But we do not find the objective correlative of that conviction until we recognise in the insensate and compunctionless Orlick a shadow image of the tender-minded and yet monstrously ambitious young hero.

What is the rationale of this elusive method? In my opinion it enabled Dickens to project a radical moral insight which anticipated the more sophisticated probings of novelists like Dostoievsky and Gide without abandoning the old-fashioned traditions of melodrama and characterisation in which he had worked for more than a quarter of a century before *Great Expectations* was published. Pip, by comparison with Raskolnikov, is a simple young man. But through the analogy Pip-Orlick, *Great Expectations* makes the same point about ambition as *Crime and Punishment*, and it is a very penetrating point indeed. In the *Brothers Karamazov* Ivan comes to recognise during the course of three tense interviews with his half-brother, Smerdyakov, how he shares with that brother a criminal responsibility for the murder of their father, although Smerdyakov alone wielded the weapon. The comparable scene in *Great Expectations* is the limekiln scene. Orlick even adopts the tone of a jealous sibling during the interview, as in the remark, "You was favoured, and he was bullied and beat." But Dickens is not a Dostoievsky. Pip does not recognise Orlick as a blood-relation, so to speak. The meaning remains submerged and is communicated to the reader through other channels than the agonised confession of a first-person narrator. Indeed, the profoundest irony of the novel is not reached until the reader realises he must see Pip in a much harsher moral perspective than Pip ever saw himself.

4

Recognition that Pip's ambition is definable under the aspect of aggression as well as in terms of the regressive desire for passive enjoyment of life's bounty depends upon the reader's willingness to work his way into the narrative from a different angle than the narrator's. The evidence for the hero's power-drive against the authority-figures, the evidence of his "viciousness" if you will, is embodied in the story in a number of ways, but a clear pattern of meaning only emerges after the reader has correlated materials which are dispersed and nominally unrelated in the story *as told*. Orlick, thus far, has been the figure whose implicit relations to the hero have constituted the chief clue to the darker meaning of Pip's career. He continues to be important in any attempt to set forth the complete case, but there are also some significant correlations to be made in which he does not figure. This is fortunate, if only to forestall the objection that the whole case depends upon an imputed resemblance between two characters whom generations of devoted readers have not, after all, found very much alike. Let us, then, present the rest of the evidence, and see whether Pip, in any sense, stands self-indicted as well as indicted for the bad company he occasionally—and most reluctantly—keeps.

We might begin with the apparently cynical remark that Pip, judged on the basis of what happens to many of the characters closely associated with him, is a very dangerous young man. He is not accident-prone, but a great number of people who move into his orbit decidedly are. Mrs. Joe is bludgeoned, Miss Havisham goes up in flames, Estella is exposed through her rash marriage to vaguely specified tortures at the hands of her brutal husband, Drummle. Pumblechook has his house looted and his mouth stuffed with flowering annuals by a gang of thieves led by Orlick. All of these characters, with the exception of Estella, stand at one time or another in the relation of patron, patroness, or authority-figure to Pip the boy or Pip the man. (Pumblechook is, of course, a parody patron, and his comic chastisement is one of the most satisfying things in the book.) Furthermore, all of these characters, including Estella, have hurt, humiliated, or thwarted Pip in some important way. All in some way have stood between him and the attainment of the full measure of his desires. All are punished.

Let us group these individual instances. Mrs. Joe, the cruel foster-mother, and Pumblechook, her approving and hypocritical relation by marriage, receive their punishment from the hands of Orlick. Mrs. Joe hurts Pip and is hurt in turn by Orlick. Pip has the motive of revenge—a lifetime of brutal beatings and scrubbings inflicted by his sister—but Orlick, a journeyman who does not even lodge with the Gargerys, bludgeons Mrs. Joe after she has provoked a quarrel between him and his master. If we put together his relative lack of motive with his previously quoted remarks at the limekiln and add to these Pip's report of his own extraordinary reaction upon first hearing of the attack—"With my head full of George Barnwell, I was at first disposed to believe that *I* must have had some hand in the attack upon my sister, or at all events that as her near relation, popularly known to be under obligations to her, I was a more legitimate object of suspicion than anyone else"—we arrive at an anomalous situation which can best be resolved on the assumption that Orlick acts merely as Pip's punitive instrument or weapon.

With regard to Pumblechook's chastisement, the most striking feature is not that Orlick should break into a house, but that he should break into Pumblechook's house. Why not Trabb's? One answer might be that Trabb has never stood in Pip's light. Pumblechook's punishment is nicely proportioned to his nuisance value for Pip. Since he has never succeeded in doing him any great harm with his petty slanders, he escapes with a relatively light wound. Although we are told near the end of the novel that Orlick was caught and jailed after the burglary, we are never told that Pip reported Orlick's murderous assault on him or his confessions of his assault on Mrs. Joe to the police. Despite the fact that there is enough accumulated evidence to hang him, Orlick's end is missing from the book. Actually, it seems that Orlick simply evaporates into thin air after his punitive role has been performed. His case needs no final disposition because he has only existed, essentially, as an aspect of the hero's own far more problematic case.

Estella receives her chastisement at the hands of Bentley Drummle. How does this fit into the pattern we have been exploring? In the first place, it can be shown that Drummle stands in precisely the same analogical relationship to Pip as Orlick does. Drummle is a reduplication of Orlick at a point higher on the social-economic scale up which Pip moves with such rapidity through the first three-quarters of the novel. Drummle, like Orlick, is a criminal psychopath. At Jaggers's dinner party the host, a connoisseur of criminal types, treats Drummle as "one of the true sort," and Drummle demonstrates how deserving he is of this distinction when he tries to brain the harmless Startop with a heavy tumbler.

But the most impressive evidence that Orlick and Drummle are functional equivalents is supplied by the concrete particulars of their description. To an extraordinary degree, these two physically powerful, inarticulate, and dark-complexioned villains are presented to the reader in terms more often identical than similar. Orlick, again and again, is one who lurks and lounges, Drummle is one who lolls and lurks. When Pip, Startop, and Drummle go out rowing, the last "would always creep in-shore like some uncomfortable amphibious creature, even when the tide would have sent him fast on his way; and I always think of him as coming after us in the dark or by the back-water, when our own two boats were breaking the sunset or the moonlight in mid-stream." When Startop walks home after Jaggers's party, he is followed by Drummle but on the opposite side of the street, "in the shadow of the houses, much as he was wont to follow in his boat." The other creeper, follower and amphibian of *Great Expectations* is Orlick, whose natural habitat is the salt marsh, who creeps his way to the dark landing below Pip's apartment to witness the return of Magwitch from abroad, who creeps behind Biddy and Pip as they walk conversing on the marshes and overhears Pip say he will do anything to drive Orlick from the neighbourhood, who appears out of the darkness near the turnpike house on the night Pip returns from Pumblechook's to discover that his sister has been assaulted, and who, finally, creeps his way so far into Pip's private business that he ends by acting as agent for Compeyson, Magwitch's—and Pip's—shadowy antagonist.

Like Orlick, Drummle is removed from the action suddenly; Pip is given no opportunity to settle old and bitter scores with him. In the last chapter we hear that he is dead "from an accident consequent on ill-treating a horse." This is the appropriate end for a sadist whose crimes obviously included wife-beating. But more important to the present argument is our recognition that Drummle has been employed to break a woman who had, in the trite phrase, broken Pip's heart. Once he has performed his function as Pip's vengeful surrogate he can be assigned to the fate he so richly deserves.

Mrs. Joe beats and scrubs Pip until she is struck down by heavy blows on the head and spine. Pumblechook speaks his lies about him until his mouth is stuffed with flowers. Estella treats his affections with cold contempt until her icy pride is broken by a brutal husband. In this series Orlick and Drummle behave far more like instruments of vengeance than like three-dimensional characters with understandable grudges of their own. In terms of my complete argument, they enact an aggressive potential that the novel defines, through patterns of analogy and linked resemblances, as belonging in the end to Pip and to his unconscionably ambitious hopes.

When Miss Havisham bursts into flames, there is no Orlick or Drummle in the vicinity to be accused of having set a match to her. In the long series of violence which runs through *Great Expectations* from the beginning to end, this is one climax of violence that can be construed as nothing more than accidental. And yet it is an accident which Pip, on two occasions, has foreseen. Before Miss Havisham burns under the eye of the horror-struck hero, she has already come to a violent end twice in his hallucinated fantasies—in Pip's visionary experiences in the abandoned brewery, where he sees Miss Havisham hanging by the neck from a beam. He has this vision once as a child, on the occasion of his first visit to Satis House, and once as an adult, on the occasion on his last visit, just a few minutes before Miss Havisham's accident occurs. What are we to make, if anything, of these peculiar hallucinatory presentiments and of the coincidence by which they come true?

The child first sees his patroness hanging from a beam after his first hour of service with her. At this point the novel dwells at length on his keen awareness that he has been cruelly treated, generalises on the extreme sensitiveness of children to injustice, and describes how Pip in utter frustration vents his injured feelings by kicking a wall and twisting his own hair. In these passages it seems to me that the reader is being prepared to interpret Pip's immediately ensuing hallucination as the child's further attempt to discharge his anger and grief against his adult tormenter. In fantasy Pip punishes a woman whom in fact he cannot disturb in any way, and, by hanging her, attempts to destroy the threat to his peace and security which she represents. This interpretation excludes the possibility of a super-natural element in the experience; the novel provides abundant evidence that the imagination of a child operating under a

great stress of emotion is possessed of a hallucinatory power. When Pip
carries stolen provisions to Magwitch on the marshes, his guilt-ridden imagination effects a transformation of the countryside through which he
passes, until even gates, dykes, banks, cattle and a signpost seem to him to
be pursuing him and crying out his guilt. Pip's hallucination, then, is an
imaginative fantasy which both projects and disguises the boy's desire to
punish his employer and to destroy her baleful power over him.

Pip experiences no recurrence of the hallucination during the long
years of an association with Miss Havisham based on his mistaken assumption that she is the sole author of his good fortunes. The fantasy returns
only after his eyes have been opened to the fact that nothing has come to
him from Miss Havisham except unhappiness. On that last visit to Satis
House he learns definitely of Estella's marriage. With this information
the last link between him and his former employer snaps. The false fairy
godmother kneels to ask forgiveness for her crimes against him, and the
duped hero offers forgiveness sincerely, if sadly. Nevertheless, as Pip
strolls through the ruins of the estate he is not able to refrain from brood-
ing over Miss Havisham's "profound unfitness for this earth," and when
he walks into the chilly, twilit brewery building he is not able to prevent
the return of the old hallucination of Miss Havisham hanging from the
beam. We are told that this was owing to the revival of a childish association. But surely the episode represents more than a curious psychological
detail. It is profoundly right that the fantasy should return at a time when
he can see in complete clarity and detail how his connection with Miss
Havisham has hurt him. It is profoundly right that he should forgive the
false patroness and yet not forgive her, behave generously toward her and
yet feel deeply that she has no right to live, treat her with some degree of
melancholy affection, yet hate her also in the depths of his being.

We need not deny Dickens the insight necessary to the imagining of
so ambivalent a response in the hero of his great novel. And we should
not commit the anachronism of demanding that this response be defined in the novel analytically and self-consciously—that the hero
should tell us, "I forgave Miss Havisham as fully as I could, but continued
to think how well it would have been for me if she had never set foot on
this earth." Pip's ambivalence is embodied dramatically. It must be
known not as it is talked about, but as enacted. A man forgives a woman,
then hallucinates her death by hanging. A man watches a woman burst
into flames, then leaps bravely to her rescue, but in the course of describing this rescue is forced to remark, "We were on the ground struggling like desperate enemies."

How do these hallucinations, the second followed immediately by
Miss Havisham's fatal accident, add to the burden of the hero's guilt? The
answer is obvious. Because Pip's destructive fantasy comes true in reality,
he experiences the equivalent of a murderer's guilt. As though he had the
evil eye, or as though there were more than a psychological truth in the

old cliché, "if looks could kill," Pip moves from the brewery, where he has seen Miss Havisham hanging, to the door of her room, where he gives her one long, last look—until she is consumed by fire. But here the psychological truth suffices to establish imaginative proof that Pip can no more escape untainted from his relationship to the former patroness than he can escape untainted from any of his relationships to characters who have held and used the power to destroy or hamper his ambitious struggles. In all these relationships the hero becomes implicated in violence. With Estella, Pumblechook, and Mrs. Joe, the aggressive drive is enacted by surrogates linked to the hero himself by ties of analogy. With Miss Havisham the surrogate is missing. Miss Havisham falls victim to the purely accidental. But the "impurity" of Pip's motivation, as it is revealed through the device of the recurrent hallucination, suggests an analogy between that part of Pip which wants Miss Havisham at least punished, at most removed from this earth for which she is so profoundly unfit, and the destroying fire itself.

5

In this essay I have argued that Dickens's novel defines its hero's dream of great expectations and the consequences stemming from indulgence in that dream under the two aspects of desire and will, of regressive longing for an excess of love and of violent aggressiveness. In the unfolding of the action these two dramas are not presented separately. Instead they are combined into Dickens's most complex representation of character in action. Pip is Dickens's most complicated hero, demonstrating at once the traits of criminal and gull, of victimiser and victim. He is victimised by his dream and the dream itself, by virtue of its profoundly antisocial and unethical nature, forces him into relation with a world in which other human beings fall victim to his drive for power. He is, in short, a hero sinned against and sinning: sinned against because in the first place the dream was thrust upon the helpless child by powerful and corrupt figures from the adult world; a sinner because in accepting for himself a goal in life based upon unbridled individualism and indifference to others he takes up a career which *Great Expectations* repeatedly, through a variety of artistic means, portrays as essentially criminal.

After Magwitch's death, Pip falls a prey to brain fever. During his weeks of delirium it seems to me that his hallucinations articulate the division in his character between helpless passivity and demonic aggressiveness. Pip tells us he dreamed "that I was a brick in the house wall, and yet entreating to be released from the giddy place where the builders had set me; that I was a steel beam of a vast engine clashing and whirling over a great gulf, yet that I implored in my own person to have the engine stopped, and my part in it hammered off." It is tempting to read these images as dream logic. The hero-victim cries for release from his unsought position of height and power, but cannot help himself from functioning as a moving part of a monstrous apparatus which seems to sustain itself from a plunge into the abyss only through the continuous expenditure of destructive force. In the narrative's full context this vast engine can be taken to represent at one and the same time the demonic side of the hero's career and a society that maintains its power intact by the continuous destruction of the hopes and lives of its weaker members. In the latter connection we can think of Magwitch's account of his childhood and youth, and of the judge who passed a death sentence on thirty-two men and women, while the sun struck in through the courtroom windows making a "broad shaft of light between the two-and-thirty and the judge, linking them both together." But to think of the engine as a symbol of society is still to think of Pip. For Pip's career enacts his society's condition of being—its guilt, its sinfulness, and in the end, its helplessness to cleanse itself of a taint "of prison and crime."

When Pip wakes up from his delirium he finds himself a child again, safe in the arms of the angelic Joe Gargery. But the guilt of great expectations remains inexpiable, and the cruelly beautiful original ending of the novel remains the only possible "true" ending. Estella and Pip face each other across the insurmountable barrier of lost innocence. The novel dramatises the loss of innocence, and does not glibly present the hope of a redemptory second birth for either its guilty hero or the guilty society which shaped him. I have already said that Pip's fantasy of superabundant love brings him at last to a point of alienation from the real world. And similarly Pip's fantasy of power brings him finally to a point where withdrawal is the only positive moral response left to him.

The brick is taken down from its giddy place, a part of the engine is hammered off. Pip cannot redeem his world. In no conceivable sense a leader, he can only lead himself into a sort of exile from his society's power centres. Living abroad as the partner of a small, unambitious firm, he is to devote his remaining life to doing the least possible harm to the smallest number of people, so earning a visitor's privileges in the lost paradise where Biddy and Joe, the genuine innocents of the novel, flourish in thoughtless content.

[*Great Expectations*]*   Robert Garis

Great Expectations, I suggest, means more than Dickens's explicit intentions achieved and therefore more than he knew. Its deepest and most interesting meanings are unconscious ones. But these unconscious mean-

*Reprinted from **The Dickens Theatre** (Oxford; The Clarendon Press, 1965), by permission of Oxford University Press. © Oxford University Press 1965.

ings are successful meanings: they are genuinely created and achieved and brought to unity and harmony in a living work of art. Dickens could only "express" these meanings whereas we can "know" them: or rather he could express them whereas we can only know them. *Great Expectations* is the one novel by Dickens that is a deeply and organically imagined criticism of life. It is the theatrical rendering of a story which contains, deep within itself, a symbolic structure of deep imagination, in comparison with which the plots of all Dickens's other novels stand revealed as conscious structural contraptions to support consciously contrived theatrical scenes and rhetorical arguments. The plot of *Great Expectations* resembles that of Dickens's other novels by virtue of his continuing predilection for lurid conventional theatricalities: disguises, thrilling discoveries, long-lost secrets, midnight encounters, and the like. But these familiar theatrical elements are in *Great Expectations* motivated and organized from within, rather than constructed and assembled for overt theatrical or argumentative purposes. They grow into a living thing, a genuine fable, which comes to be a vision and a criticism of life, not a series of rhetorical "points" but a harmonious and organically alive work of the imagination. Indeed, the lack of rhetorical argument in *Great Expectations* is the first evidence of its essentially organic nature.

Every reader will have observed that, though this novel touches on the law, on prison, on mechanical behaviour of all kinds—familiar Dickensian themes—it is oddly uninterested in making a rhetorical attack upon these social evils. The theatrical mode of seeing and performing this material closely resembles Dickens's methods in *Bleak House*, with the single difference that these evils are not the objects of explicit critical attack in *Great Expectations*. Wemmick will be a sufficient example. He is one of the most brilliantly rendered of Dickens's mechanical men: his "post-office" face, his collection of "portable property," his organized inhumanity to Jaggers's clients, and, of course, his double life—these are virtual distillations of Dickens's earlier efforts in this direction. Yet nothing is clearer than that we are never asked by the prose to want all this to be changed. I do not mean to suggest merely that we like Wemmick the way he is, because he so vividly performs his own nature—as in *Bleak House* no one would (in the theatrical context) want Mr. Vholes to be changed, because he performs his Vholes-like nature so well and with such fresh inventiveness at every moment. With Mr. Vholes we can combine this attitude quite comfortably with another attitude: that of wanting the world to be different, of wanting nobody to have to be like Mr. Vholes, of wanting Richard Carstone to be saved from the clutches of "respectable men" like Mr. Vholes—and we take this latter attitude in easy obedience to the audibly insistent rhetoric of criticism in the theatrical artist's voice. But with Mr. Wemmick there is no such rhetoric. Nor with Mr. Jaggers, Mr. Pumblechook, Mr. Trabb, Mrs. Pocket.

The meaning of *Great Expectations* is correspondingly different from the meaning of the other mature novels. *Bleak House, Hard Times, Little Dorrit, Our Mutual Friend*—all these portray a world in which human freedom and happiness is threatened by wrong systems, wrong institutions, bad habits, bad values, bad people. And the portrait of this world becomes Dickens's rhetorical instrument for attacking these wrongs. But *Great Expectations* offers a new portrait. Dickens's new insight discovers a world in which human freedom and happiness are frustrated not by social wrongs, not by bad habits, but by the opposite, by the best and most demanding ideals of society. Pip is frustrated by people and by habits and by values which he, Dickens, and the reader all take to be good rather than bad. Moreover, the final statement of the significance of Pip's experiences articulates a moral attitude which we agree is good. Yet we feel that it is also a frustrating attitude, and the tone of the whole work confirms us in this opinion. Dickens's new insight into his world, in short, is an embodiment of Freud's theme in one of his most important works, *Civilization and its Discontents*.

I have argued that if we should stop to think about the curious emptiness of Pip's response to Biddy's marriage, it would immediately occur to us that the response is not in the least surprising, since we have known all along that Pip is like that, that something is missing in him. We have also known the identity of that something, though we may never have named it consciously. One name for it would be "force of will," but a more accurate and illuminating word is "libido." We have known from the beginning of the novel that what is missing from Pip's life is any free expression of libido, and that it is missing because it is held in contempt and horror by the ideals of the civilization within which Pip tries to make a life for himself. It must have been for this reason that Dickens was drawn to the characterization, as he was earlier drawn to Arthur Clennam and was later to Eugene Wrayburn. But *Great Expectations* differs from the novels which surround it. Although Pip is, beneath the surface of the novel, known to us as "the man without will, the man who cannot act," yet on the surface of the novel he is defined as "the man who wanted and acted wrongly." *Great Expectations* is the deepest of Dickens's visions of the discontents of civilization because of this unemphasized contradiction: the traditional moralization of its surface allowed Dickens unconsciously to render in the structure of his story itself that final pessimism about the possibility of human happiness which, in combination with his regretfully humorous acceptance of this condition, is his deepest criticism of life.

Who, then, is Pip? What is he like? Pip speaks of himself as being "morally timid and very sensitive" and gives a reason for it: "My sister's bringing up had made me sensitive" (8:57). But "within myself, I had sustained, from my babyhood, a perpetual conflict with injustice." We hear of these things at an early point in the narrative when Estella has just humiliated Pip. His response is classic: "I got rid of my injured feelings for the time, by kicking them into the brewery wall, and twisting them out of my hair, and then I smoothed my face with my sleeve, and came from behind the gate. The bread and meat were acceptable, and the beer was warming and tingling, and I was soon in spirits to look about me" (8:58). The young animal returns to the hope of free expression of impulse by means of the bread and meat which operate directly on the animal spirits through the animal body. But it is the animal body which had been insulted before— "And what coarse hands he has! And what thick boots!" And the meat and bread had been given "as insolently as if [he] were a dog in disgrace" (8:57).

Here is the hero, and now a few elementary facts about his circumstances. His home had been "sanctified" by a "giant" of a man who is emasculated by fear of his own capacity for violence. In the first long discussion between Pip and Joe Gargery, Joe puts this fear into significant language:

> "And last of all, Pip—and this I want to say very serous to you, old chap—I see so much in my poor mother, of a woman drudging and slaving and breaking her honest hart and never getting no peace in her mortal days, that I'm dead afeerd of going wrong in the way of not doing what's right by a woman, and I'd fur rather of the two go wrong the t'other way, and be a little ill-conwenienced myself. I wish it was only me that got put out, Pip; I wish there warn't no Tickler for you, old chap; I wish I could take it all on myself; but this is the up-and-down-and-straight on it, Pip, and I hope you'll overlook shortcomings." (7:45)

That this is the clearest possible instance of civilization producing discontent is a point that Dickens enforces by what follows: "Young as I was, I believe that I dated a new admiration of Joe from that night. We were equals afterwards, as we had been before; but afterwards, at quiet times when I sat looking at Joe and thinking about him, I had a new sensation of feeling conscious that I was looking up to Joe in my heart" (7:ibid).

The net result of this "new admiration" is to perpetuate the injustice of the Tickler and at the same time to frustrate any animal conflict with that injustice. The image of gentle Joe sanctifies the home at the same time as it inhibits free expression of impulse; and when we read later that Pip has lost the early vision of the forge as "the glowing road to manhood and independence" (14:100) we are in no moral perplexity about this "miserable" change.

Into Pip's discontent at the forge breaks the promise of great expectations—freedom, release, money. Pip can become a gentleman and he can win Estella. The dream here is perfectly ambiguous: the new money will make it possible to conquer the animal completely, the coarse hands and thick boots, the coarse and common flesh of the blacksmith; but it is also a gift of energy and potentiality. It leads to self-subduing work (the study with Mr. Pocket which Pip undergoes so dutifully and so successfully). But Pip hopes it will also magically confer at the end a new influx of free animal energy, the possibility of free expression of libido: Pip's money will win Estella. The unapproachable Estella, however, proves to be a deeply frustrating riddle: she herself is a product of "the old wild violent nature" of her criminal mother and father, and she can be possessed only by "heavy" brutish Bentley Drummle, whom she hates and who beats her. Pip remains a gentlemanly friend, with whom she holds familial, affectionate, and genteel converse.

All this is doubly confirmed by the fact that the great expectations are discovered to derive from the wild and violent Magwitch who eats like a dog (3:16), makes a mechanical animal sound when moved by gentle sentiments (ibid.), is like a 'terrible beast' (39:304), and lays on Pip's shoulder a hand which "might be stained with blood." (39:306). Once the source of the money is discovered, Pip is instantly sure that he "can take no further benefits from" Magwitch and this seems perfectly correct from the point of view of "civilization." Legally speaking, Magwitch's money is immoral money when it is in England; and it is implied that Herbert (who also finds convicts a "degraded and vile sight") shares Pip's conviction that the money must not be used. Pip's heart softens towards Magwitch, to be sure, but not until Magwitch's appearance and manner, too, have softened; indeed, the gentle old man whom Pip loves at the end is simply not a violent wild beast but another version of gentle Joe. Pip had pleased the convict at first by his gentleness and his childish sense of honour, his decency, that is by virtue of his "civilization"; but we know of the fear that played so important a part in this childish honour. When Magwitch returns, he is delighted that he has "made a gentleman," and he watches Pip's style as if it were an exhibition. Pip has learned this lesson well, too, and actually has the good manners and decent refined instincts which Magwitch likes to see, and which amount to civilization. But even before Magwitch has softened, Pip's loyalty to Magwitch amounts to the moral obligation of not betraying a man who loves him and depends on him and who will virtually commit suicide if Pip lets him down. Again civilization wins out, but there is blood-fear too. The violence of the convict, the blood on his hands, figure both as a horror and a lure. Blood and violence produce power and satisfaction and are in fact in this story the only means towards fruition. But violence is a deceptive lure in two senses: the power offered is useless because it comes through blood, and the violence itself disappears into the final gentleness of Magwitch's demeanour and behaviour before Pip, so to speak, has a chance to face it and accept it.

Through the whole story, Pip is always called on for the special kind of hard work that goes to make up this civilization. When Miss Havisham orders Pip to "play" in her presence, the irony would seem sufficiently obvious, and the ambiguity of Pip's "service" for Miss Havisham is in fact very richly worked out. What he is asked to do requires difficult self-control and deliberate application (the fascination of the house adds to the tension, to the pressure on Pip, who must retain his obedient good manners in this weird atmosphere), yet he is made to feel embarrassed and clumsy in accepting the wages for this really difficult work. With Miss Havisham, indeed, he is always "working." When he discovers the facts of his great expectations, civilization demands that he forgive Miss Havisham rather than hate her. He manages to produce only a mild reproach before his "better nature" comes into evidence: "It was a weak complaint to have made, and I had not meant to make it." (44:341). And in the next breath he is pleading with Miss Havisham to do the decent thing by Mr. Matthew Pocket, and to continue his own secret financial support of Herbert. A few chapters later, when Miss Havisham asks him to forgive her, he is ready with the touchingly honourable reply: "There have been sore mistakes; and my life has been a blind and thankless one; and I want forgiveness and direction far too much, to be bitter with you." (49:377). Soon afterwards Pip has the "work" of rescuing Miss Havisham from the flames.

Here, then, is the basic fable of *Great Expectations* and the vision of life and criticism of life which it embodies. It is the story of a hopeful young man with a strong animal body and powerful desires who is called on at every turn to display, in the commonest actions of his everyday life, the ideals of the civilization into which he was born: continual self-restraint, self-control, forgiveness of enemies, fortitude in withstanding—not heroic combat, which would be invigorating—but boredom and frustration and insult. He is this perfect model of moral deportment because he is "morally timid and very sensitive"—because he is so utterly persuaded of the validity of these ideals that he never finds any adequate opportunity for expressing, or even recognizing, his own interests and his own self. Although he has within himself "sustained . . . a perpetual conflict with injustice," this conflict, because his civilization never offered him a vocabulary for articulating it, was always turned against himself. In his youth it took the form of "kicking [his] injured feelings into the brewery-wall, and twisting them out of [his] hair"; when he grows up he inevitably turns his frustrations against himself in the form of continual remorse and guilt. Looking everywhere around him and in particular at the people responsible for his continued frustrations, he can find no one to blame: but this is true only because he is imbued with the moral obligation of understanding and forgiving. Moreover, there is no conceivable alternative to his sense of horror and repulsion about the one source of power apparently available in this civilization: blood, wildness, and violence. It never occurs to him that these horrors are really "human," that they are in any way worthy of respect. Pip is an obedient child of civilization; the fact that he is also a human animal, with many and complex impulses which breed animal needs and glamorous hopes and great expectations—this fact leads to the melancholy, mildly humorous acceptance of the world's insufficiency which is the novel's guiding tone and final meaning.

Crime and Fantasy in
Great Expectations°

Albert D. Hutter

1

"Hold your noise!" cried a terrible voice, as a man started up from among the graves at the side of the church porch. "Keep still, you little devil, or I'll cut your throat!"[1]

The terrible voice belongs to Abel Magwitch. He descends upon Pip and the reader alike with tremendous suddenness and ferocity. Here, at the very outset of the novel, Magwitch bursts into Pip's thoughts like some imagined ogre of childhood, rising from "the distant savage lair from which the wind was rushing," rising from the marshes, starting up from among the Pirrip graves. "You young dog," he tells Pip, licking his lips, "what fat cheeks you ha' got. . . . Darn Me if I couldn't eat 'em" (1:3). He goes on to describe the young man with him ("in comparison with which young man I am a Angel"):

> That young man hears the words I speak. That young man has a secret way pecooliar to himself, of getting at a boy, and at his heart, and at his liver. It is in wain for a boy to attempt to hide himself from that young man. A boy may lock his door, may be warm in bed, may tuck himself up, may draw the clothes over his head, may think himself comfortable and safe, but that young man will softly creep and creep his way to him and tear him open. I am a keeping that young man from harming of you at the present moment, with great difficulty. I find it wery hard to hold that young man off of your inside. (1:4–5)

This opening incident is the basis for what Dickens called "the grotesque tragicomic conception," the relationship between Pip and Magwitch which inspired the book and which achieves a pivotal surprise in chapter 39 when Magwitch returns.[2] Magwitch's reappearance in *Great Expectations* gives literal substance to the guilt and fears that haunt Pip from the opening chapter. Throughout the novel Pip's chance association with the convict overshadows his other relationships, his aspirations and pretensions.

At first Pip's terror and guilt over robbing a file and "wittles" appear

°Reprinted by permission of the author from *Psychoanalysis and Literary Process*, edited by Frederick Crews (Cambridge, Mass.: Winthrop Publishers, Inc., 1970).

to be the exaggerations of childhood. His terror is conveyed to the reader through surprise—as when Magwitch first appears, or when Pip opens his door to find "a party of soldiers with their muskets: one of whom held out a pair of handcuffs to me, saying, 'Here you are, look sharp, come on!'" (4:31). Yet there is enough humor in Dickens's description to distance our identification with Pip. We perceive Magwitch's exaggeration in describing his horrific young man; Pip cannot. As the novel progresses, however, the first encounter with Magwitch takes on overtones that mystify and disturb us as much as they do the protagonist.

Pip betrays Joe for the first time in the act of stealing Joe's file, and as a result he is tormented by guilt.[3] Later the file mysteriously turns up in the hands of a stranger who uses it as a swizzle stick to stir his rum and water. Although Pip is now older, and apprenticed to Joe, he still responds to this stranger and to the file itself as he had first responded to the convict. He thinks of "the strange man taking aim at me with his invisible gun" and of "the guility coarse and common thing" his own convict associations have been. He dreads that the file will reappear when he least expects it (as in fact Magwitch does reappear in chapter 39), and he dreams of it "coming at me out of a door, without seeing who held it," until he screams himself awake (10:83).

Instead of the file, Magwitch's broken leg-iron turns up six chapters later as the weapon used to assault Mrs. Joe. Pip's immediate reaction to this crime is: "I was at first disposed to believe that *I* must have had some hand in the attack upon my sister" (16:128), and he continues to feel responsible for the assault.[4] By now the file has become an obsession and a barrier between him and Joe. Pip's attempts to rationalize the theft and the necessity for keeping it secret are self-contradictory and unnecessarily defensive: "the secret was such an old one now, had so grown into me and become a part of myself, that I could not tear it away. In addition to the dread that, having led up to so much mischief, it would be now more likely than ever to alienate Joe from me if he believed it, I had a further restraining dread that he would not believe it . . ." (16:130).

Through his guardian in London, a criminal lawyer, Pip continues to be thrown in contact with a world that he associates with Magwitch and that taints even his pursuit of Estella. Thus at one point when he is waiting for Estella, immediately after a tour through Newgate, he frantically tries to beat the prison dust from his clothes. Instead, the aura of prison clings to him: "I consumed the whole time in thinking how strange it was that I should be encompassed by all this taint of prison and crime; that, in my childhood out on our lonely marshes on a winter evening I should have first encountered it; that, it should have reappeared on two occasions, starting out like a stain that has faded but not gone; that, it should in this new way pervade my fortune and advancement." (32:285)

Magwitch proves to be not only Pip's benefactor but also the father of Estella. We don't know this until chapter 50; we simply feel an inexplicable weight of criminality on Pip. But even when Pip's connections with Magwitch are finally accounted for, his sense of criminality and guilt remains unappeased and unexplained. His hatred and disgust toward Magwitch linger on in peculiarly unresolved ways. Pip's immediate response to the returned convict, like his later rejection of Magwitch's money,[5] is absolute: "The abhorrence in which I held the man, the dread I had of him, the repugnance with which I shrank from him, could not have been exceeded if he had been some terrible beast" (39:346).

The hero's initial fears of Magwitch are tied to an equally powerful hatred of him. The process of repressing this hatred and learning to love his benefactor is only partially successful. In childhood Pip tries to soothe his fears by imagining Magwitch transported or dead (19).[6] When he reappears, Pip quarters him elsewhere and soon hopes to ship him out of the country again. As Pip realizes that he is the cause of Magwitch's illegal return, he fancies himself "in some sort, as his murderer" (41:370). Pip seems capable of loving Magwitch only to the degree that Magwitch is helpless and endangered. Pip's solicitude is suspect when he comments, "it was dreadful to think that I could not be sorry at heart for his being badly hurt, since it was unquestionably best that he should die" (54:483–84). And in a peculiar, if suggestive, incident Pip believes himself to be suspected of carrying poison to Magwitch.[7] It is very unlike Dickens to introduce this suspicion and then to drop it completely. As minor as the incident is, it reinforces our sense of Pip's lingering hostility toward Magwitch. This seems, in fact, the only way of accounting for it.

The relationship between Pip and Magwitch is obviously central to our understanding of the novel. A literal summary of its progress, however, does not adequately account for its power. Although we know that Dickens first conceived the novel in terms of these two figures and their effect on each other, we don't know why they so fascinated him. Pip's own reaction to Magwitch far exceeds anything Magwitch does to him; the haunting fear and hatred in their first encounter affect Pip throughout the novel, lingering in ways that Dickens himself may have been unaware of (as in the "poisoning incident"). Dickens's evident incapacity to provide an explanation for Pip's continuing guilt suggests that for both Pip and Dickens himself, the Pip-Magwitch relationship has deep unconscious roots. Magwitch, I believe, must be understood as Pip's father— or, more specifically, as that aspect of the father that both threatens and terrifies a child.

A number of passages strongly imply this relationship. "As I never saw my father or my mother," Pip tells us in chapter 1, "and never saw any likeness of either of them . . . my first fancies regarding what they were like, were unreasonably derived from their tombstones" (1:1). One paragraph later, Magwitch leaps at Pip from among the tombstones marking his parents' graves. And the chapter closes with Magwitch moving back toward the dead: "As I saw him go . . . he looked in my young eyes as if he were eluding the hands of the dead people, stretching up cautiously out of their graves, to get a twist upon his ankle and pull him in" (1:5). When Magwitch returns from the colonies and Pip recoils from him, Magwitch makes it quite clear how he sees their relationship: "Look'ee here, Pip. I'm your second father. You're my son—more to me nor any son" (39:346).

What is crucial here is not simply the suggestion or actual statement of a father-son relationship, but the context of that relationship—the fear and guilt that so intensely accompany these two scenes. Magwitch threatens to overwhelm Pip, either by brute force or by love. Socially, Magwitch first drags Pip into the mud of his own attempted escape, makes him a criminal accomplice, and then goes to an opposite extreme of elevating Pip as high as his money will carry the boy. Imagery relating to phallic strength and fear of castration pervades these scenes with Magwitch and suggests the source of their intensity. For example, Magwitch's return is heralded by a detailed account of the weather:

> It was wretched weather; stormy and wet, stormy and wet; mud, mud, mud, deep in all the streets. . . . So furious had been the gusts, that high buildings in town had had the lead stripped off their roofs; and in the country, trees had been torn up, and sails of windmills carried away; and gloomy accounts had come in from the coast, of shipwreck and death. . . . We lived at the top of the last house, and the wind rushing up the river shook the house that night, like discharges of cannon or break-ings of a sea. When the rain came with it and dashed against the win-dows, I thought . . . that I might have fancied myself in a storm-beaten light-house. . . . the staircase lamps were blown out; . . . [and] through the black windows (opening them ever so little was out of the question in the teeth of such wind and rain) I saw that the lamps in the court were blown out, and that the lamps on the bridges and the shore were shud-dering, and that the coal fires in barges on the river were being carried away before the wind like red-hot splashes in the rain. (39:339–40)

The repeated references to objects torn, pulled out at their roots, stripped, and blown out, attacking the doors, windows, and passages of Pip's house, suggest a personal assault. Later Pip admits, "In every rage of wind and rush of rain, I heard pursuers . . . I began either to imagine or recall that I had had mysterious warnings of this man's approach" (39:350). The language of these warnings implies that Magwitch's strength is phallic and that he threatens Pip with both castration and a sexual attack on the passages of Pip's body. Thus Pip pulls back from Magwitch as if "he had been some terrible beast," or, even more specifi-cally: "I recoiled from his touch as if he had been a snake." And again: "At a change in his manner as if he were even going to embrace me, I laid a hand upon his breast and put him away" (39:347, 342). The first words Magwitch utters offer to slice Pip open, and Magwitch goes on to specify a few internal organs (heart and liver) on which he has particular designs.

Magwitch's "young man" has similar aims, and is likely to appear even when Pip has locked his door and is safely tucked in bed; and Magwitch's emissary in chapter 10 possesses the alarming phallic powers of "an invisible gun" forever pointed at Pip, as well as the stolen file. It was this file that reappeared in Pip's nightmare, held by some invisible hand (10:83). That hand is surely Magwitch's, and in chapter 39 we find that Magwitch "laid his hand on my shoulder. I shuddered at the thought that for anything I knew, his hand might be stained with blood" (348).

At the height of his anxiety over the storm Pip hears the sound of a church clock striking eleven, and Magwitch makes his appearance: "I was listening, and thinking how the wind assailed and tore it, when I heard a footstep on the stair." And Pip adds: "What nervous folly made me start, and awfully connect it with the footstep of my dead sister, matters not" (39:340). It actually matters a great deal. Like the reference to Pip's carrying poison to Magwitch, this peculiar suggestion is made and then dropped. There is no apparent reason for Dickens to introduce it, and there is no apparent use made of it once it has been introduced. But I suggest that it intimates an unconscious connection between Magwitch, Joe, and Mrs. Joe: they enact various parental attitudes of an Oedipal triangle centering on Pip. Moreover, the pervasive sense of crime in the novel may be traced back, through the association with Magwitch, to the original crimes Pip commits: the theft of Joe's file, and the robbing of Mrs. Joe.

Mrs. Joe is represented in the most forbidding terms: "She was tall and bony, and almost always wore a coarse apron, fastened over her figure behind with two loops, and having a square impregnable bib in front, that was stuck full of pins and needles" (2:7). That bib is the very essence of her as a woman: it makes her literally "impregnable," and minimizes the effect of anything stuck into her. It is against this formidable foster mother that Pip commits his first crime. He robs her, stealing at dawn into her kitchen pantry, probing into jars, uncovering dishes, and finally escaping with her "beautiful round compact pork pie" (2:15). This intimation of an incestuous entering and robbing of the mother is developed in Pip's own guilt over the impending act when he comments: "I was in mortal terror of the young man who wanted my heart and liver; I was in mortal terror of my interlocutor with the iron leg; I was in mortal terror of myself, from whom an awful promise had been extracted" (2:14). Most importantly, the first "crime" against Mrs. Joe is magnified into a genuine assault on her by Orlick, later in the novel. Julian Moynahan has suggested that Orlick (and later, Bentley Drummle) "enact an aggressive potential that the novel defines, through patterns of analogy and linked resemblances, as belonging in the end to Pip and to his unconscionably ambitious hopes."[8] He shows that Orlick commits the crime for which Pip has all the justification. Although he also shows that Orlick enacts an aggressively sexual side of Pip in his pursuit of Biddy, he does not see the attack on Mrs. Joe in this light.[9] The emphasis on the weapon, Mrs. Joe's falling and bleeding, and the subsequent, inexplicable propitiation of Orlick all suggest, however, that this attack carries strong sexual overtones. Particular attention is directed to the weapon used—"something blunt and heavy"—which turns out to be Magwitch's old leg-iron. And Pip laments: "It was horrible to think that I had provided the weapon, however undesignedly, but I could hardly think otherwise" (16:129, 130).

Once the assault has been carried out, Mrs. Joe is a changed woman. She no longer torments Pip or Joe, and she positively plays up to Orlick: "I confess that I expected to see my sister denounce him, and that I was disappointed by the different result. She manifested the greatest anxiety to be on good terms with him, was evidently much pleased by his being at length produced, and motioned that she would have him given something to drink. . . . and there was an air of humble propitiation in all she did, such as I have seen pervade the bearing of a child towards a hard master" (16:133).[10]

Her hardness and lack of femininity have been assaulted and broken down with a vengeance. It is as if the formidable bib and forbidding air were themselves symbolic of the taboos of incest, and had been pierced by Orlick—but at a price. Mrs. Joe soon dies, while Pip's guilt continues to grow. Hearing Magwitch and thinking of Mrs. Joe, with the fearful storm raging outside, Pip brings an unconscious thread of the novel to a climax. Those footsteps arouse Pip's guilty conscience. Someone has come to avenge the crime against his dead sister.

To understand why that avenger is Magwitch—and not, for example, Joe, who is husband to Mrs. Joe and a more obvious father to Pip—we must recognize that ambivalent attitudes toward a single father have been split apart in this novel and divided between at least two father figures, Joe and Magwitch. Freud wrote:

> The relation of the boy to the father is, as we say, an "ambivalent" one (that is, composed of conflicting feelings of tenderness and hostility). In addition to the hate which wants to remove the father as a rival, a measure of tenderness for him also exists as a rule. Both attitudes of mind combine to produce identification with the father: the boy wants to be in his father's place because he admires him and wants to be like him, and also because he wishes to put him out of his way. At a certain moment the child comes to understand that the attempt to remove the father as a rival would be punished by the father with castration.[11]

In the imaginative world of Pip's childhood Magwitch is the castrating father—the "pirate," the "snake," the "terrible beast" come to cut the organs out of little Pip. The "measure of tenderness" and "admiration" for the father are concentrated on Joe. As a result Joe is virtually feminized in his relations with Pip. The theft of his phallic file and its surrender to

Magwitch dramatize Joe's weakness; they also locate the father's power—and potential for revenge—in Magwitch's hands.

Pip tells us that he always treated Joe as "a larger species of child, and as no more than my equal" (2:7). Before he is exposed to Miss Havisham, before he develops his love for Estella and his social aspirations, Pip knows a kind of pastoral bliss beside Joe, emulating his work in the forge. Whenever he sees Joe after he has left for London, he is reminded of the "larks" they were to have had together and of the old quiet life by the forge that he has lost. He first describes Joe as "a mild, good-natured, sweet-tempered, easy-going, foolish, dear fellow—a sort of Hercules in strength, and also in weakness" (2:6). Later he writes, "Joe laid his hand upon my shoulder with the touch of a woman. I have often thought him since like the steam-hammer, that can crush a man or pat an eggshell, in his combination of strength with gentleness" (18:151–52). In dealing with Orlick Joe displays his most effective steam-hammer qualities, and Pip is lost in admiration: "if any man in that neighbourhood could stand up long against Joe, I never saw the man" (15:122). Only Joe's egg-shell tenderness, however, is directed toward Pip. At times this aspect of the blacksmith is carried to a ludicrous extreme. For example, at Mrs. Joe's funeral we find "Poor dear Joe, entangled in a little black cloak tied in a large bow under his chin . . . seated apart at the upper end of the room" (35:302).

A small boy's relationship to his father is defined between the polarities of killing and replacing him or submitting fully to his power. In the latter case he may solve the problem of incest and consequent fear of the father by deciding to take the mother's role himself, even imagining that he will bear the father's child.[12] This solution, clearly not part of Dickens's conscious intention, is nevertheless suggested at two points in the text. The comic and sad encounter between Joe and Pip in London is occasioned by a message from Miss Havisham. Joe comes down to London to pass it on, receives an uncomfortable welcome from Pip, and is made awkward and formal in his turn. But he is determined to relate his conversation with Miss Havisham. She had asked if he were in correspondence with Mr. Pip. "Having had a letter from you, I were able to say 'I am.' (When I married your sister, Sir, I said 'I will'; and when I answered your friend, Pip, I said, 'I am.')" (27:241). The comic allusion to a marriage comments ironically on Pip's coolness toward Joe: they have scarcely any contact now, and their once close union has been dissolved. Unconsciously, it suggests that their former tie was a kind of marriage.

Much earlier in the novel, when Pip and Joe are on the closest of terms, Pip scrawls out another letter for Joe. They are alone together, and Pip is learning how to write:

мI dеEr JO i opE U r krWitE wEll i opE i shAl soN B haBelL 4 2
teeDge U JO aN ThEN wE shOrl B sO glOdd aN wEn i M preNgtD 2 u
JO woT larX aN blEvE ME inF xn PiP" (7:47).

Unlike such extra letters as the "r" in "krWitE" (which helps to reproduce a dialect sound in pronouncing the word), the "g" in "preNgtD"
seems wholly gratuitous. But it makes the phrase look more like "preg-
nant to you" than "prenticed to you."

One further piece of textual evidence may help to demonstrate the
unconscious splitting of attitudes toward the father in *Great Expectations*. Some twenty years ago there was an exchange of articles between
John Butt and Humphry House. Butt had published Dickens's outline or
plan for the conclusion of *Great Expectations*. He and House debated the
exact dating of the plan and the use Dickens made of it. At one point, convinced by House's argument, Butt changed his earlier position and argued that the plan applied only to the final episodes of the novel: "Other
details help to confirm this view. Miss Havisham's lover was originally
named 'Compey,' and so the name stands in Chapter 42 of the Wisbech
MS. Later Dickens changed the name to 'Compeyson,' and we can watch
him in the act of adding the last three letters to the name in the manuscript of Chapter 45."[13] "Compeyson" is also the form that appears in the
manuscript plan: "Compeyson. How brought in?" Butt writes: "But
Compeyson had been 'in' from the beginning of the novel, and he had
been actively shadowing Pip and Magwitch from the first chapter of the
final stage. Moreover Dickens had 'brought in' his relationship to Miss
Havisham while he was still calling him 'Compey.' 'How brought in' must
therefore refer to something else, and to what else can it refer but to
Compeyson's part in the scene of Magwitch's capture?"[14] Butt's scholarship raises still another question: why should Dickens bother to change
the name of this character at all, and what, if any, relationship does this
have to the climactic scene on the river? The answer, I believe, lies in the
unconscious meaning of the added suffix, and more generally in
Compeyson's role as another of Pip's alter egos, like Orlick.

Compeyson is a confidence man, selfishly abusing the trust and love
he inspires by posing as a gentleman, while Pip looks back on his own expectations and aspirations to be a gentleman as criminally selfish.
Compeyson betrays Miss Havisham; Miss Havisham tries to dupe Pip,
abusing both Estella and Pip in her desire for revenge. But most importantly, Compeyson's relationship to Magwitch is a projection of Pip's unconscious response to his benefactor. We have seen that Pip reveals a
desire for Magwitch's death along with his terror of him. Compeyson
tries to destroy Magwitch and is destroyed in turn.

When Pip aids Magwitch's attempted escape, late in the novel, he
nervously comments on the convict's calm: "One would have supposed
that it was I who was in danger, not he . . ." (54:479). With the steamer

bearing down upon them, Magwitch is apprehended from a customs galley, and he responds by reaching across and seizing a muffled figure shrinking back in a corner of the galley. The figure is Compeyson, who has pursued Magwitch and betrayed him. At that instant the steamer hits the two boats. These events occur so swiftly that Pip is struck by a blow and stunned unconscious during Compeyson's fight with Magwitch:

> Still in the same moment, I saw the face [i.e., Compeyson's] tilt backward with a white terror on it that I shall never forget, and heard a great cry on board the steamer and a loud splash in the water, and felt the boat sink from under me.
>   It was but for an instant that I seemed to struggle with a thousand mill-weirs and a thousand flashes of light; that instant past, I was taken on board the galley. (54:481)

Pip's struggle coincides exactly with the struggle between Magwitch and Compeyson. Magwitch later tells Pip that he and Compeyson "had gone down, fiercely locked in each other's arms, and that there had been a struggle under water, and that he had disengaged himself, struck out, and swam away" (54:482–83). The simultaneity of the two events suggests a confusion between Pip and Compeyson which the plot as a whole reinforces.

Compeyson is thus a kind of scapegoat-Pip. Once he has been disposed of, Pip feels much closer to Magwitch: "for now my repugnance to him had all melted away" (54:483).[15] It seems reasonable to suppose that Dickens played with the name "Compey" until he found a variation that sounded right, satisfying his unconscious sense of Compey's role in the novel. "Compey" is a patricidal "son," on whom the father takes appropriate vengeance.

Following this scene on the river the novel moves swiftly toward its conclusion. Magwitch dies in prison, and in the following chapter Pip contracts a fever.[16] He falls into a coma and appears to hallucinate:

> . . . that I often lost my reason, that the time seemed interminable, that I confounded impossible existences with my own identity; that I was a brick in the house wall, and yet entreating to be released from the giddy place where the builders had set me; that I was a steel beam of a vast engine, clashing and whirling over a gulf, and yet that I implored in my own person to have the engine stopped, and my part in it hammered off; that I passed through these phases of disease, I know of my own remembrance, and did in some sort know at the time. That I sometimes struggled with real people, in the belief that they were murderers, and that I would all at once comprehend that they meant to do me good, and would then sink exhausted in their arms, and suffer them to lay me down, I also knew at the time. But, above all, I knew that there was a constant tendency in all these people—who, when I was very ill, would present all kinds of extraordinary transformations of the human face, and would be much di-

lated in size—above all, I say, I knew that there was an extraordinary tendency in all these people, sooner or later, to settle down into the likeness of Joe. (57:500–501)

Pip then wakes up to find Joe at his bedside, nursing him back to health.

Julian Moynahan believes that Pip's hallucinations "articulate the division in his character between helpless passivity and demonic aggressiveness."[17] It is possible to be still more specific. All the images in this passage refer to the dualities we have associated with Magwitch and Joe, and to the response they elicit from Pip. The important quality of the first image would appear to be the giddy height that frightens Pip, possibly suggesting erection. Each of the final two images unmistakably shows Pip repudiating his "rise," his power within the vast engine, and begging instead for a symbolic castration: "to have the engine stopped, and my part in it hammered off." The next hallucination locates these fears more specifically: he dreams of struggling with murderers who turn out to be friends. In the preceding three chapters Magwitch has murdered Compeyson and Pip has responded with a greater trust and love for the convict than he had previously shown. In the hallucination the murderers-turned-friends look more and more like Joe. The fantasy anticipates the transition to a waking state, as Pip gradually focuses on his nurse, and it also reduplicates in miniature the larger transition of the novel: having left Joe, fought against Magwitch, and been reconciled to him, he is now about to return to Joe's care.

The final reflection is astonishingly specific. It shows that these pendulum swings of the novel reflect Pip's struggle with a powerful phallic father (Magwitch) and his desire to submit to a passive love of the much gentler Joe. "The human face" behaves like a human phallus: it transforms itself by dilating in size, by expanding and then contracting until it finally settles "down into the likeness of Joe."

The solution Pip seeks at the close of the novel is a figurative self-castration and a return to a childhood state of absolute dependence on Joe:

> I was slow to gain strength, but I did slowly and surely become less weak, and Joe stayed with me, and I fancied I was little Pip again.
>
> For, the tenderness of Joe was so beautifully proportioned to my need, that I was like a child in his hands. He would sit and talk to me . . . in the old unassertive protecting way . . . He did everything for me except the household work, for which he had engaged a very decent woman . . . (57:505)

When Pip is able to leave London,

> an open carriage was got into the Lane, Joe wrapped me up, took me in his arms, carried me down to it, and put me in, as if I were still the small helpless creature to whom he had so abundantly given of the wealth of his great nature. . . . and I laid my head on Joe's shoulder, as I had laid it

long ago when he had taken me to the Fair or where not, and it was too much for my young senses. (57:505–6)

When he feels Joe once again growing distant with him, he accuses his own callous independence:

> Ah! Had I given Joe no reason to doubt my constancy, and to think that in prosperity I should grow cold to him and cast him off? Had I given Joe's innocent heart no cause to feel instinctively that as I got stronger, his hold upon me would be weaker . . . ? (57:509)

Pip actually repeats a state of infancy when, with the father watching, he demonstrates his ability to walk: "See, Joe! I can walk quite strongly. Now, you shall see me walk back by myself" (57:509). When Joe answers him as "sir," Pip devises a regressive means of recapturing their lost intimacy:

> The last word ['sir'] grated on me; but how could I remonstrate! I walked no further than the gate of the gardens, and then pretended to be weaker than I was, and asked Joe for his arm (57:509)

Although the final chapter of *Great Expectations* has Pip leaving for Egypt and not returning for eleven years, we feel that the real close of the novel occurs with his return to Joe and Biddy. Pip had hoped to propose marriage to Biddy, but this would have been a strange marriage, smacking of a child-parent relationship. He intends to ask her if she "can receive me like a forgiven child (and indeed I am as sorry, Biddy, and have as much need of a hushing voice and a soothing hand) . . ." (57:511). Biddy ends by marrying Joe and becoming in a sense Pip's mother. Thus in the final chapter, when Pip returns after eleven years to surprise Joe and Biddy, he finds an infant "Pip" in his place:

> There, smoking his pipe in the old place by the kitchen firelight, as hale and as strong as ever, though a little grey, sat Joe; and there, fenced into the corner with Joe's leg, and sitting on my own little stool looking at the fire, was—I again!
> "We giv' him the name of Pip for your sake, dear old chap," said Joe, delighted when I took another stool by the child's side . . . (59:521)

2

Magwitch's function in the novel cannot be defined purely in terms of a threatening, paternal relationship with Pip. He is also a victim of society, the product of an expanding materialist economy that was itself criminally negligent of the lower classes it exploited. Magwitch's life history is a parable of Victorian economic life: he had been deserted from earliest memory, left to fend for himself, and forced into stealing merely in order to survive. He is seen as dirty, dangerous, and a hardened criminal by those who have shaped him and who wish to keep him at a distance—in prison or transported (42:passim).

It seems fitting, then, that he should be particularly associated with dirt. When Pip first sees him he is "smothered in mud" (1:2); he calls himself a "dung-hill dog"; he fights Compeyson in a muddy ditch, twice escapes, and is twice captured in the mud flats of a Thames swamp; and he makes his reappearance in London when there is "mud, mud, mud, deep in all the streets" (39:346, 339). One critic comments: "Mud is a peculiarly appropriate symbol for the class of society that Magwitch represents—the downtrodden and oppressed of life, all those victims of injustice whom society has tried to submerge. It is a natural image of the social dunghill in which violence and rebellion are fomented. . . ."[18] "Dunghill" is a well-chosen term, as Magwitch's effect on Pip is often described as one of soiling or staining.

In fact, the ideas and images associated with Magwitch—dirt, lack of self-control (revealed in his excesses of temper and revenge, of love for Pip), money and gifts—all partake of the psychoanalytic complex of anality.[19] It is not that Magwitch is himself an "anal personality" but rather that he evokes the particular range of associations originating in a child's attitude toward his feces. These images tell us that money is dirty, that a blatant need for it is demeaning, and that making it is itself a process that stains or pollutes. This attitude toward money certainly pervades Pip's snobbery, if not snobbery in general. The snob's poses of not soiling his hands, of holding his head high, and of turning up his nose are all characteristically "anal."

Pip turns down Magwitch's first gift, the two pound notes sent via another convict, with an obvious disgust for the dirt and foul associations he automatically attributes to them: "two fat sweltering one-pound notes that seemed to have been on terms of the warmest intimacy with all the cattle markets in the county" (10:83). Such language indicates a further basis for Pip's revulsion toward Magwitch's second gift, the money of his great expectations. We have seen the unconscious association suggested earlier, linking Magwitch with a threatening image of the father. There is also the Victorian social stigma normally attached to dealings with or dependency on a criminal, and that stigma itself stresses an association between money and feces (the "dust piles" in *Our Mutual Friend*), which was strongly felt in the period and still more strongly defended against.

Jaggers's response to Magwitch, and to the poor and criminal classes in general, is characteristic of Victorian society's "successful" repression of the basis of its own wealth and expectations. Not accidentally, Jaggers is also a model of the anal personality—highly ordered, obstinate, and compulsively clean. His ritualistic cleanliness leaves the constant smell of "scented soap" on his hands, and leads to a scene like this:

> . . . he washed his clients off, as if he were a surgeon or a dentist. He had a
> closet in his room, fitted up for the purpose, which smelt of the scented
> soap like a perfumer's shop. It had an unusually large jack-towel on a

roller inside the door, and he would wash his hands, and wipe them and dry them all over this towel, whenever he came in from a police-court or dismissed a client from his room. When I and my friends repaired to him at six o'clock next day, he seemed to have been engaged on a case of a darker complexion than usual, for, we found him with his head butted into this closet, not only washing his hands, but laving his face and gargling his throat. And even when he had done all that, and had gone all round the jack-towel, he took out his penknife and scraped the case out of his nails before he put his coat on. (26:226–27)

This ritual defines the nature and basis of his self-control and moral fastidiousness. The normal requirements of his working day, his contact with clients, the law, prisons, people in general constantly threaten to soil him—much as Pip feels his existence strangely stained after leaving Jaggers's office or visiting Newgate, and feels this stain about to pollute his meeting with Estella. Jaggers's office is in Little Britain. The pollution of his daily life and his response to it are a microcosm of the business world of nineteenth-century Britain.

Like any successful figure in that world, Jaggers is also highly aggressive, but he is careful to keep his aggression under strict control. Jaggers's obvious exaggerations are built on the most sacred economic and ethical clichés of the period. The ambitious man of the era hoped to "rise" in the world, to thrust himself to the top of his economic and social group, yet he tried not to appear competitive, crude, ungentlemanly. The adjective "manly," as it was used by the Victorians, contained both aspects of this idea: male strength and power, plus a self-imposed restraint: "There are many tests by which a gentleman may be known; but there is one that never fails—How does he *exercise power* over those subordinate to him? How does he conduct himself towards women and children? . . . Strength, and the consciousness of strength, in a righthearted man imparts a nobleness to his character; but he will be most careful how he uses it. . . . Gentleness is indeed the best test of gentlemanliness."[20]

The sense of conflict and repression built into such terminology mirrors the conflict at work in Jaggers and the world he symbolizes. The very physical appearance of the lawyer simultaneously asserts his masculinity and denies it: "He was a burly man of an exceedingly dark complexion, with an exceedingly large head and a corresponding large hand. . . . He was prematurely bald on the top of his head, and had bushy black eyebrows that wouldn't lie down, but stood up bristling. His eyes were set very deep in his head, and were disagreeably sharp and suspicious. He had . . . strong black dots where his beard and whiskers would have been if he had let them" (11:87). We are very aware of hair on his face which bristles with assertion, and we are even more aware of hair which isn't there—the early baldness on a large head, the heavy beard which is kept back. His moral posture strikes the same note. As Wemmick repeatedly tells us, Jaggers is "always so high"—a phrase which implies his moral superiority and associates it with male power. Dickens's portrayal of Jaggers reveals the enormous discomfort occasioned by the lawyer's moral positions and clarifications. When he cross-examines Wopsle or disposes of a client he asserts himself to a point of total domination, but always with a strict self-control that seems to deny the assertiveness. When Pip comes to remonstrate with him, Jaggers immediately puts Pip on the defensive by absolving himself of any involvement, any interest at all. "Don't commit yourself . . . and don't commit any one. You understand—any one. Don't tell me anything. I don't want to know anything" (40:360). This phallic assertion and its immediate repression, characteristic of Jaggers and of the language of economic power in the period generally, are epitomized in Jaggers's most distinctive gesture. He throws out his great forefinger, and then bites it "accusingly."

Jaggers affects Pip in many ways that suggest a legitimized, and consequently a less overtly frightening, version of Magwitch. He is Magwitch's agent and spokesman for a good part of the novel. He distributes Magwitch's money to Pip and in the process he cleans it up until the time when Pip discovers its (dirty) source. As Pip's guardian, he behaves like a chiding, disapproving father. Between them Magwitch and Jaggers suggest opposite but related sides to Victorian economic life—the dirty and the clean, the criminal and the legitimate.

Their shared qualities offer additional insight into Pip's hallucinations in chapter 57. There Pip feels himself giddily exposed, first as a brick and then as a steel beam of a vast engine, and begs to be removed from his height, to have the engine stopped and his "part in it hammered off" (57:500). We can now see that his fear of phallic assertiveness and desire for symbolic castration have two related meanings. They signal, in his personal life, a shift in attitude toward the father, a movement from Magwitch to Joe. But the sense of a vast whirling engine or great housewall in which he has been placed is also his and our sense of society as a whole. Julian Moynahan writes that "the hero-victim cries for release from his unsought position of height and power, but cannot help himself from functioning as a moving part of a monstrous apparatus. . . . In the narrative's full context this vast engine can be taken to represent at one and the same time the demonic side of the hero's career and a society that maintains its power intact by the continuous destruction of the hopes and lives of its weaker members."[21] The imagery of Pip's hallucinations and even Moynahan's own language suggest an identical unconscious basis for individual and social attitudes in the novel. "The monstrous apparatus" is powerful and male, and its fierceness destroys what Moynahan aptly terms "its weaker members." Just as Pip fears to assert himself against Magwitch (and suffer the fate of Compeyson), so he fears to assert himself in society, to find work, to succeed, and to abuse the lower classes as society itself has abused Magwitch. The underlying pattern of phallic aggression and fear of castration is present in a social as well as a personal reading of this passage.

Jaggers's goal would seem to be total self-reliance: sufficient control over those people and objects around him to ensure his safety, his own freedom of action, and ultimately his dissociation from any human emotion. His actions exaggerate and parody the popular notions of self-reliance and self-help of the period. The "self-made man" is a man who owes his success to no one, who has perfect control over his own movements, over what he takes in and what he releases. In psychoanalytic terms the concept suggests an individual's desire for mastery of his body and of his very existence: he has made (created) himself. The adult solution to problems of independence and economic self-reliance will be excessively important to a man whose childhood contains conflict over related issues. Similarly, in a society where children grow up in competition with strong fathers (where the family structures tend to be markedly patriarchal), and where great stress is placed on cleanliness, toilet-training, and self-control, the family and business structures will be mutually reinforcing.

Financial independence thus becomes of paramount importance, whereas "any class of men that lives from hand to mouth will ever be an inferior class. They will necessarily remain impotent and helpless."[22] To avoid this impotence Smiles urges "the virtue of self-denial, than which nothing is so much calculated to give strength to the character."[23] The ideal of an economically independent man is attained by an adult version of toilet training, as Smiles's language makes clear:

> Economy, at bottom, is but the spirit of order applied in the administration of domestic affairs: it means management, regularity, prudence, and the avoidance of waste. . . .
> Economy also means the power of resisting present gratification for the purpose of securing a future good, and in this light it represents the ascendency of reason over the animal instincts.[24]

Smiles's thought reveals a combination of anal and genital attitudes that seems particularly Victorian. Helplessness and impotence result from a lack of wealth; self-denial gives strength and power to the individual. As he reminds his readers at one point, there are two classes of men: "those who have saved, and those who have spent."[25] The latter waste their power, the former are the industrial monarchs of society. Steven Marcus has shown how this "economic" mode of thought was part of the official Victorian doctrine of sexuality. Marcus describes Dr. William Acton's warnings against masturbation, concluding that Acton's apparently scientific advice is essentially fantasy, built on fear of sexuality:

> The fantasies that are at work here have to do with economics; the body is regarded as a productive system with only a limited amount of material at its disposal. And the model on which the notion of semen is formed is

clearly that of money. Science, in the shape of Acton, is thus still expressing what had for long been a popular fantasy: up until the end of the nineteenth century the chief English colloquial expression for the orgasm was
"to spend." . . . Furthermore, the economy envisaged in this idea is based
on scarcity and has as its aim the accumulation of its own product.[26]

Marcus goes on to suggest two ideas behind this Victorian fantasy: the
fear of poverty and the tendency to regard the human body as a machine.

Dickens's novels demonstrate the pervasiveness of both ideas. Wills,
gifts, hidden paternity, and recurrent great expectations are the con-
cretely financial rewards lavished on his heroes, while economic disaster
leads characters from every social class—Little Nell, Betty Higden, or
the financial giant, Merdle—to death. Dorothy Van Ghent has shown
that the mechanical view of people as things or parts of things and the ani-
mation of the inanimate inform the vision of *Great Expectations*, and are
prominent as early as *Martin Chuzzlewit*.[27] Both Jaggers and Magwitch
share in this mechanization: Jaggers forces Wemmick into a fixed pose of
reticence known as his "post-office mouth"; and he is himself mechani-
cally ritualistic in his cleanliness and in the accusatory gesture of his
forefinger—a gesture that finally comes to stand for him. Magwitch virtually incorporates Pip as an extension of himself in his financial desire to
"make a gentleman" out of the mire of his own life,[28] to clean and gild the
degradation felt while accumulating money: "I mustn't see my gentleman a footing it in the mire of the streets; there mustn't be no mud on *his*
boots" (40:357).

Psychoanalysis tells us that a child's first notion of his feces are that
they are a part or extension of himself. With a boy they become associated in his mind with that part of himself he most fears to lose—the
penis—and are thus closely linked to fears of castration. Holding on to
feces, in a later stage of development, may result from an overwhelming
fear of castration; if the Oedipal conflict strongly reinforces such fears,
the solution may be to regress to an earlier mode of thought and an earlier
conflict, to substitute feces for penis and hold on to the former as a means
of protecting the latter. But psychoanalysis has shown that reversal is
often used defensively in neurotic thought, and an opposite solution may
also be used for the same problem: threatened with a fear of castration,
the neurotic decides to give in, to relinquish the penis or to go back to the
anal substitute and relinquish wealth.[29]

In *Great Expectations* the powerful and threatening fathers also control the source of Pip's wealth. We have already seen that Pip desires to be
rid of both Magwitch and Jaggers but avoids open conflict with them. Fear-
ing castration, he seeks a regressive solution—appeasement of the father
along with denial of his own aggressive, incestuous wishes. So, too, he
seeks to adopt an aloof and genteel attitude toward material possession,
the attitude of the inept Matthew and Herbert Pocket, and finally he re-

nounces altogether the money proffered by Magwitch. The business of a gentleman, it would seem, is no business at all, a denial of money-making which ought to lead to a denial of money itself—to poverty. The unconscious wish behind this aspect of the novel is a desire to reverse society's imposed pattern of phallic competition and economic control—to be generous, disinterested, and wholly above such competition.

And this is precisely how Dickens resolves Pip's business career. He credits Pip with one disinterested act: setting up Herbert Pocket in business. Pip rejects Magwitch's money with all its unpleasant associations, but he manages to spend a portion of it on Herbert before he is made aware of those associations. The investment is sound. Pip can roll up his sleeves and go to work for Clarriker's, he can give up his independence and work for someone else, knowing all the time that he himself has created his employer. He is a self-made man. This act guarantees his own power while asserting his disinterestedness and lack of manipulation. The hero's realized expectations with Clarriker's gratify a wish for independence and success which is everywhere in the novel, beginning with its title, but the wish is gratified by what seems a deus ex machina. Pip achieves his expectations too easily, without actually suffering the price they appear to demand.

Pip's problems are caricatured and overcome in the portrayal of Wemmick. At work Wemmick is dominated by his employer, who places him in the outer office and makes him screen anyone who enters. His eating habits here epitomize the role he must adopt: "Wemmick was at his desk, lunching—and crunching—on a dry hard biscuit; pieces of which he threw from time to time into his slit of a mouth, as if he were posting them" (24:213). Everyone who enters and leaves the office is carefully checked and dealt with in the same manner. Wemmick turns himself into a machine in order to eat, to receive or give directions, to dispose of people and property. His ideal is to turn all possessions into portable property. At Walworth he has similarly built a fortress home, complete with drawbridge, whose entrances are narrow and protected, and are now under his exclusive control. Wemmick's identification with his snug retreat is the reverse of Pip's sense of exposure in his rooms on the evening of Magwitch's return. By controlling the entries and passages of his house Wemmick implicitly takes full control over himself.

The main difference between Wemmick's home and his office is his reversal of roles toward Jaggers and his own father. As Wemmick tells Pip, "Walworth is one place, and this office is another. Much as the Aged is one person, and Mr. Jaggers is another" (36:315). The extreme contrast between Wemmick's father ("the Aged" or "Aged Parent") and Jaggers is strikingly similar to the split for Pip between his guardian-benefactor and Joe. Whereas Joe is good-hearted and tender (and intellectually and socially Pip's inferior), Wemmick's father is simply senile. This gives the son full control over him. What is euphemistically described as "the great nightly ceremony" is a ritual prepared by Wemmick presumably for his father's benefit:

> Proceeding into the Castle again, we found the Aged heating the poker, with expectant eyes, as a preliminary to the performance of this great nightly ceremony. Wemmick stood with his watch in his hand until the moment was come for him to take the red-hot poker from the Aged, and repair to the battery. He took it, and went out, and presently the Stinger went off with a bang that shook the crazy little box of a cottage as if it must fall to pieces . . . Upon this the Aged—who I believe would have been blown out of his arm-chair but for holding on by the elbows—cried out exultingly, "He's fired! I heered him!" (25:224–25)

The hot poker, the gun, the explosion all emphasize the potency of Wemmick, who organizes the ceremony and fires the weapon—while his father grabs his chair for dear life. This scene may be a comic inversion of a primal scene. Instead of a boy's witnessing his parents copulating, and being terrified by what he takes to be their violence, the son himself now performs the "great nightly ceremony," and with parental approval. What is perfectly clear from the passage is an inversion of power from father to son. Wemmick is ideally tender and considerate of the Aged, and the Aged is ideally weakened and dependent on his son. There is no conflict because the Aged's senility is a most effective form of castration.

With Jaggers, Wemmick is another man, or son; he dramatically alters and splits his personality. While he and Pip are dining at Jaggers' home, Pip tries "catching his eye now and then in a friendly way. But it was not to be done. He turned his eyes on Mr. Jaggers whenever he raised them from the table, and was as dry and distant to me as if there were twin Wemmicks and this was the wrong one." (48:420). As they are about to leave a transformation takes place:

> Even when we were groping among Mr. Jaggers's stock of boots for our hats, I felt that the right twin was on his way back; and we had not gone half a dozen yards down Gerrard Street in the Walworth direction before I found that I was walking arm-in-arm with the right twin, and that the wrong twin had evaporated into the evening air.
>
> "Well!" said Wemmick, "that's over! He's a wonderful man, without his living likeness; but I feel that I have to screw myself up when I dine with him—and I dine more comfortably unscrewed." (48:423)

Wemmick can afford to be gentle and tender with his parent for the same reasons that Pip can afford to be "disinterested" in his position at Clarriker's; both are aware of their ultimate influence and control. Wemmick's exaggerated splitting of personalities between home and office is not only a profound comment on the gulf between moral and economic demands in the period, but also a filial strategy far more successful than Pip's. The aspects of Pip's psychic plight that must remain painfully repressed are made comically accessible to us through Wemmick. This is true, for example, of the very language used to describe Wemmick's father: "The Aged . . . might have passed for some clean old chief of a savage tribe, just oiled" (37:321). The basis of humor here is the treatment of what would normally be a symbol of potency and domination (the chief of a savage tribe) as if he were a harmless ("clean," "old") sexual tool ("just oiled"). The surprising and clever description is a "bribe," an inducement to allow a release of aggression against a father figure.[30] And the humor also lets us enjoy the mechanization of a human being (oiled like a tool) which is so frightening at other points in the novel.

Pip's fortunate solution to his financial problems, however, is neither comic nor successful. It is rather symptomatic of Dickens's own difficulty in trying to offer a viable alternative to the social ills he has described. The overt solution to Pip's great expectations is ill prepared and unconvincing, while the implied solution is regressive: the appearance of a little Pip back at the forge, tended by Joe and by a new, loving Mrs. Joe, and with all the problems of economic competition and social identity comfortably reserved for a distant point in the future.

This ultimate failure to suggest radical reform prompted Humphry House to call the book "the clearest artistic triumph of the Victorian bourgeoisie on its own special ground." House accused Dickens of shirking "the implications of the reconciliation with Joe and Biddy," and of trying to assure us that "Pip is the same decent little fellow after all: but what if he had had no Herbert to fall back on . . . ? Dickens . . . takes Pip's new class position as established, and whisks him off to the East, where gentlemen grow like mushrooms." Yet House defends the ending aesthetically because the book "is the sincere, uncritical expression of a time when the whole class drift was upwards and there was no reason to suppose that it would ever stop being so. The social ideals of Pip and Magwitch differ only in taste."[31]

I disagree. On the level of characterization, Dickens is quite critical of the upward class-drift of his society. The pressure of expectations tends to divide characters, to induce a separation between an external pose of correct aloofness and a covert aggression aiming at wealth and social supremacy. The few characters who fail to evidence this split— Matthew Pocket, for example—are dominated and lifeless. In *Great Expectations* the "correct" attitudes of the period have nothing like the emotional force of its criminality. Jaggers may manage, with great effort, to keep his hands clean of this criminal stain, but his success is hardly held up for emulation. Yet Dickens, for reasons that have never been satisfactorily explained, could not pursue the logic of his own implicit critique, either here or elsewhere in his works and life. His reactionary support of Carlyle in the Governor Eyre case, his contradictory positions on prison reform,[32] and his surprising repudiation of labor unions in *Hard Times*

(1854) are characteristic turnabouts, attempts to deny the reform whose necessity he had demonstrated. The ending of *Great Expectations* is typical precisely because it is inconsistent. But why this ambivalence?

The case of *Hard Times* suggests a possible answer. *Hard Times* is as oriented toward social criticism and social reform as any novel Dickens wrote. It castigates industrial society as a whole and raises the common industrial worker to the status of hero. But when the workers' grievances seem to lead them to a justified and total revolt, Dickens introduces an inept caricature of a union organizer to discredit the obvious solution. In a chapter entitled "Men and Brothers," he contrasts the short and twisted figure of Slackbridge "with the great body of his hearers in their plain working clothes." Slackbridge "was above the mass in very little but the stage on which he stood. In many great respects he was essentially below them. He was not so honest, he was not so manly. . . ."[33] The imagery emphasizes Slackbridge's lack of masculinity, his shortness, his twistedness, and his "mongrel dress,"[34] in comparison with the upright, "manly" workers in the hall. At the same time it emphasizes and deplores Slackbridge's attempt to raise and assert himself, either literally on the podium or by urging the men to crush their "masters" in a strike. The passage repudiates a rebellion against the industrial masters by denigrating the phallic power ("slack bridge") of the would-be leader of the rebellion, by implying castration or impotence as the necessary result of such a desire. Dickens here upholds the implicit contradiction in Victorian manliness. For the workers whom he idealizes, it means both strength *and* repression of that strength.

The clean, enduring, and self-controlled nature of his hero, Stephen Blackpool, reinforces this ideal. Stephen refuses to strike and is ostracized by his "brothers." In the following chapter, entitled "Men and Masters," Stephen also tries to maintain his independence from his overbearing employer, Mr. Bounderby. Implicitly he is seeking an equilibrium of ambivalent forces toward a father figure. Dickens is unwilling to have him either revolt entirely or become Bounderby's tool. Thus Stephen emerges as the epitome of "manliness," whose practical consequence is paralysis—he cannot revolt and he cannot work for Bounderby. In the end he leaves Coketown, is falsely accused of theft, and dies from his fall into the Old Hell Shaft.

The dissatisfying outcome of *Great Expectations* reflects not only Dickens's personal ambivalence but the unconscious contradictions of Victorian society with regard to money, the lower classes, and the upward class-drift described by Humphry House. In this shared ambivalence lies the power as well as the limitation of Dickens's novel. It is felt throughout Pip's personal history and in the social allegory of his great expectations. Dickens offers us a profound insight into the psychology underlying Victorian social attitudes—a psychology he seems to have fully shared.

3

The attempt to resolve social conflict in *Great Expectations* is only one of the problems of its final chapter. Dickens had submitted the last installment to Bulwer-Lytton, and allowed himself to be persuaded into a radical revision of the ending.[35] In its original (draft) version Pip's chance meeting with Estella simply leaves him with a sense that "suffering . . . had given her a heart to understand what my heart used to be" (59:523). Bentley Drummle has died, but Estella has remarried. In the published ending Estella has not remarried, and there is a clear suggestion of a future marriage to Pip. Pip finds her in Miss Havisham's old ruined garden, they part hand in hand, and Pip sees "no shadow of another parting from her" (59:526).

Our preference for one version or the other depends upon more than the plausibility of Pip's marriage to Estella. In order to accept the second ending we must take a wish, an impossible dream, as fact. Until the final chapter Dickens has made us feel Pip's hopeless idealization of a woman raised for revenge, raised—as Estella herself realizes—incapable of normal affections.

Dickens's heroines are always incomplete women. As his hero discovers the pretty young thing of his dreams to be a vacuous, spoiled child he attains a measure of self-understanding but is never reconciled to feminine imperfection. Rather, the woman herself is implausibly perfected, or simply replaced—as Dora Spenlow is replaced by Agnes Wickfield in *David Copperfield*. The very names of Dickens's heroines, culminating with the ironic Rosa Bud of *Edwin Drood*, suggest a self-parody of his tendency to create female china dolls. In *Great Expectations* Dickens seems particularly aware of his own limitations: instead of attempting to transform or eliminate Estella—at least until the final chapter—he uses her to dramatize Pip's self-delusion.

Dickens never really tries to portray Estella's emotions. She has been the object of other people's hopes and ideals, perhaps understanding them but incapable of a full response. "It seems," she tells Pip, "that there are sentiments, fancies—I don't know how to call them—which I am not able to comprehend. When you say you love me, I know what you mean, as a form of words; but nothing more. You address nothing in my breast, you touch nothing there" (44:390). Estella is Dickens's finest study of a beautiful and desired woman because she is seen so exclusively from without. She is created by those around her—by Miss Havisham, for whom she is an instrument of revenge, a more beautiful and invulnerable version of herself; and by Pip, for whom she is the ultimate great expectation, the princess awarded him by his fairy godmother. The second ending is dissonant because we suddenly see Estella from within, as really having a personality, and we are asked to believe that Pip's attitude toward her is completely altered.

From their first meeting, however, Pip's attraction for Estella is bound to a sense of her inaccessibility. "She seemed much older than I," he says on first meeting her, " . . . and beautiful and self-possessed; and she was as scornful of me as if she had been one-and-twenty, and a queen" (8:59). Pip thus becomes obsessed with what he cannot have, and finds himself incapable of pursuing a more satisfactory love. When he later contrasts Biddy and Estella, he realizes that "Biddy was never insulting, or capricious . . . ; she would have derived only pain, and no pleasure, from giving me pain; she would far rather have wounded her own breast than mine. How could it be, then, that I did not like her much the better of the two?" (17:140).

The answer is that his strongest attachments can only be maintained where there is little or no prospect of fulfillment. Only when Estella announces that she will marry Bentley Drummle does Pip make his own declaration. During this meeting, Pip admits that he has always loved her, has seen her everywhere ("on the river, on the sails of the ships, on the marshes, in the clouds . . .") and insists on the fact that "you must have done me far more good than harm, let me feel now what sharp distress I may" (44:393). But it is distress he has sought all along with Estella, and he fully indulges himself in it in this scene. He concludes: "In what ecstasy of unhappiness I got these broken words out of myself, I don't know. The rhapsody welled up within me, like blood from an inward wound, and gushed out. I held her hand to my lips some lingering moments, and so I left her. But ever afterwards, I remembered—and soon afterwards with stronger reason—that while Estella looked at me merely with incredulous wonder, the spectral figure of Miss Havisham, her hand still covering her heart, seemed all resolved into a ghastly stare of pity and remorse" (44:393). The passage is particularly revealing in two ways. First, its use of contradictory language exposes the logic behind Pip's passion. Unhappiness, his own rejection, is really a part of what he seeks in Estella and the basis for his "ecstasy." Second, the transition from Estella to Miss Havisham suggests a substitution of one for the other.

Estella and Miss Havisham become interchangeable. Throughout this scene Pip finds Estella uncomprehending or unresponsive to his words, while marking their profound effect on Miss Havisham. Later, Miss Havisham sends for Pip to beg his forgiveness.[36] In the process she undergoes a transformation, and sees herself as she once was in the period before her disaster. She is changed from an old hag to a woman, as Pip himself notes: "There was an earnest womanly compassion for me in her new affection" (49:432). Pip leaves her, walks into the old brewery, and sees a vision of her hanging from a beam (434). This is a repetition of an earlier vision (8:68), and in both cases Pip had previously been bitterly wounded by Estella's treatment of him. Yet he never maligns Estella or wishes her ill; rather, his vengeance is projected onto Miss Havisham.[37] And not only his vengeance, but his passion. His vision so disturbs him that he returns to check on Miss Havisham, and as he is about to leave he sees her burst into flame: "I saw a great flaming light spring up. In the same moment I saw her running at me, shrieking, with a whirl of fire blazing all about her, and soaring at least as many feet above her head as she was high" (49:434).

Pip covers her with his coats and the tablecloth, closes with her, and finds that "we were on the ground struggling like desperate enemies, and that the closer I covered her, the more wildly she shrieked and tried to free herself; . . . I still held her forcibly down with all my strength, like a prisoner who might escape; and I doubt if I even knew who she was, or why we had struggled . . . Assistance was sent for, and I held her until it came, as if I unreasonably fancied (I think I did) that if I let her go, the fire would break out again and consume her (49:434–35). Although her dress is burned, she is covered in a white sheet and cotton and still has "something of her old ghastly bridal appearance" (435). She repeats three phrases over and over, asking Pip in the last to forgive her: "I leaned over her and touched her lips with mine, just as they said, not stopping for being touched, 'Take the pencil and write under my name, "I forgive her"'" (49:436).

This change of heart and desire to be forgiven are similar to Mrs. Joe's behavior following her beating. As she sought to propitiate Orlick, so Miss Havisham continues to beg Pip's pardon. And as with the attack on Mrs. Joe, there is a sense here of sexual assault: Miss Havisham is shrieking and "inflamed." Pip holds her, covers her with his own body on the ground, and keeps her there even after the flames have gone out, for the fire within her may "break out again."

Miss Havisham and Estella are opposite versions of a single woman: the latter a virgin (unobtainable) ideal, the former a debased sexual object. Their exaggerated contrast is typically Victorian, yet it is rooted in a universal repression of childhood. All boys are forced, with varying success, to divorce sexual longing from a tender respect for their mothers. A common unconscious strategy is to imagine two figures, a "whore" sexually possessed by the father and an ideally spiritual "virgin."[38] Fairy tales display this split by depicting a disgusting old hag and a beautiful princess. And the world of Satis House is seen, especially by the boy Pip, as a fairyland where Miss Havisham is the presiding deity and Estella is the princess and the reward.[39]

On his first visit to Satis House Pip is met by Estella, who leads him to Miss Havisham's door and leaves him by himself in the dark hall. "This was very uncomfortable, and I was half afraid. However, the only thing to be done being to knock at the door, I knocked, and was told from within to enter." He goes into a room lighted entirely by candles, and discovers

in an arm-chair, with an elbow resting on the table and her head leaning on that hand, . . . the strangest lady I have ever seen, or shall ever see.

She was dressed in rich materials . . . all of white. . . . But, I saw that everything within my view which ought to be white, had been white long ago, and had lost its lustre, and was faded and yellow. I saw that the bride within the bridal dress had withered like the dress, and like the flowers, and had no brightness left but the brightness of her sunken eyes. I saw that the dress had been put upon the rounded figure of a young woman, and that the figure upon which it now hung loose, had shrunk to skin and bone. Once, I had been taken to see some ghastly waxwork at the Fair, representing I know not what impossible personage lying in state. Once, I had been taken to one of our old marsh churches to see a skeleton in the ashes of a rich dress, that had been dug out of a vault under the church pavement. Now, waxwork and skeleton seemed to have dark eyes that moved and looked at me. I should have cried out, if I could. (8:60–61)

Symbols of purity and beauty (whiteness, the bridal dress, the rounded body of a young woman) are seen in terms of decay—yellowing, withering, shrinking, sinking—and finally death itself. With its repeated emphasis on the wedding and the physical changes in Miss Havisham, this rotting of dress and body ultimately makes itself felt as sexual decay. It carries a disgust which contradicts all the symbols of the wedding. The clocks are stopped *before* the marriage which never occurred, and everything Miss Havisham does, and is, emphasizes that the marriage was never consummated. This insistence on the fact that no marriage took place, together with the repeated imagery of sexual decay, suggests that the frozen clocks, the wedding cake and dress are products of reversal and denial.[40] Miss Havisham's literal story and symbolic trappings tell us that her existence has been defined by Compeyson's betrayal. The unconscious implication is that she has been sexually rotted by Compeyson. As fairy godmother to Pip, her physical and symbolic qualities derive from the same source as the old hag's ugliness in fairy tales: she is an extreme caricature of the sexually desired mother whom the child must vilify in order to reject.

Compeyson's role as "son" is as crucial here as it was in the climactic scene of Magwitch's capture. His betrayal of Miss Havisham is felt, at its deepest level, as the son's sexual betrayal of the mother. It is related to Pip's robbery of Mrs. Joe and Pip's later "grappling" with the burning Miss Havisham. In this sense Compeyson is a surrogate for Pip with Miss Havisham, much as Orlick was a surrogate for Pip in the attack on Mrs. Joe. The language describing Compeyson's betrayal once again bears this out. Pip tells us that Miss Havisham "had the appearance of having dropped, body and soul, within and without, under the weight of a crushing blow" (8:64). Miss Havisham herself refers to her "wretched breast when it was first bleeding from [the] stabs" inflicted by Compeyson (38:329). And her brother Arthur has a similar vision of her when he tells Compeyson, "'she's standing in the corner at the foot of the bed, awful mad. And over where her heart's broke—*you* broke it!—there's drops of blood'" (42:376).

The speaker in this last quotation is Magwitch, who is retelling to Pip what he overheard Arthur tell Compeyson. The complicated history of this piecemeal and thrice-removed narration of Miss Havisham's love affair with Compeyson is in sharp contrast to the climactic scene of Compeyson's final betrayal of Magwitch and his death. The contrast suggests that maternal relations in the underlying Oedipal conflict of the novel are far more repressed than the father conflicts described above. This is felt more generally in the absence of character or its complete distortion in all the major female figures. Mrs. Joe is seemingly unmotivated in her ill-treatment of Pip or her sudden reversal after being attacked, while Joe's sensibilities are delicately portrayed throughout (and particularly in scenes such as his visit to Pip in London). For all his coarseness Magwitch's character is strongly felt, whereas Estella is emotionally vacant. Miss Havisham is the richest creation among the women in the novel, and this richness is a direct result of her powerful unconscious appeal and of the conscious repression used to mask this appeal. Caricature here derives from a particularly strong degree of repression.

This view of Dickensian caricature may be clarified if it is contrasted with a more naked and less successful portrayal of a similar underlying fantasy. We have examined the passages in chapter 8 of *Great Expectations* in which Pip first enters Satis House, meets the beautiful and queen-like Estella, is guided down dark passages of the house, and is left alone to enter a room without a trace of sunlight. The vision of whiteness and glitter that first greets him gives way to a sense of decay, and to the wizened, frightful figure of Miss Havisham seated in a chair. Compare this to the portion of *Hard Times* in which the hero, Stephen Blackpool, is seen entering his own home. Stephen is first accompanied by Rachael, an idealized woman who refuses to become his wife and who is an earlier and more saccharine version of Estella. After leaving her, Stephen proceeds home, lights his way by candle upstairs through the passages of a dark shop, and enters his own darkened room. He stumbles against something:

> As he recoiled, looking down at it, it raised itself up into the form of a woman in a sitting attitude. . . .
>
> Such a woman! A disabled, drunken creature, barely able to preserve her sitting posture by steadying herself with one begrimed hand on the floor, while the other was so purposeless in trying to push away her tangled hair from her face, that it only blinded her the more with the dirt upon it. A creature so foul to look at, in her tatters, stains and splashes, but so much fouler than that in her moral infamy, that it was a shameful thing even to see her. (1.x.52)

The woman is Stephen's wife. A former friend of Rachael's when Stephen courted and married her, she has gradually become degraded and debauched (1.xiii.64). There is an unconscious logic to this sequence of events: the woman with whom the hero has sexual relations is seen as corrupted and corrupting. She becomes both a "dead woman" and a "demon" (1.xii.62). The woman who remains a loyal, platonic comrade through the years is gradually elevated to the status of angel (1.xiii.68). Stephen broods over the fact that his relations with Rachael are restricted and subjugated to "the infamous image" of his wife: "Filled with these thoughts—so filled that he had an unwholesome sense of growing larger, of being placed in some new and diseased relation towards the objects among which he passed, of seeing the iris round every misty light turn red—he went home for shelter." (1.xii.63). The "sense of growing larger" implies erection: his aggressiveness and anger against his wife grow out of his sexual desire. This desire is seen as "unwholesome" and "diseased," tainting the objects around him, turning the very area in which he walks into one of the red lanterns, of lust. His subsequent temptation to poison his whore of a wife (1.xiii) carries the same sexual force. If she should swallow the poison (as he hopes and fears), he will be responsible for poisoning (i.e., polluting) her, and he himself will be polluted by the act. But when he returns home, he finds Rachael by his wife, a heavenly force to minister to her and to protect him from temptation. The entire scene reads like a soap opera; Stephen cries out to Rachael, "Thou art an Angel. Bless thee, bless thee! . . . Thou changest me from bad to good. . . . it may be, thou hast saved my soul alive!" (1.xiii.68), and he kneels before her. The chapter concludes: "As the shining stars were to the heavy candle in the window, so was Rachael, in the rugged fancy of this man, to the common experiences of his life" (1.xiii.69).

This imagery is repeated in the scene of Stephen's death, in the chapter entitled "The Starlight" (3.vi.201). Stephen has been crushed and mangled by a blatant symbol of destructive female sexuality—he falls into a deep, treacherous hole known as the "Old Hell Shaft." His rescue suggests a fetus being pulled from the womb: as he is extricated from the pit, attention focuses on a long rope, straining as it is wound coil upon coil, finally pulling him up in a bucket: "A low murmur of pity went round the throng, and the women wept aloud, as this form, almost without form, was moved very slowly from its iron deliverance, and laid upon the bed of straw. At first, none but the surgeon went close to it. He did what he could in its adjustment on the couch . . . (3.vi.206). And this chapter, too, concludes with a contrast between the ugly pit from which he has been delivered and the heavenly quality of Rachael, the angelic virginal woman, whom Stephen sees in the stars.[41]

The constant juxtaposition of Rachael and Mrs. Blackpool, with the contrasting imagery of angelic virginity and debased whoredom, has the same unconscious roots as the creations of Estella and Miss Havisham. But the latter are far more disguised in their conscious characterization and their relations with the hero. Whereas there seems to be no distance between Stephen's feelings for Rachael and the author's perception of them, Dickens makes us aware of the inherent problems in Pip's obsessive idealization of Estella. Similarly, while the sense of disgust attached to Blackpool's wife is fully indulged, the entire presentation of Miss Havisham is oblique and stylized. What might have been crude melodrama has been rendered artistically successful by the heightened work of psychic disguise.

Until the close of *Great Expectations* Dickens works brilliantly within the limits posed by his underlying assumptions about women. But at this point the ability to operate on two contradictory levels breaks down: he is unable to sustain an unconscious Oedipal fantasy in a significantly disguised form. The sexually charged "burning" scene between Miss Havisham and Pip anticipates Estella's debasement in her marriage to the brutal Bentley Drummle. The fantasy of possessing the mother, which results in the death of Miss Havisham, is then followed by a fight and an implicit murder of the son by the father (Compeyson's death on the river) and by Pip's own illness. From this point until its close the emotional force of the novel is nostalgic, implying a regressive, infantile solution rather than the adult solutions of economic independence and marriage.

One element of nostalgia has already been discussed: Pip's quite conscious desire to remain weak and childish with Joe after his illness, and his discovering himself again as Little Pip in the final chapter. The language of these last pages plays sentimentally on direct references to his boyhood: "Now let me go up and look at my old little room, and rest there a few minutes by myself," Pip tells Joe and Biddy before parting (58:520). Eleven years later he returns to touch "the latch of the old kitchen door," to see Joe "in the old place by the kitchen firelight" and to see himself again "on my own little stool" (59:521).

Nostalgia, particularly at the close of Dickens's novels, suggests a desire to return to a pre-Oedipal state, free of conflict and at one with the mother. This is perhaps most clearly seen at the end of *Barnaby Rudge*. The idiot-hero, Barnaby, is described by his mother as a "loving child to me—never growing old or cold at heart, but needing my care and duty in his manly strength as in his cradletime." After the death of his villainous father, Barnaby achieves that state which every Dickens hero desires with varying degrees of explicitness or completeness: "Never was there a lighter-hearted husbandman, a creature more popular with young and old, a blither or more happy soul than Barnaby; and though he was free to ramble where he would, he never quitted Her, but was for evermore her stay and comfort."[42] The exalted "Her" is Barnaby's mother.

This implicit solution is achieved, somewhat less obviously, through Pip's thwarted proposal to Biddy, who becomes a loving mother to Little Pip. Mrs. Joe is replaced by a woman who has implicitly loved Pip prior to her attachment to his foster father, Joe. A "family romance" is thus suggested in which Pip "allows" the marriage of his own parents. Early in the novel Pip described his harsh treatment by Mrs. Joe in terms of "the ridgy effect of a wedding-ring, passing unsympathetically over the human countenance" (7:55). He rejoices when at the end, Biddy puts her "good matronly hand with which she had touched [the hand of Little Pip], into mine. There was something in the action and in the light pressure of Biddy's wedding-ring, that had a very pretty eloquence in it" (59:521). That eloquent gesture, with all three of their hands touching, symbolizes the ideal relationship toward which Pip seeks a return. He could have been Biddy's lover and husband; through Little Pip he is both Biddy's son and her first "lover."

Biddy is Dickens's cure for the close of the novel. He originally seemed about to use her as he used Agnes Wickfield in *David Copperfield*: as a sisterly friend to the hero, in love with him throughout, who is discovered in time to console him with a love as much maternal as it is marital. Instead, while struggling with the insoluble problem of disposing satisfactorily of Estella, Dickens reveals in the use of Biddy and Little Pip the novel's deepest wish for regression.

This pronounced regressiveness does not, of course, make *Great Expectations* an aesthetic failure, but it does suggest inherent limits in Dickens's art and possibly in the terms of Victorian art in general.[43] Dickens's limitations are the very basis of his ingenuity: repression demands a constant succession of bizarrely brilliant psychic improvisations. If *Great Expectations* is his finest novel, this may be because its incredibly intricate devices of plot and symbolism enabled him to imply here, more clearly than elsewhere, that beneath the hero's manifest guilt there lies a deeper guilt, felt but never articulated.

The trend of recent Dickens criticism has been to emphasize guilt and pervasive darkness in his work, particularly in his later novels. Moreover, critics like J. Hillis Miller have seen in these novels Dickens's increasingly mature perception both of his own attitudes and weaknesses and of the inherent contradictions of his age. If Dickens's world seems to take on a darker hue, we are told, it is because he has grown up, because he has rejected the infantile solutions of his early works. Miller sees "a reorientation toward the future and toward the free human spirit itself as the only true sources of value."[44]

We have seen, however, that Dickens's mature achievement is very much enmeshed in the child-parent relationships that occupy his earlier plots. Those relationships have been more deeply embedded in the late novels, provided with a form that gives scope to the underlying fantasies without giving them away. Dickens's success as a popular writer was based on his continued ability to transmit fantasies of universal appeal and power; his achievement as an artist grew with his varied and more prolonged exploration of these themes.

In *Great Expectations* the pervasive guilt and criminality, the bizarre women and the frustrated love of the hero consistently resonate on several levels. Pip's fears and desires extend to all of the novel's relationships, its minor characters, its comedy and caricature, and even to the business context of Little Britain and the socially shared attitudes toward women. The social dimension of *Great Expectations* cannot be ignored, but does not in itself account for the novel's power. Dickens has created a richly suggestive story of individual growth that reveals the deepest wishes and conflicts of its hero, of its author, and of an age to which we still respond.

Notes

1. Charles Dickens, *Great Expectations*, ed. Louis Crompton (Indianapolis and New York, 1964), p. 2; copyright © 1964 by the Bobbs-Merrill Company, Inc.; reprinted by permission of the publisher. All references are to this edition; chapter and page numbers appear in parentheses following quotations.

2. John Forster, *The Life of Charles Dickens*, ed. A. J. Hoppé, 2 vols. (London, 1966), 2:284–85.

3. Pip admits that "My state of mind regarding the pilfering . . . did not impel me to frank disclosure; . . . It was much upon my mind (particularly when I first saw him looking about for his file) that I ought to tell Joe the whole truth. Yet I did not, and for the reason that I mistrusted that if I did, he would think me worse than I was" (6:42–43).

4. Because he is Mrs. Joe's closest relation, and because of his obligations to her, Pip assumes that he was "a more legitimate object of suspicion than any one else" (16:128). This is certainly a peculiar piece of reasoning. Later Pip is horrified at having inadvertently provided the weapon (16:130).

5. A powerful social stigma, of course, was attached to accepting money from a convict. The conscious moral force of the novel, however, rejects such prejudice and moves us toward an acceptance and love of Magwitch. Dickens reveals that Magwitch's wealth was earned quite legally in New South Wales (39:347–48). But to the very last Pip refuses to think of taking money from him. When Magwitch hints that Pip will have the money after his death, Pip still rejects the thought and realizes with relief that Magwitch's possessions would be forfeited to the Crown (54:passim).

6. "My comfort was, that it happened a long time ago, and that he had doubtless been transported a long way off, and that he was dead to me, and might be veritably dead into the bargain" (19:158).

7. "The daily visits I could make him were shortened now, and he was more strictly kept. Seeing, or fancying, that I was suspected of an intention of carrying poison to him, I asked to be searched before I sat down at his bedside" (56:496–97).

8. Julian Moynahan, "The Hero's Guilt: The Case of *Great Expectations*," reprinted in *Assessing Great Expectations*, ed. Richard Lettis and William E. Morris (San Francisco, 1960), 163.

9. In his attack on Mrs. Joe and the robbery-assault of Pumblechook, "Orlick acts merely as Pip's instrument or weapon" (Moynahan, "The Hero's Guilt," 161). Here, Moynahan's own language inadvertently suggests a sexually aggressive meaning to Orlick's role.

10. The "bearing of a child" and "a hard master" are suggestive of pregnancy and erection.

11. Sigmund Freud, "Dostoevsky and Parricide," *The Standard Edition of The Complete Psychological Works of Sigmund Freud*, ed. James Strachey, *et al.* (hereafter abbreviated *S.E.*), 24 vols. (London, 1953–66), 14:309–32.

12. See, for example, Freud's discussion of the "complete" Oedipus complex in "The Ego and the Id," *S.E.*, 19:12–59. The tendencies toward replacement of the mother via identification derive from what Freud termed the "inverted negative" response (34). Two of Freud's longer case histories deal with versions of this response: the analysis of Schreber, "Psycho-Analytic Notes on an Autobiographical Account of a Case of Paranoia (Dementia Paranoides)," *S.E.* 12:9–82; and the "Wolf-man" case, "From the History of an Infantile Neurosis," *S.E.*, 17:7–122.

13. John Butt, "Dickens's Plan for the Conclusion of *Great Expectations*," *The Dickensian*, 45 (Spring 1949), 78.

14. Butt, "Dickens's Plan," 79.

15. As I have mentioned, however, his love for Magwitch is still ambivalent and takes peculiar turns. In the paragraph following this quotation Pip reasons that it was best that Magwitch die.

16. In Dickens's next novel, *Our Mutual Friend*, Eugene Wrayburn is beaten and nearly killed at the point where he seems to contemplate seducing the heroine. He, too, suffers a coma and prolonged illness and is then nursed by the heroine, whom he marries. Clearly Wrayburn is being punished for his would-be sins, and his illness and recovery signify expiation and a process of spiritual rebirth. This characteristically Dickensian pattern seems to be behind Pip's illness. The scene acted out between Compeyson and Magwitch is repeated here: Pip, the cause of Magwitch's return and therefore of his death, suffers punishment and a kind of death in his turn. He will then be reborn into Joe's arms.

17. Moynahan, "The Hero's Guilt," 166.

18. John H. Hagan, Jr., "The Poor Labyrinth: The Theme of Social Justice in Dickens's *Great Expectations*," reprinted in Lettis and Morris, *Assessing Great Expectations*, 84.

19. See particularly Freud's "Character and Anal Erotism," *S.E.*, 9:169–75, and "On the Transformations of Instinct as Exemplified in Anal Erotism," *S.E.*, 17:127–33; and Otto Fenichel, *The Psychoanalytic Theory of Neurosis* (New York, 1945), 278–84, 487–88.

20. Samuel Smiles, *Self Help; With Illustrations of Character, Conduct, and Perseverance* (Chicago, 1881), 440–41.

21. Moynahan, "The Hero's Guilt," 167.

22. Smiles, *Self Help*, 324.

23. Smiles, 322.

24. Smiles, 327.

25. Smiles, 324.

26. Steven Marcus, *The Other Victorians* (New York, 1966), 22. Marcus approaches nineteenth-century medical bias through Freudian insight. But it is worth noting that Freud himself was practicing psychoanalysis before 1900, and he occasionally reflects prevalent Victorian prejudices. For example, his theory of the "actual neuroses" (see "On the Grounds for Detaching a Particular Syndrome from Neurasthenia Under the Description 'Anxiety Neurosis,'" *S.E.*, 3:90–115) seems to reflect an unfounded prejudice against masturbation and coitus interruptus.

27. Dorothy Van Ghent, "The Dickens World: A View from Todgers's," in *The Dickens Critics*, ed. George Ford and Lauriat Lane (Ithaca, 1961), 213–32, and *"Great Expectations": Form and Function in the English Novel* (New York, 1961), 125–38.

28. Magwitch says to Pip, "I tell it, fur you to know as that there hunted dung-hill dog wot you kep life in, got his head so high that he could make a gentleman—and, Pip, you're him!" (39:346).

29. In Freud's "Wolf-man" case (see above, note 12) his patient had been seduced by an elder sister and he had responded with a mental reversal of the trauma, even feeling considerable guilt at his own (imagined) aggression toward that sister. He had witnessed intercourse between his parents, had felt it as an act of violence, and yet in his subsequent fantasies of the act had adopted his mother's role. He developed an anal fixation as part of his inverted solution to the Oedipus complex. Feces were imagined as substitutes for children and for the penis, and one memory sounds as if it had been lifted from *Great Expectations:* the subject's father gave his sister "two large bank notes" which were unconsciously interpreted as a sexual gift, an act of intercourse (83).

Pip's relationship with Joe implies a desire—like that of Freud's subject—to replace the mother. Magwitch's violent and dirty reappearance, accompanied by imagery of the storm raging against the apertures and passages of Pip's rooms, is suggestive of "anal rape." Magwitch's wealth, epitomized by the "fat sweltering one-pound notes," provides the weapon for assaulting and appropriating Pip, who feels himself "pursued by the creature who had made me" (40:365). The unconscious implications here remain pertinent to Pip's whole social initiation and to his eventual repudiation of his fortune and implicit withdrawal from any form of economic competition. In this novel of social consciousness and growth, father-son relationships are critical because they determine social identity in a world dominated by men.

30. See generally Freud's "Jokes and Their Relation to the Unconscious," *S.E.,* 8, and particularly p. 132.

31. Humphry House, *The Dickens World* (London, 1965), 156–57.

32. Philip Collins thoroughly discusses this question in *Dickens and Crime* (London, 1965).

33. Charles Dickens, *Hard Times,* ed. George Ford and Sylvère Monod (New York: Norton, 1966), 105–6. Citations by book, chapter, and page are in parentheses following quotations.

34. He was also described by Dickens as "shabby-genteel," although this was removed from the proofs (see p. 256, note 106.3 in the Norton Critical Edition cited in note 33). The phrase implies that Slackbridge is a false gentleman, much like Compeyson.

35. The original ending was first reprinted and discussed by Forster, *Life of Charles Dickens,* 2 (1966), 289 and 441n.

36. See 49:430. In the final chapter Estella makes the same request and receives virtually the same answer (59:525).

37. Moynahan, "The Hero's Guilt," 163–65, shows that this vengeance is also due Miss Havisham in her own right. Moynahan sees Bentley Drummle as Pip's vengeful surrogate in Drummle's cruel treatment of Estella (161–62).

38. See Freud's "Contributions to the Psychology of Love," especially Parts I and II: "A Special Type of Choice of Object Made by Men," and "On the Universal Tendency to Debasement in the Sphere of Love" (*S.E.,* 11:165–90).

39. Both Estella and Miss Havisham are seen as "queens" by Pip (8:59; 29:253), and Miss Havisham is twice referred to as his "fairy godmother" (169, 170).

The name "Satis House" is itself an ironic comment on the lack of satisfactions to be obtained there (see especially 8:59). It "had a great many iron bars to it. Some of the windows had been walled up; of those that remained, all the lower were rustily barred. There was a court-yard in front, and that was barred" (8:57). The physical qualities of the house emphasize that it was once used; its entries and openings were once clear and have since been covered, barred, rusted. The same sense is conveyed by its "rank garden" and old brewery: once active and fermenting, the brewery's liquids have dried, its "uses and scents . . . have evaporated" (8:67). These symbols imply a former sexual access or "entry," subsequent decay, and a continued taboo against Pip's entry. Estella warns Pip, "Better not try to brew beer there now, or it would turn out sour, boy" (59). The entire place is barricaded against robbers (7:54).

40. Some aspects of Miss Havisham's implied sexuality are less affected by a defensive reversal—like her feeding unseen in the night and a "ravenous intensity" in her affection for Estella (29:261, 258).

41. Rachael's frequent association with the stars provides another connection with "Estella."

42. Charles Dickens, *Barnaby Rudge* (London, 1961), Chapter 17:137; and Chapter the Last, 634.

43. However, Dickens's persistent tendency to split women into absolute categories of good and bad, virgin and whore, makes him something of an aesthetic conservative. Thackeray's portrayal of Becky Sharp and Amelia Sedley, in *Vanity Fair*, was a radical attack on this established Victorian attitude toward women. Becky becomes little more than a highclass whore, but retains the author's interest and much of his sympathy, while Dobbin is forced to devalue Amelia before their marriage can take place. In *Henry Esmond*, Thackeray dwelt on the hero's love for his foster mother, and received a strong Victorian reaction: "The reviewer . . . in *Blackwood's Magazine* wrote: 'Our most sacred sympathies are outraged and our best prejudices shocked by the leading feature of this tale.' The *Athenaeum's* reviewer was more explicit: Esmond's marriage to Rachel , he wrote, 'affects us somewhat like a marriage with his own mother. All the previous emotions of the piece return to haunt us.' . . . The *Athenaeum's* man was right: we are in the presence of a kind of incest . . ." (From Walter Allen's "Afterword" to the Signet edition [New York, 1964] of *The History of Henry Esmond, Esq.*, 473).

Several of Hardy's major novels attempt to confront Victorian prejudice toward women, and in Tess and Sue Bridehead he deals explicitly with the problems attached to a woman who has been sexually "soiled." Eliot and Meredith partake of this same exploration, which seems to culminate in the work of D. H. Lawrence. In the period surrounding the growth of psychoanalysis there is thus a growing self-awareness and a movement toward breaking down set sexual attitudes. Dickens's incapacity to challenge feminine stereotypes may help to account for his peculiar lack of direct influence on major writers of this century.

44. J. Hillis Miller, *Charles Dickens: The World of His Novels* (Cambridge, Mass., 1958), 333. Miller maintains that Dickens has moved from a dependence on "the child-parent relation as an escape from isolation" in the early novels to "the more adult solution of romantic love" in *David Copperfield*. From *Bleak House* through *Our Mutual Friend* he traces the further development of an "adult view" of love (as denial and sacrifice).

Repetition, Repression, and Return: *Great Expectations* and the Study of Plot°

Peter Brooks

What follows is intended primarily as a discourse on plot, a concept which has mostly gone unhonored in modern criticism, no doubt because it appears to belong to the popular, even the commercial side of litera-

°Reprinted from *New Literary History* 11 (1980): 503–26 by permission of the editors and the Johns Hopkins University Press. An expanded version of this essay can be found in Peter Brooks, *Reading for the Plot* (New York: Vintage Books, 1985), 113–42.

ture. "Reading for the plot," we were taught, is a low form of activity. Long caught in valuations set by a criticism conceived for the lyric, the study of narrative has more recently found its way back to a quasi-Aristotelian view of the logical priority of plot in narrative forms. In the wake of Russian Formalism, French "narratology" has made us sensitive to the functional logic of actions, to the workings of sequence and trans-formation in the constitution of recognizable narrative units, to the presence of codes of narration that demand decoding in consecutive, ir-reversible order.[1] Plot as I understand it, however, suggests a focus some-what more specific than the questions of structure, discourse, and narrativity addressed by most narratology. We may want to conceive of plot less as a structure than as a structuring operation, used, or made nec-essary, by those meanings that develop only through sequence and suc-cession: an interpretative operation specific to narrative signification. The word *plot*, any dictionary tells us, covers a range of meanings, from the bounded piece of land, through the ground plan of a building, the chart or map, the outline of a literary work, to the sense (separately de-rived from the French *complot*) of the scheme or secret machination, to the accomplishment of some purpose, usually illegal. All these meanings, I think, usefully cohere in our common sense of plot: it is not only the out-line of a narrative, demarcating its boundaries, it also suggests its inten-tion of meaning, the direction of its scheme or machination for accom-plishing a purpose. Plots have not only design, but intentionality as well.

Some narratives clearly give us a sense of "plottedness" in higher de-gree than others. Our identification of this sense of plottedness may pro-vide a more concrete and analyzable way into the question of plots than an abstract definition of the subject, and a way that necessarily finds its focus in the readership of plot, in the reader's recognition of the need for structuring interpretative operations. The motive for plotting, the need for a sense of plot, may ultimately lie in the desire to recuperate pure suc-cessivity, passing time: a search, not so much for redemption *from* time, but redemption *of* time as the possible medium of significance. This may already suggest the predominant importance of the end as that moment which illuminates, and casts retrospective meaning on the middle, and indeed defines the beginning as a certain desire tending toward the end. If the promised end may once have offered an arrest of time in the time-less, in a secularized world the resonance of the end has increasingly be-come the anticipated echo of the individual human death. Thus Walter Benjamin can claim that "death is the sanction of everything the story-teller has to tell," because only at the moment of death does life acquire authoritative meaning and become transmissible. The problem for "man in the middest," to use Frank Kermode's term, is how to find that end and beginning that will give a significant closure, the closure on which de-pends meaning: that knowledge of death, Benjamin maintains, which is denied to us in terms of our own lives, and which precisely we seek in the fictions of others.[2] How do we find significant plots for our lives; how do we make them *narratable*? This is the problem to which I want to make an approach, and I will in a moment call upon Freud's speculations about how we understand our transit from birth to death, in *Beyond the Pleasure Principle*, as a source of illumination which may suggest the value of a psychoanalytically informed textual criticism.

The problems of closure, authority, and narratability show up in particularly acute form in any autobiographical narration. As Sartre succinctly puts it in *Les Mots*, to narrate himself to himself, he had to become "my own obituary." Whatever of an autobiographical account can be enclosed between beginning and end must have margins outside, margins of leftover "life" which allow the narrating I to objectify and look at the narrated I, and to see the plotted middle as shaped by its provisional start and finish. In the fictional pseudoautobiography that is *Great Expectations*—my text of reference here, one that gives in the highest degree the sense of plottedness and the impression that its central meanings depend on the working-out of the plot—Dickens adopts the strategy of taking a "life" and creating the demarcations of a "plot" within it. The novel will indeed be concerned with finding a plot and losing it, with the precipitation of the sense of plottedness around its hero, and his eventual "cure" from plot. The novel images in its structure the kind of structuring operation of reading that plot is.

1

Great Expectations is exemplary for a discourse on plot in many respects, not least of all for its beginning. For what the novel chooses to present at its outset is precisely the search for a beginning. As in so many nineteenth-century novels, the hero is an orphan, thus undetermined by any visible inheritance, apparently unauthored. While there may be sociological and sentimental reasons to account for the high incidence of orphans in the nineteenth-century novel, clearly they present an author with the greatest possible opportunity to create all the determinants of plot within his text, to profit from what Gide called the "lawlessness" of the novel by starting with an undefined, rule-free character and then bringing the law to bear upon him—creating the rules—as the text proceeds. With Pip, Dickens begins as it were with a life which is for the moment precedent to plot, and indeed necessarily in search of plot. Pip when we first see him is in search of the "authority"—the word stands in the second paragraph of the novel—that would define and justify—authorize—the plot of his ensuing life.

The authority to which Pip refers here is that of the tombstone which bears the names of his parents, the names which have already been displaced, condensed, and superseded in the first paragraph, where Pip describes how his "infant tongue" (literally, a speechless tongue: a catachresis which points to a moment of emergence, of transition into language) could only make of the name, Philip Pirrip, left to him by the dead parents, the monosyllabic Pip. "So, I called myself Pip, and came to be called Pip."[3] This originating moment of Pip's narration and his narrative is a self-naming which already subverts whatever authority could be found in the text of the tombstones. The process of reading that text is described by Pip the narrator as "unreasonable," in that it interprets the appearance of the lost father and mother from the shape of the letters of their names. The tracing of the name—which he has already distorted in its application to self—involves a misguided attempt to remotivate the graphic symbol, to make it directly mimetic, mimetic specifically of origin. Loss of origin, misreading, and the problematic of identity are bound up here in a manner that will need further investigation later on. The question of reading and writing—of learning to decipher and to compose texts—is persistently thematized in the novel.[4]

The decipherment of the tombstone text as confirmation of loss of origin—as unauthorization—is here at the start of the novel the prelude to Pip's cogito, the moment in which his consciousness seizes his existence as other, alien, forlorn:

> My first most vivid and broad impression of the identity of things, seems to me to have been gained on a memorable raw afternoon towards evening. At such a time I found out for certain, that this bleak place overgrown with nettles was the churchyard; and that Philip Pirrip, late of this parish, and also Georgiana wife of the above, were dead and buried; and that Alexander, Bartholomew, Abraham, Tobias, and Roger, infant children of the aforesaid, were also dead and buried; and that the dark flat wilderness beyond the churchyard, intersected with dykes and mounds and gates, with scattered cattle feeding on it, was the marshes; and that the low leaden line beyond was the river; and that the distant savage lair from which the wind was rushing, was the sea; and that the small bundle of shivers growing afraid of it all and beginning to cry, was Pip.
> "Hold your noise!" cried a terrible voice.

The repeated verbs of existence—"was" and "were"—perform an elementary phenomenology of Pip's world, locating its irreducible objects, and leading finally to the individual subject as other, as aware of its existence through the emotion of fear, fear which then appears as the origin of voice, or articulated sound, as Pip begins to cry: a cry which is immediately censored by the command of the convict Magwitch, the father-to-be, the fearful intrusive figure of future authorship who will demand of Pip: "Give us your name."

The scenario is richly suggestive of the problem of identity, self-consciousness, naming, and language which will accompany Pip throughout the novel, and points to the original decentering of the subject in regard to itself. For purposes of our study of plot, it is important to note how this beginning establishes Pip as an existence without a plot at the very moment of occurrence of that event which will prove to be decisive for the plotting of his existence, as he will discover only two-thirds of the way through the novel. Alien, unauthorized, self-named, at the point of entry into the language code and the social systems it implies, Pip will in the first part of the novel be in search of a plot, and the novel will recount the gradual precipitation of a sense of plot around him, the establishment of portents of intentionality.

Schematically, we can identify four lines of plot that begin to crystallize around the young Pip, the Pip of Part One, before the arrival of his "Expectations":

1. Communion with the convict/criminal deviance.
2. Naterally wicious/bringing up by hand.
3. The dream of Satis House/the fairy tale.
4. The nightmare of Satis House/the witch tale.

These plots, we will see in a moment, are paired as follows: $2/1 = 3/4$. That is, there is in each case an "official" and censoring plot standing over a "repressed" plot. In terms of Pip's own choices, we could rewrite the formula: $3/4//2/1$. When the Expectations are announced by Jaggers at the end of Part One, they will apparently coincide with Pip's choices ("My dream was out; my wild fancy was surpassed by sober reality" [chap. 18]), and will thus appear to take care of the problem of plot. But this will be so only on the level of official plots; the Expectations will in fact only mask further the true problem, the status of the repressed plots.

I choose the term *communion* for the first plot because its characteristic symbolic gesture is Pip's pity for the convict as he swallows the food Pip has brought him, a moment of sympathetic identification which focuses a series of suggestive sympathies and identifications with the outlaw: the bread and butter which Pip puts down his leg, which makes him walk like the chained convict; Mrs. Joe's belief that he is on his way to the Hulks; Pip's flight from the Christmas dinner table into the arms of a soldier holding out handcuffs, to give a few examples. Pip is concerned to assure "his" convict that he is not responsible for his recapture, a point he conveys in a mute exchange of glances which the convict understands, and which leads him to make a public statement in exoneration of Pip, taking responsibility for stealing the food. This in turn provokes an overt statement of community with the outlaw, which comes from Joe: "We don't know what you have done, but we wouldn't have you starved to death for it, poor miserable fellow creatur.—Would us, Pip?" (chap. 5).

The fellowship with the convict here stated by Joe will remain with Pip, but in a state of repression, as what he will later call "that spell of my childhood" (chap. 16)—an unavowable memory. It finds its official, adult, repressive version in the conviction—shared by all the adults in

Pip's life, with the exception of the childlike Joe—that children are naturally depraved and need to be corrected, kept in line with the Tickler,
brought up by hand lest their natural willfulness assert itself in plots that
are deviant, transgressive. Pumblechook and the Hubbles, in their
Christmas dinner dialogue, give the theme a choric statement:

> "Especially," said Mr. Pumblechook, "be grateful, boy, to them
> which brought you up by hand."
> Mrs. Hubble shook her head, and contemplating me with a mourn-
> ful presentiment that I should come to no good, asked, "Why is it that the
> young are never grateful?" This moral mystery seemed too much for the
> company until Mr. Hubble tersely solved it by saying, "Naterally wi-
> cious." Everybody then murmured "True!" and looked at me in a partic-
> ularly unpleasant and personal manner. (Chap. 4)

The nateral wiciousness of children legitimates communion with the outlaw, but legitimates it as that which must be repressed, forced into other
plots—including, as we shall see, "binding" Pip as an apprentice.

The dream of Satis House is properly a daydream, in which "His Maj-
esty, the Ego" pleasures himself with the fantasy of social ascension and
gentility. Miss Havisham is made to play the role of Fairy Godmother, her
crutch become a magic wand, explicitly evoked twice near the close of
Part One.[5] This plot has adult sanction, its first expression comes from
Pumblechook and Mrs. Joe when they surmise that Miss Havisham intends to "do something" for Pip, and Pip comes to believe in it, so that
when the "Expectations" arrive he accepts them as the logical fulfillment
of the daydream, of his "longings." Yet to identify Satis House with the
daydream is to perform a repression of all else that Satis House suggests
and represents—all that clusters around the central emblem of the rotting bride cake and its crawling things. The craziness and morbidity of
Satis House repose on desire fixated and become sadistic, on a deviated
eroticism which has literally shut out the light, stopped the clocks, and
made the forward movement of plot impossible. Satis House, as the circular journeys of the wheelchair to the rhythm of "Old Clem" may best suggest, constitutes repetition without variation, a collapsed metonymy
where cause and effect have become identical, the same-as-same. It is significant that when Pip returns from his first visit to Satis House, he responds to the interrogations of Pumblechook and Mrs. Joe with an
elaborate lie—the story of the coach, the flags, the dogs fighting for
"weal" cutlets from a silver basket—a fantasy which we can read as his response to what he calls a "smart without a name, that needed counterac-
tion" (chap. 8). All the attempts to read Satis House as a text speaking of
gentility and social ascension may be subverted from the outset, in the
passage which describes Pip's first impression of Miss Havisham, which
reads in part:

> It was not in the first few moments that I saw all these things, though I saw more of them in the first moments than might be supposed. But, I saw that everything within my view which ought to be white, had been white long ago, and had lost its lustre, and was faded and yellow. I saw that the bride within the bridal dress had withered like the dress, and like the flowers, and had no brightness left but the brightness of her sunken eyes. . . . Once, I had been taken to see some ghastly waxwork at the Fair. . . . Once, I had been taken to one of our old marsh churches to see a skeleton. . . . Now, waxwork and skeleton seemed to have dark eyes that moved and looked at me. I should have cried out, if I could. (Chap. 8)

The passage records the formation of a memory trace from a moment of unmastered horror, itself formed in repetition of moments of past visual impression, a trace which forces its way through the mind without being grasped by consciousness, and which is refused outlet in a cry. Much later in the novel, Pip—and also Miss Havisham herself—will have to deal with the return of this repressed.

We have, then, a quadripartite scheme of plots, organized into two pairs, each with an official plot, or interpretation of plot, standing over a repressed plot. The scheme may lead us in the first instance to reflect on the place of repression as one of the large "orders" of the novel. Repression plays a dominant role in the theme of education which is so important to the novel, from Mrs. Joe's bringing up by hand, through Mrs. Wopsle's aunt's schoolroom, to Mr. Pocket's career as a "grinder" of dull blades (while his own children meanwhile are "tumbling up"). Bringing up by hand in turn suggests Jaggers's hands, representation of accusation and the Law, which in turn suggest all the instances of censorship in the name of high authorities evoked from the first scene of the novel onward: censorship is repression in the name of the Law.[6] Jaggers's sinister hand-washings point to the omnipresent taint of Newgate, which echoes the earlier presence of the Hulks, to which Mrs. Joe verbally assigns Pip. Then there is the moment when Pip is "bound" as apprentice blacksmith before the magistrates, in a scene of such repressive appearance that a well-meaning philanthropist is moved to hand Pip a tract entitled *To Be Read in My Cell*. There is a constant association of education, repression, criminality, the fear of deviance. We might note in passing Dickens's capacity to literalize the metaphors of education—"bringing up by hand," "grinding"—in a manner that subverts the order that ought to assure their figural validity. The particularly sinister version of the *Bildungsroman* presented by *Great Expectations* derives in some measure from the literalization of metaphors pertaining to education and upbringing. Societal repression and censorship are of course reinforced by Pip's own, his internalization of the Law and the denial of what he calls the "old taint" of his association with the criminal. The whole theme of gentility, as represented by the Finches of the Grove, for instance, or the punishment of Trabb's boy, consistently suggests an aggressivity based on denial. One could reflect here on the splendid name of Pip's superfluous valet: the Avenger.

The way in which the Expectations are instituted, in seeming realization of the Satis House dream, comprehends "bringing up by hand" (the other official plot) in that it includes the disciplines necessary to gentility: grinding with Mr. Pocket, lessons in manners from Herbert, learning to spend one's time and money in appropriate gentlemanly pursuits. There is in this manner a blurring of plot lines, useful to the processes of wish fulfillment in that education and indeed repression itself can be interpreted as agencies necessary to the pursuit of the dream. Realization of the dream permits acceptance of society's interpretations, and in fact requires the abandonment of any effort at personal interpretation: Pip is now enjoined from seeking to know more about the intentions of his donor, disallowed the role of detective which so much animates him in Part Three of the novel—when the Expectations have proved false—and is already incipiently present in Part One.

Taking our terminology from the scene where Pip is bound as apprentice, we may consider that education and repression operate in the novel as one form of "binding": official ways of channeling and tying up the mobile energies of life. It is notable that after he has become apprenticed to Joe, Pip goes through a stage of purely iterative existence—presented in chapter 14—where the direction and movement of plot appear to be finished, where all life's "interest and romance" appear shut out as by a "thick curtain," time reduced to a repetitive durance. Conversely, when the Expectations have arrived, and Miss Havisham is apparently identified as the fairy-tale donor, and the Satis House plot appears securely bound, Pip need only wait for the next stage of the plot to become manifest. Yet it is clear that for the reader, neither binding as an apprentice (first accomplishment of an upbringing by hand) nor the tying up of Satis House as a fairy-tale plot constitutes valid and adequate means of dealing with and disposing of the communion with the convict and the nightmare of Satis House. The energy released in the text by its liminary "primal scene"—in the graveyard—and by the early visits to Satis House, creating that "smart without a name," simply are not and cannot be bound by the bindings of the official, repressive plots. As readers we know that there has been created in the text an intensive level of energy that cannot be discharged through these official plots.

In fact, the text has been working simultaneously to bind these disavowed energies in other ways, ways over which Pip's ego, and the societal superego, have no control, and of which they have no knowledge, through repetitions which, for the reader, prepare an inevitable return of the repressed. Most striking are the periodic fragmentary returns of the convict-communion material: the leg iron used to bludgeon Mrs. Joe, guns firing from the Hulks to signal further escapes, and especially the reappearance of Joe's file, the dramatic stage property used by

Magwitch's emissary in a "proceeding in dumb show . . . pointedly addressed at me." His stirring and tasting his rum and water "pointedly at" Pip suggests the establishment of an aim (Pip calls his proceeding "a shot"), a direction, an intention in Pip's life: the first covert announcement of another plot which will come to govern Pip's life, but of course misinterpreted as to its true aim. With the nightmare energies of Satis House, binding is at work in those repetitive journeys around the rotting bride cake, suggestive of the reproduction or working through of the traumatic neurotic whose affects remain fixed on the past, on the traumatic moment which never can be mastered. These energies can never be plotted to effective discharge. The compulsive repetition that characterizes every detail of Satis House allows us to perceive how the returns of the convict-communion suggest a more significant repetitive working through of an unmastered past. In both cases—but ultimately with different results—the progressive, educative plots, the plots of advancement, are threatened by a repetitive process obscurely going on underneath and beyond them. We sense that forward progress will have to recover markings from the beginning.

2

In my references to repetition and return as a process of "binding," I have had in mind a model of the text suggested by the model of the mental apparatus speculatively elaborated by Freud in *Beyond the Pleasure Principle*.[7] Freud's essay takes its departure from the compulsion to repeat that can be noticed in children's games, in literature (the literature of "the uncanny"), in the dreams of traumatic neurotics, which return again and again to the moment of trauma, to relive its pain, in apparent contradiction to the wish-fulfillment theory of dreams. Freud is led to postulate that the repetition compulsion constitutes an effort to "bind" mobile energy, to master the flood of stimuli that have breached the shield of the psychic apparatus at the moment of trauma, in order to produce the quiescent cathexis that allows the pleasure principle to assert its dominance in the psychic economy, and to lead energy to orderly and efficient discharge. Repetition as binding is hence a primary act, prior to the operations of the pleasure principle and more "primitive": it works to put affect into serviceable, controllable form. In analytic work, the repetition compulsion becomes particularly sensible in the transference, where patients display the need to reenact, reproduce, and work through repressed material as if it were present, rather than simply recollecting it as belonging to the past. Past history, lost to conscious memory, reproduces itself as an unmastered force in the present. To patients, the compulsion to repeat, to bind the unmastered past, speaks of a daemonic power, which for Freud (as in the literature of the uncanny) indicates the presence of the instinctual. Since for Freud the nature of the instinctual is radically conservative—an inherent urge to restore a prior state of affairs, which means essentially a return to the quiescence of the inorganic—repetition eventually speaks of the death instinct, of the fact that "the aim of all life is death." Yet the drive to return to death must conform itself to that divergence from an immediate return to quiescence which has been programmed into the organism as its response to outside stimuli: the death aimed at must be the right, the proper death, achieved through the complication of a detour, avoiding short circuit. The conflict of the death instincts and the self-preservative life instincts—Eros— provides a self-regulating economy where each set of instincts is dependent on the other, where the organism lives in order to die, but to die its proper death, which means that it follows a detour and a vacillating rhythm, with new beginnings in resistance to the impending end, in its movement to the end.

Of the complex intentions presiding over the composition of *Beyond the Pleasure Principle*, one appears to be a desire to consider how life is narratable, that is, how and why it has beginning and end, and how these are related in a pattern of extension with closure, which seems to be the requisite of talking about the shape or meaning of a life, about the plot of life. Freud's essay may offer a model suggestive of how narrative both seeks and delays its end. In particular, his concept of repetition seems fully pertinent, since repetition of all sorts is the very stuff of literary meanings, the basis of our creative perception of relation and interconnection, the means by which we compare and combine in significant patterns and sequences, and thus overcome the meaninglessness of pure contiguity. In the narrative text, repetition constitutes a *return*, a calling-back, or a turning-back, which enables us to perceive similarity in difference, consequence in contiguity, metaphor in metonymy. Since they are both calling-back and turning-back, repetitions may be seen as both returns to and returns of: for instance, returns to origins and returns of the repressed. The study of repetition as return can lead us to think about how the text speaks of its drive toward its end, and how the accomplishment of this drive must proceed through detour and vacillation, the textual middle, thereby enabling us to understand the end in relation to the beginning. Repetition, while speaking of the end, does so in such a manner—through its shuttlings back and forth—as to delay the end and to confer shape on the detour of the middle.

Freud's model seems in general pertinent to what I have been saying about the repetition and binding of Pip's official and repressed plots: their energy is being bound, overtly or covertly according to the case, and thus put into serviceable form within the textual economy. In particular, it may offer some illumination of the novel's middle—that place of mysterious necessity, which must be of a certain length in order to accomplish its processes—which is most notably characterized by the *return*. Literally, it is Pip's return from London to his hometown which appears as the organizing device of the whole of the London period, the time of the Expectations and their aftermath. Pip's returns are always ostensibly undertaken to make reparation to the neglected Joe, an intention never realized, and always implicitly an attempt to discover the intentions of the putative donor in Satis House, to bring her plot to completion. Yet the returns also always bring his regression, in Satis House, to the status of the "coarse and common boy" (chap. 29) whose social ascension is hallucinatorily denied, his return to the nightmare of unprogressive repetition, and, too, a revival of the repressed convict association, the return of the childhood spell. Each return suggests that Pip's official plots, which seem to speak of progress, ascent, and the satisfaction of desire, are in fact subject to a process of repetition of the yet unmastered past, the true determinant of his life's direction.

The pattern of the return is established in Pip's first journey back from London in chapter 28. The decision to visit Joe is quickly thrown into the shade by the presence on the stagecoach of two convicts, one of whom Pip recognizes as the man of the file and the rum and water, Magwitch's emissary. There is a renewed juxtaposition of official, genteel judgment on the convicts, voiced by Herbert Pocket—"What a vile and degraded spectacle"—and Pip's inward avowal that he feels sympathy for their alienation. On the roof of the coach, seated in front of the convicts, Pip dozes off while pondering whether he ought to restore the two one-pound notes which the convict of the file had passed him so many years before. Upon regaining consciousness, the first two words he hears, continuing his dream thoughts, are: "Two one-pound notes." There follows the convict's account of his embassy from "Pip's convict" to the boy who had saved him. Although Pip is certain that the convict cannot recognize him, so changed in age, circumstance, and even name (since Herbert Pocket calls him "Handel"), the dreamlike experience forces a kind of recognition of a forgotten self, refound in fear and pain: "I could not have said what I was afraid of, for my fear was altogether undefined and vague, but there was a great fear upon me. As I walked on to the hotel, I felt that a dread, much exceeding the mere apprehension of a painful or disagreeable recognition, made me tremble. I am confident that it took no distinctness of shape, and that it was the revival for a few minutes of the terror of childhood" (chap. 28). The return to origins has led to the return of the repressed, and vice versa. Repetition as return becomes a reproduction and reenactment of infantile experience: not simply a recall of the primal moment, but a reliving of its pain and terror, suggesting the impossibility of escape from the originating scenarios of childhood, the condemnation forever to replay them.

This first example may stand for the other returns of the novel's middle, which all follow the same pattern, which all double return to with return of, and which show Pip's ostensible progress in the world to be subverted by the irradicable presence of the convict-communion and the Satis House nightmare. It is notable that toward the end of the middle—as the novel's denouement approaches—there is an acceleration in the rhythm of these returns, as if to affirm that all the clues to Pip's future, the forward movement of his plot, in fact lie in the past. Repetition as return speaks as a textual version of the death instinct, plotting the text, beyond the seeming dominance of the pleasure principle, toward its proper end, imaging this end as necessarily a time before the beginning. Even Pip's attempted escape with Magwitch, his voyage out to another land and another life, will lead him back, in the Thames estuary, to marsh country like his own, to the horizontal perspectives and muddy tidal flats that are so much a part of our perception of him during childhood.

We must come back in a moment to return, repetition, and the death instinct. First a word should be said about the novel's recognition scene, the moment at which the latent becomes manifest, the repressed convict plot is forcibly brought to consciousness, a scene which decisively enacts both a return of the repressed and a return to the primal moment in childhood. The recognition scene of chapter 39 is preceded by two curious paragraphs at the end of chapter 38 in which Pip the narrator suggests that the chapter he has just written, concerning his frustrated pursuit of Estella, constitutes, on the plane of narration itself, a last binding of that plot in its overt version, as a plot of romance, and that now he must move on to a deeper level of plot—reaching further back—which subsumes as it subverts all the other plots of the novel: "All the work, near and afar, that tended to the end had been accomplished." That this long-range plot is presented as analogous to "the Eastern story" in which a heavy slab of stone is carved out and fitted into the roof in order that it may fall on "the bed of state in the flush of conquest" seems in coded fashion to suggest punishment for erotic transgression, which we may want to read as return of the nightmare plot of Satis House, forcing its way through the fairy tale, speaking of the perverse, sadistic eroticism which Pip has covered over with his erotic object-choice—Estella, who in fact represents the wrong choice of plot and the danger of short circuit. To anticipate later revelations, we might note that Estella will turn out to be approximately Pip's sister—natural daughter of Magwitch as he is Magwitch's adoptive son—which lends force to the idea that she, like so many Romantic maidens, is marked by the interdict, as well as the seduction, of incest, which, as the perfect androgynous coupling, is precisely the short circuit of desire.[8]

The scene of Magwitch's return operates for Pip as a painful forcing through of layers of repression, an analogue of analytic work, compelling Pip to recognize that what he calls "that chance encounter of long ago" is no chance and cannot be assigned to the buried past, but must be repeated, reenacted, worked through in the present. The scene replays numerous details of their earlier encounter, and the central moment of recognition comes as a reproduction or reenactment of the novel's primal scene, played in dumb show, a mute text which the more effectively stages recognition as a process of return to the inescapable past:

> Even yet I could not recall a single feature, but I knew him! If the wind and the rain had driven away the intervening years, had scattered all the intervening objects, had swept us to the churchyard where we first stood face to face on such different levels, I could not have known my convict more distinctly than I knew him now, as he sat in the chair before the fire. No need to take a file from his pocket and show it to me; no need to take the handkerchief from his neck and twist it round his head; no need to hug himself with both his arms, and take a shivering turn across the room, looking back at me for recognition. I knew him before he gave me one of those aids, though, a moment before, I had not been conscious of remotely suspecting his identity. (Chap. 39)

The praeterition on which the passage is constructed—"no need . . . no need"—marks the gradual retrieval of the buried past as its involuntary present repetition. The passage offers the most striking example of the fact, already encountered in Pip's "returns," that key moments of Pip's life bring back the past not simply as recollection, but as reproduction: as a living-through of the past as if it were present. This corresponds to Freud's discovery—recorded in the essay, "Remembering, Repeating and Working-Through"—that repetition and working through of material from the past as if it were an active force in the present come into play when recollection properly speaking is blocked by resistance.[9] It becomes clear that the necessity for Pip to repeat and work through everything associated with his original communion with Magwitch is a factor of his "forgetting" this communion: a forgetting which is merely conscious. The reader has undergone a similar process through textual repetition and return, one which has had the function of not permitting him to forget.

The scene of Magwitch's return is an important one for any study of plot since it so well demonstrates how such a novelist as Dickens can make plotting the central vehicle and armature of meaning in the narrative text. All the issues raised in the novel—social, ethical, interpretative— are here simultaneously brought to climax through the peripety of the plot. Exposure of the "true" plot of Pip's life brings with it instantaneous consequences for all the other "codes" of the novel, as he recognizes with the statement, "All the truth of my position came *flashing* on me; and its disappointments, dangers, disgraces, consequences of all kinds" (chap. 39—my italics). The return of the repressed—the repressed as knowledge of the self's other story, the true history of its misapprehended desire—forces a total revision of the subject's relation to the orders within which it constitutes meaning.

As Magwitch's unanswerable questions to Pip—on the origins of his property, the means of his social ascent—force home to him, Pip has covered over a radical lack of original authority. Like Oedipus, he does not know where he stands. The result has been the intrusion of an aberrant, contingent authorship—Magwitch's—in the story of the self. That it should be the criminally deviant, transgressive plot that is shown to have priority over all the others stands within the logic of the model derived from *Beyond the Pleasure Principle*, since it is precisely this plot that most markedly constitutes the detour from inorganic quiescence: the arabesque of the narratable. One could almost derive a narratological law here: the true plot will be the most deviant. We might be tempted to see this deviant arabesque as gratuitous, the figure of pure narration. Yet we are also allowed to remotivate it, for the return of the repressed shows that the story Pip would tell about himself has all along been subverted by the more complex history of unconscious desire, unavailable to the conscious subject but at work in the text. Pip has in fact misread the plot of his life.

3

This misreading of plots and the question of authority may serve to return us to the question of reading with which the novel began. Pip's initial attempt to decipher his parents' appearance and character from the letters traced on their tombstones has been characterized as "childish" and "unreasonable." Pip's decipherment in fact appears as an attempt to motivate the arbitrary sign, to interpret signs as if they were mimetic and thus naturally tied to the object for which they stand. Deriving from the shape of the letters on the tombstones that his father "was a square, stout, dark man, with curly hair," and that his mother was "freckled and sickly," for all its literal fidelity to the graphic trace, constitutes a dangerously figural reading, a metaphorical process unaware of itself, the making of a fiction unaware of its status as fictionmaking. Pip is here claiming natural authority for what is in fact conventional, arbitrary, dependent on interpretation.

The question of texts, reading, and interpretation is, as we earlier noted, consistently thematized in the novel: in Pip's learning to read (using that meager text, Mrs. Wopsle's aunt's catalogue of prices), and his attempts to transmit the art of writing to Joe; the expressive dumb shows between Pip and Joe; messages written on the slate, by Pip to Joe, and then (in minimum symbolic form) by the aphasic Mrs. Joe; the uncanny text of Estella's visage, always reminding Pip of a repetition of something else which he cannot identify; Molly's wrists, cross-hatched with scratches, a text for the judge, and eventually for Pip as detective, to decipher; Mr. Wopsle's declamations of *George Barnwell* and *Richard III*. The characters appear to be ever on the watch for ways in which to textualize the world so that they can give their readings of it: a situation thematized early in the novel, at the Christmas dinner table, as Pumblechook and Wopsle criticize the sermon of the day and propose other "subjects":

> Mr. Pumblechook added, after a short interval of reflection, "Look at Pork alone. There's a subject! If you want a subject, look at Pork!"
>
> "True, sir. Many a moral for the young," returned Mr. Wopsle; and I knew he was going to lug me in, before he said it, "might be deduced from that text."
>
> ("You listen to this," said my sister to me, in a severe parenthesis.)
>
> Joe gave me some more gravy.
>
> "Swine," pursued Mr. Wopsle, in his deepest voice, and pointing his fork at my blushes, as if he were mentioning my christian name; "Swine were the companions of the prodigal. The gluttony of Swine is put before us, as an example to the young." (I thought this pretty well in him who had been praising up the pork for being so plump and juicy.) "What is detestable in a pig, is more detestable in a boy."
>
> "Or girl," suggested Mr. Hubble.
>
> "Of course, or girl, Mr. Hubble," assented Mr. Wopsle, rather irritably, "but there is no girl present."
>
> "Besides," said Mr. Pumblechook, turning sharp on me, "think what you've got to be grateful for. If you'd been born a Squeaker—"
>
> "He *was*, if ever a child was," said my sister, most emphatically.
>
> Joe gave me some more gravy.
>
> "Well, but I mean a four-footed Squeaker," said Mr. Pumblechook. "If you had been born such, would you have been here now? Not you—"
>
> "Unless in that form," said Mr. Wopsle, nodding towards the dish.
>
> (Chap. 4)

The scene suggests a mad proliferation of textuality, where literal and figural switch places, where any referent can serve as an interpretant, become the sign of another message, in a wild process of semiosis which seems to be anchored only insofar as all texts eventually speak of Pip himself as an unjustified presence, a presence demanding interpretation.

We are constantly warned that texts may have no unambiguous referent and no transcendent signified. Of the many examples one might choose in illustration of the status of texts and their interpretation in the novel, perhaps the most telling is the case of Mr. Wopsle. Mr. Wopsle, the church clerk, is a frustrated preacher, ever intimating that if the Church were to be "thrown open," he would really "give it out." This hypothetical case never coming to realization, Mr. Wopsle is obliged to content himself with the declamation of a number of secular texts, from Shakespeare to Collin's Ode. The Church indeed remains resolutely closed (we never in fact hear the word of the preacher in the novel, only Mr. Wopsle's critique of it), and Mr. Wopsle "has a fall": into playacting. He undertakes the repetition of fictional texts which lack the authority of that divine word he would like to "give out." We next see him playing *Hamlet,* which is of course the text par excellence about usurpation, parricide, lost regal authority, and wrong relations of transmission from generation to generation. Something of the problematic status of textual authority is suggested in Mr. Wopsle's rendition of the classic soliloquy: "Whenever that undecided Prince had to ask a question or state a doubt, the public helped him out with it. As for example; on the question whether 'twas nobler in the mind to suffer, some roared yes, and some no, and some inclining to both opinions said "toss up for it"; and quite a Debating Society arose" (chap. 31). From this uncertainty, Mr. Wopsle has a further fall, into playing what was known as "nautical melodrama," an anonymously authored theater played to a vulgar public in the Surreyside houses. When Pip attends this performance, there occurs a curious mirroring and reversal of the spectacle, when Mr. Wopsle himself becomes the spectator, fascinated by the vision, in the audience, of what he calls a "ghost" from the past—the face of the novel's hidden arch-plotter, Compeyson. The vision leads to a reconstruction of the chase and capture of the convicts from the early chapters of the novel, a kind of analytic dialogue in the replay of the past, where Mr. Wopsle repeatedly questions: "You remember?" and Pip replies: "I remember it very well. . . . I see it all before me." The replay evokes an intense visual, hallucinatory reliving of a charged moment from the past:

> "And you remember that we came up with the two in a ditch, and that there was a scuffle between them, and that one of them had been severely handled and much mauled about the face, by the other?"
> "I see it all before me."
> "And that the soldiers lighted torches, and put the two in the centre, and that we went on to see the last of them, over the black marshes, with the torchlight shining on their faces—I am particular about that; with the torchlight shining on their faces, when there was an outer ring of dark night all about us?" (Chap. 47)

By an apparently gratuitous free association, from Mr. Wopsle's play-acting, as from behind a screen memory, emerges a drama on that "other stage": the stage of dream, replaying a past moment which the characters have never exorcised, that moment of the buried yet living past which insists on repeating itself in the present.

Mr. Wopsle's career as a whole may be seen to be exemplary of a general movement in the novel toward recognition of the lack of authorship and authority in texts: textures of codes without ultimate referent or hierarchy, signs cut loose from their apparent motivation, capable of wandering toward multiple associations and of evoking messages that are entirely other, and that all speak eventually of determinative histories from the past. The original nostalgia for a founding divine word leads to a generalized scene of writing, as if the plotting self could never discover a decisive plot, but merely its own arbitrary role as plot-maker. Yet the arbitrary is itself subject to an unconscious determinant, the reproductive insistence of the past history.

Mr. Wopsle's career may stand as a figure for Pip's. Whereas the model of the *Bildungsroman* seems to imply progress, a leading forth, developmental change, Pip's story—and this may be true of other nineteenth-century educative plots as well—becomes more and more as it nears its end the working through of past history, an attempted return to the origin as the motivation of all the rest, the clue to what must else appear, as Pip puts it to Miss Havisham, a "blind and thankless life" (chap. 49). The past needs to be incorporated *as past* within the present, mastered through the play of repetition in order for there to be an escape from repetition: in order for there to be difference, change, progress. In the failure ever to recover his own origin, Pip comes to concern himself with the question of Estella's origin, searching for her patronymics where knowledge of his own is ever foreclosed. Estella's story in fact eventually links all the plots of the novel: Satis House, the aspiration to gentility, the convict identity, "naterally wicious" (the status from which Jaggers attempted to rescue her), bringing up by hand, the Law. Pip's investigation of her origins as substitute for knowledge of his own has a certain validity in that, we discover, he appeared originally to Magwitch as a substitute for the lost Estella, his great expectations a compensation for the impossibility of hers: a chiasmus of the true situation. Yet when Pip has proved himself to be the successful detective in this quest, has uncovered the convergence of lines of plot that previously appeared distinct, indeed has proved more penetrating even than Jaggers, he discovers the knowledge he has gained to be radically unusable. When he has imparted his knowledge to Jaggers and Wemmick, he arrives at a kind of standoff, between what he has called his "poor dreams" and the deep plot he has now exposed. As Jaggers puts it to him, there is no gain to be had from knowledge. We are in the heart of darkness, and the articulation of its meaning must simply be repressed. In this novel full of mysteries and occult connections, detective work turns out to be both necessary and useless. It can offer no comfort and no true illumination to the detective himself. Like deciphering the letters on the tombstone, it produces no authority for the plot of life.

The novel in fact toward its end records a generalized breakdown of plots: none of the schemes machinated by the characters appears to accomplish its aims. The proof *a contrario* may be the "oversuccessful" result of Miss Havisham's plot, which has turned Estella into so heartless a creature that she cannot even experience emotional recognition of her benefactress. Her plotting has been a mechanical success but an intentional failure. This appears to be articulated in her final words, in her delirium following the fire: "Towards midnight she began to wander in her speech, and after that it gradually set in that she said innumerable times in a low solemn voice, 'What have I done!' And then, 'When she first came I meant to save her from misery like mine.' And then, 'Take the pencil and write under my name, "I forgive her!"'" She never changed the order of these three sentences, but she sometimes left out a word in one or other of them; never putting in another word, but always leaving a blank and going on to the next word" (chap. 49). The cycle of three statements suggests a metonymy in search of arrest, a plot that can never find satisfactory resolution, that unresolved must play over its insistent repetitions, until silenced by death.

We confront the paradox that in this most highly plotted of novels—where Dickens performs all his thematic demonstrations through the manipulation of plot—we witness an evident subversion and futilization of the very concept of plot. If the chosen plots turn out to be erroneous, unauthorized, self-delusive, the deep plots when brought to light turn out to be unusable—criminally tainted, deviant. Plot as direction and intention in existence appears ultimately to be as evanescent as Magwitch's money, the product of immense labor, deprivation, planning, which is in the end forfeit to the Crown. Like money in its role as universal modern (capitalist) signifier as described by Roland Barthes, tied to no referent (such as land), defined only by its exchange-value, capable of unlimited metonymic circulation, the Expectations of fortune, as both plot and its aim or intention, as vehicle and object of representation, circulate through inflation to devaluation.[10]

The ultimate situation of plot in the novel may suggest an approach to the vexed question of Dickens's two endings to the novel: the one he originally wrote, and the revision substituted (at Bulwer Lytton's suggestion) that was in fact printed. As modern readers we may tend to prefer the original ending, with its flat tone and refusal of romantic expectation, and find that the revision, with its tentative promise of reunion between Pip and Estella, "unbinds" energies that we thought had been thoroughly bound and indeed discharged from the text. We may also feel that choice between the two endings is somewhat arbitrary and unimportant in that the decisive moment has already occurred before either of these finales begins. The real ending may take place with Pip's recognition and acceptance of Magwitch after his recapture—this is certainly the ethical denouement—and his acceptance of a continuing existence without plot, as celibate clerk for Clarrikers. The pages that follow may simply be *obiter dicta*.

If we acknowledge Pip's experience of and with Magwitch to be the central energy of the text, it is significant that the climax of this experience, the moment of crisis and reversal in the attempted escape from England, bears traces of a hallucinatory repetition of the childhood spell—indeed, of that first recapture of Magwitch already repeated in Mr. Wopsle's theatrical vision:

> In the same moment, I saw the steersman of the galley lay his hand on his prisoner's shoulder, and saw that both boats were swinging round with the force of the tide, and saw that all hands on board the steamer were

running forward quite frantically. Still in the same moment, I saw the prisoner start up, lean across his captor, and pull the cloak from the neck of the shrinking sitter in the galley. Still in the same moment, I saw the face disclosed was the face of the other convict of long ago. Still in the same moment, I saw the face tilt backward with a white terror on it that I shall never forget, and heard a great cry on board the steamer and a loud splash in the water, and felt the boat sink from under me. (Chap. 54)

If this scene marks the beginning of a resolution—which it does in that it brings the death of the arch-villain Compeyson and the death sentence for Magwitch, hence the disappearance from the novel of its most energetic plotters—it is resolution in the register of repetition and working through, the final effort to master painful material from the insistent past. Pip emerges from this scene with an acceptance of the determinative past as both determinative and as *past*, which prepares us for the final escape from plot. It is interesting to note that where the "dream" plot of Estella is concerned, Pip's stated resolution has none of the compulsive energetic force of the passage just quoted, but is rather a conventional romantic fairy-tale ending, a conscious fiction designed, of course, to console the dying Magwitch, but possibly also a last effort at self-delusion: "'You had a child once, whom you loved and lost. . . . She lived and found powerful friends. She is living now. She is a lady and very beautiful. And I love her!'" (chap. 56). If taken as anything other than a conscious fiction—if taken as part of the "truth" discovered by Pip's detections—this version of Pip's experience leads straight to what is worst in Dickens's revised version of the ending: the suggestion of an unbinding of what has already been bound up and disposed of, an unbinding which is indeed sensible in the rather embarrassed prose with which the revision begins: "Nevertheless, I knew while I said these words, that I secretly intended to revisit the site of the old house that evening, alone, for her sake. Yes, even so. For Estella's sake" (chap. 59). The original end has the advantage of denying to Pip's text the possibility of any new infusion of energy, any new aspirations, the undoing of anything already done, the unbinding of energy that has been bound and led to discharge.

As at the start of the novel we had the impression of a life not yet subject to plot—a life in search of the sense of plot that would only gradually begin to precipitate around it—so at the end we have the impression of a life that has outlived plot, renounced plot, been cured of it: life that is left over. What follows the recognition of Magwitch is leftover, and any renewal of expectation and plotting—such as a revived romance with Estella—would have to belong to another story. It is with the image of a life bereft of plot—bereft of movement and desire—that the novel most appropriately leaves us. Indeed, we have at the end what could appropriately be called a "cure" from plot, in Pip's recognition of the general forfeiture of plotting, his renunciation of any attempt to direct his life. Plot comes to resemble a diseased, fevered state of the organism caught in the machinery of a desire which must eventually be renounced. Plot, we come to understand, was a state of abnormality or deviance, suggested thematically by its uneasy position between Newgate and Old Bailey, between criminality and the Law. The nineteenth-century novel in general—and especially that highly symptomatic development, the detective story—regularly conceives plot as a condition of deviance and abnormality, the product of cities and social depths, of a world where *récit* is *complot*, where all stories are the result of plotting, and plotting is very much machination. Deviance is the very condition for life to be narratable: the state of normality is devoid of interest, energy, and the possibility for narration. In between a beginning prior to plot and an end beyond plot, the middle—the plotted text—has been in a state of *error:* wandering and misinterpretation.

4

That plot should prove to be deviance and error is fully consonant with Freud's model in *Beyond the Pleasure Principle*, where the narratable life of the organism is seen as detour, a deviance from the quiescence of the inorganic which has been maintained through the dynamic interaction of Eros (desire, intention, the urge toward combination and meaning) and the death instinct (the drive toward the end). What Pip at one point has called his "ill-regulated aspirations" (chap. 39) is the figure of plot as desire: Eros as the force that binds integers together in ever-larger wholes, totalizing, metaphoric, the desire for the integration of meaning. Whereas, concomitantly, repetition and return have spoken of the death instinct, the drive to return to the quiescence of the inorganic, of the nontextual. Yet the repetitions, which have served to bind the various plots, both prolonging the detour and more effectively preparing the final discharge, have created that delay necessary to incorporate the past within the present and to let us understand end in relation to beginning. Through the erotics of the text, we have inexorably been led to its end, which is precisely quiescence: to a "time after" which is an image of the "time before," to the nonnarratable. If we take a further step suggested by adducing the argument of "Remembering, Repeating, and Working Through" to that of *Beyond the Pleasure Principle* and say that repetition is a kind of remembering, and thus a way of reorganizing a story whose connective links have been obscured and lost, and if repetition speaks of the death instinct, the finding of the right end, then what is being played out in repetition is necessarily the proper vector of the drive toward the end. That is, once you've determined the right plot, plot is over. Plot itself is working-through.

Great Expectations is exemplary in demonstrating both the need for plot and its status as deviance, both the need for narration and the necessity to be cured from it. The deviance and error of plot may be necessary factors of the historicity of desire and the insistence on, and of, narrative meanings; the desire to wrest beginnings and ends from the uninterrupted flow of middles, from temporality itself; the search for that significant closure that would illuminate the sense of an existence, the meaning of life. The desire for meaning is ultimately the reader's, who must mime Pip's acts of reading, but do them better. Both using and subverting the systems of meaning discovered or postulated by its hero, *Great Expectations* exposes for its reader the very reading process itself: the way the reader goes about finding meaning in the narrative text, and the limits of that meaning as the limits of narrative.

In terms of the problematic of reading which the novel thematizes from its opening page, we could say that Pip, continuously returning toward origins in order to know the plot whose authority would lead him to the right end, never recovering origins and never finding the authoritative plot, never succeeds in going behind his self-naming to a reading of the missing patronymic. He is ever returned to a rereading of the unauthorized text of his self-given name, Pip. "Pip" sounded like a beginning, a seed. But of course when you reach the end of the name "Pip," you can return backwards, and it is just the same: a repetitive text without variation or point of fixity, a return which leads to an unarrested shuttling back and forth. The name is in fact a palindrome. In the rereading of the palindrome the novel may offer its final comment on its expectative plot.

What, finally, do we make of the fact that Dickens, master-plotter in the history of the novel, in this most tightly and consistently plotted of his novels seems to expose plot as a kind of necessary error? Dickens's most telling comment on the question may come at the moment of Magwitch's sentencing. The judge gives a legalistic and moralistic version of Magwitch's life story, his violence, his crimes, the passions that made him a "scourge to society" and led him to escape from deportation, thus calling upon his head the death sentence. The passage continues:

> The sun was striking in at the great windows of the court, through the glittering drops of rain upon the glass, and it made a broad shaft of light between the two-and-thirty [prisoners at the bar] and the Judge, linking both together, and perhaps reminding some among the audience, how both were passing on, with absolute equality, to the greater Judgment that knoweth all things and cannot err. Rising for a moment, a distinct speck of face in this way of light, the prisoner [Magwitch] said, "My Lord, I have received my sentence of Death from the Almighty, but I bow to yours," and sat down again. There was some hushing, and the Judge went on with what he had to say to the rest. (Chap. 56)

The passage is sentimental but also, I think, effective. What it does is juxtapose human plots—including those of the Law—to eternal orders which render human attempts to plot and to interpret plot not only futile, but ethically unacceptable. The greater Judgment makes human plots mere shadows. There is another end that recuperates passing human time and its petty chronologies to the timeless. Yet this other end is not visible; the other orders are not available. As Mr. Wopsle's case suggested, the divine word is barred in the world of the novel (it is suggestive that Christmas dinner is interrupted by the command to repair handcuffs). If there is a divine master-plot for human existence, it is radically unknowable.

In the absence or silence of divine master-plots, the organization and interpretation of human plots remains as necessary as it is problematic. Reading the signs of intention in life's actions is the central act of existence, which in turn legitimates the enterprise of reading for the reader of *Great Expectations*—or perhaps, vice versa, since the reading of plot within the text and as the text are perfectly analogous, mirrors of one another. If there is by the end of the narrative an abandonment of the attempt to read plot, this simply mirrors the fact that the process of narration has come to a close—or, again, vice versa. But that there should be a cure from the reading of plot within the text—before its very end—and the creation of a leftover, suggests a critique of reading itself, which is possibly like the judge's sentence: human interpretation in ignorance of the true vectors of the true text. So it may indeed be. But if the master-text is not available, we are condemned to the reading of erroneous plots, granted insight only insofar as we can gain disillusion from them. We are condemned to repetition, rereading, in the knowledge that what we discover will always be that there was nothing to be discovered. Yet the process remains necessary if we are not to be caught perpetually in the "blind and thankless" existence, in the illusory middle. Like Oedipus, like Pip, we are condemned to reinterpretation of our names. But it is rare that the name coincides so perfectly with a fullness and a negation of identity as in the case of Oedipus. In a posttragic universe, our situation is more likely to be that of Pip, compelled to reinterpret the meaning of the name he assigned to himself with his infant tongue: the history of an infinitely repeatable palindrome.

Notes

1. Most useful to me has been the work of Tzvetan Todorov, esp. *Poétique de la prose* (Paris, 1971), in English, *The Poetics of Prose*, tr. Richard Howard (Ithaca, N.Y., 1977); Roland Barthes, esp. *S/Z* (Paris, 1970), in English, *S/Z*, tr. Richard Miller (New York, 1975); and Gérard Genette, esp. "Discours du recit," in *Figures III* (Paris, 1972).

2. Walter Benjamin, "The Storyteller," in *Illuminations*, tr. Harry Zohn (New York, 1969), 94, 101. See also Frank Kermode, *The Sense of an Ending* (New York, 1967).

3. Charles Dickens, *Great Expectations* (New York, 1963), 1. My references are all to this Holt, Rinehart and Winston edition, and will henceforth be given within parentheses in the text. I will include chapter numbers to facilitate reference to other editions.

4. On the theme of reading in the novel, see Max Byrd, "'Reading' in *Great Expectations*," *PMLA*, 9, No. 2 (1976), 259–65.

5. See chap. 19: 159, 160. Miss Havisham is thus seemingly cast in the role of the "Donor" (who provides the hero with a magical agent), one of the seven dramatis personae of the fairy tale identified by Vladimir Propp in *The Morphology of the Folktale*.

6. On the role of the law as one of the formal orders of the novel, see Moshe Ron, "Autobiographical Narration and Formal Closure in *Great Expectations*," *University of Hartford Studies in Literature*, 5, No. 1 (1977), 37–66. The importance of criminality in Dickens has of course been noted by many critics, including Edmund Wilson in his seminal essay "Dickens: The Two Scrooges," in *The Wound and the Bow* (Boston, 1941).

7. A fuller exposition of this model will be found in my essay "Freud's Masterplot," *Yale French Studies*, No. 55–56 (1977–78), 280–300. *Beyond the Pleasure Principle* is found in *The Complete Psychological Works of Sigmund Freud*,18: ed. James Strachey (London, 1953), 1–64.

8. The pattern of the incestuous couple, where for the implication of the brother-sister relation serves as both attraction and prohibition, has been noted by several critics. See esp. Harry Stone, "The Love Pattern in Dickens' Novels," in *Dickens the Craftsman*, ed. Robert B. Partlow, Jr. (Carbondale and Edwardsville, 1970), and Albert J. Guerard, *The Triumph of the Novel* (New York, 1976), 70. *Great Expectations* gives particular weight to the role of the Father as source of the Law: Magwitch, assuming in different registers the role of father both to Estella and to Pip, becomes, not a figure of authority, but a principle of pure interdiction.

9. "Remembering, Repeating, and Working-Through" [*Erinnern, Wiederholen und Durcharbeiten*], *Works*, 12: 145–56.

10. See *S/Z*, tr. Richard Miller, 39–40.

"In Primal Sympathy": *Great Expectations* and the Secret Life[*]   Elliot L. Gilbert

In his Preface to the first edition of *Martin Chuzzlewit*, a novel which in a number of significant ways resembles the later, more mature *Great Expectations*, Charles Dickens declares that he set out to write the earlier book "with the design of exhibiting, in various aspects, the commonest of all vices."[1] Always a purveyor of mysteries, a lover of secrets, Dickens declines to be more explicit about the exact nature of the vice he means his story to illustrate, but his biographer, John Forster, leaves no doubt in the matter. *Martin Chuzzlewit* is designed, Forster writes, "to show, more or less by every person introduced, the number and variety of humours and vices that have their root in selfishness."[2]

Selfishness is indeed a common vice, perhaps too common, too ubiquitous to be the main theme of any particular work of fiction. One might even argue that novels cannot be written on any other subject. And it is true that if by selfishness Dickens means nothing more than a general preoccupation with private ambition and personal appetite, then such a theme hardly seems special enough to require mention in a preface.

[*]Reprinted by permission from *Dickens Studies Annual: Essays in Victorian Fiction* 11 (1983): 89–113. © AMS Press, Inc.

What is clear from *Martin Chuzzlewit*, however, and even clearer from *Great Expectations*, is that for Dickens the term "selfishness" had a much broader significance, was in an important way associated with the nineteenth century's well-known effort to redefine, in every area of human experience, the concept of self; was in fact a name for what the novelist plainly saw as the master social, political, economic, and metaphysical problem of the age.

In his perception of those years as a time of nearly pathological individualism and self-consciousness, Dickens was certainly correct, for toward the end of the eighteenth century, people had begun—more widely and more intensely than they had ever done before—to lead secret lives. I do not mean by this term that a whole civilization suddenly embarked on a clandestine and licentious career of the sort celebrated in the anonymous autobiography, *My Secret Life*. (Though such a career would come to be seen by many Victorians as an inevitable result of the radical turn-of-the-century redefinition of self.) Instead, I mean to identify by the phrase "secret life" that dramatic turning inward, that interiorization of reality, with its consequent emphasis on the private experience of the individual, so characteristic of late eighteenth- and early nineteenth-century romanticism.

Nor do I mean to suggest that such turning inward, such a determination to live a secret life, is a uniquely nineteenth-century phenomenon. Intense individualism, with its assertion of the primacy of the inner life, has appeared in one form or another in all ages. Christianity is the form this impulse most memorably took two thousand years ago; "the heresy of the free spirit" is the way one scholar designates the same concept in its medieval manifestation;[3] and Cartesian philosophy, concerned as it is above all with "a subject receiving experience,"[4] is a powerful seventeenth-century version of this idea.

Nevertheless, the late eighteenth- and early nineteenth-century celebration of self was unique in at least one way. Where previous upsurges of individualism had always had to move against the grain of prevailing, solidly authoritarian political and social structures, romantic emphasis on the sovereignty of the inner life could draw support from a growing perception of that sovereignty in many areas of human experience. Thus, where a literary critic is able to explain nineteenth-century poetic theory by stating that "to receive true glimpses of the real nature of things, the human mind must, at least temporarily, withdraw its attention from practical mundane affairs and concentrate it upon the inner life."[5] Alexis de Tocqueville can use virtually the same language to define the new American democracy, saying of it that "every man finds his belief within himself . . . [and] all his feelings are turned in on himself."[6] The century of Dickens is, then, more universally, more all-pervasively a century of self than any age had ever been before, and it is for this reason that the novelist devoted not just one book but, in some way or other, every book he ever wrote to examining the consequences, both good and bad, of living what I have called a secret life.

Perhaps the most troublesome consequence of the romantic theory of self stems, ironically, from one of that theory's greatest strengths: its emphasis on what Coleridge called "the shaping spirit of imagination." "To the romantic poets," Masao Miyoshi writes in *The Divided Self,* "the imagination is a mode of transcending raw reality, a means of overcoming the world as given. . . . The imagination is here [an] active agent, shaping the world as it finds it, creating it anew with each vision. The world as given is continually being transformed into a Higher Reality of the poet's own making."[7] Not concealed by the generally approving tone of this passage is the metaphysical perilousness of the procedure Miyoshi describes. For it is clear that one inevitable result of the interiorization of reality sanctioned by romanticism must be an undermining of the autonomous, independent reality left behind, must involve a questioning of the very existence of such an autonomous reality.

This problem had early been foreseen in the pre-romantic philosophy of Bishop Berkeley and in the even more influential writings of David Hume, for whom, as one commentator has remarked, "the existence of an external world with fixed properties [was] really an unwarranted assumption."[8] And these ideas had, again, a currency far beyond the interests of philosophers and poets. Wordsworth, we know, famously described a period in his childhood when "I was unable to think of external things as having external existence, and I communed with all that I saw as something not apart from but inherent in my own immaterial nature. Many times while going to school have I grasped at a wall or tree to recall myself from this abyss of idealism to the reality." But only a few years later, Tocqueville was discussing this same withdrawal from reality as a practical political problem, declaring as a prime weakness of democracy that it "makes men forget their ancestors, clouds their view of their descendants, and isolates them from their contemporaries. Each man is forever thrown back on himself alone, and there is a danger that he may be shut up in the solitude of his own heart."[9]

Nothing more clearly testifies to the nineteenth century's preoccupation with "the abyss of idealism" than the number and the range of the images it created to illustrate its fear of a solipsistic isolation from the world. Premature burial, for example, was the fate Edgar Allan Poe obsessively reserved for characters "shut up in the solitude of their own hearts." Prisons were another major symbol of the pathological internalization of experience, Walter Pater, for one, finding all of life reduced to the "impressions of the individual in his isolation, each mind keeping as a solitary prisoner its own dream of a world." Just as powerfully, the silence and ultimately the disappearance of God were signs for Victorians of a serious loss of connection with any authoritative reality independent of the self. "I am on fire within," cries the self-absorbed, guilt-ridden protagonist of Tennyson's "The Palace of Art," "There comes no murmur of reply"; words echoed by the narrator of Robert Browning's "Porphyria's Lover" as he clings hour after hour to the body of the mistress he has murdered: "And thus we sit together now, / And all night long we have not stirred, / And yet God has not said a word!" Perhaps most curious and idiosyncratic is Thomas Carlyle's employment of eating as a metaphor for the solipsistic interiorization of reality, the conversion of an autonomous universe into one more element of self, the imposition of one person on another. "The least blessed fact one knows of," writes Carlyle in *The French Revolution,* "on which necessitous mortals have ever based themselves, seems to be the primitive one of Cannibalism: That *I* can devour *Thee.*"

The proliferation of such images in nineteenth-century literature— burial alive, imprisonment, silence, cannibalistic consumption— suggests how deeply the age was obsessed with selfishness in the broadest sense of that word, how much it feared the darker and more uncontrollable consequences of what I have called the secret life. Victorian writers began, Miyoshi declares, "with the knowledge of the Romantic failure in self-discovery,"[10] and a major strain of Victorian culture may thus be characterized as an intensive effort to reverse, or at least to slow, the inward journey romanticism had so hopefully begun.

One comparatively naive attempt at such a reversal is already hinted at in Wordsworth's grasping at a wall or tree to recall himself from his solipsistic self-absorption, an act reminiscent of Dr. Johnson refuting Berkeley by kicking a stone. There is a certain innocent appeal in these gestures, gestures which, in the face of profound epistemological scepticism, simply assert as self-evident the reality of the external universe. Another well-known instance of such bluff British empiricism can be found in John Ruskin's essay on the Pathetic Fallacy. There, in response to the statement of a philosopher that "everything in the world depends upon his seeing or thinking of it, and that nothing, therefore, exists but what he sees or thinks of," Ruskin considers it entirely sufficient to declare that there is "something the matter" with the man and to denounce him for his "egotism, selfishness, shallowness, and impertinence." More sophisticated, though not—finally—more responsive to the challenge of romantic inwardness, is the philosophy of positivism, a dominant intellectual force in England from the middle of the nineteenth century. For the positivist, to quote one commentator, the "final point of reference is the reality of the natural world, the objective world as in itself it really is, apart from the mediating human consciousness."[11] Carlyle, with a very different philosophical outlook, also counsels escape from self into an objective universe of action. In *Sartor Resartus,* he urges those who would seek their inner natures to turn outward, work in the world, and discover themselves in their own products.

These and many other responses to romantic subjectivity make up the familiar picture of Victorian thought and culture. The responses were of two basic kinds. First, there were those which attempted, at every level, to deny if not the existence then the priority of the secret life. Victorian culture was in many ways a surface phenomenon, with artifacts elaborately decorated to conceal their function, clothing ingeniously cut to conceal the female form, a complex code of conduct designed to suppress sexuality, and a hierarchy of social virtues at the summit of which stood respectability.

The second kind of Victorian response to romanticism consisted of frenetic activity in the world, an unprecedented busyness whose deepest metaphysical intention was to permit escape from the self into some independent reality, into a much-desired otherness. The intention may have been reasonable, but the method was fatally flawed; for, unavoidably, in building in the world the Victorians built in their own image. Inevitably, English industrialism imposed English forms on nature and English colonialism imposed English values on other races. It was precisely in this that the pathos of the nineteenth-century dilemma lay. For in seeking to avoid the romantic trap of subjectivity and self, the Victorians chose to subordinate their inner lives to a seemingly objective materialism in which, in the end, they were able to find only their own selves again.

Charles Dickens, born when the influence of romanticism was at its peak, and later to be the great popular novelist of the high Victorian period, lived and worked at the junction of these two powerfully opposed cultural ideas, and achieved the success he did in part because he knew how to give these ideas vivid and dramatic expression and, just as importantly, because he was able, especially in his later work, to provide a plausible resolution of such seemingly irreconcilable philosophical positions. Much of the drama in the novels takes the form of the opposition of two very different kinds of characters. In the first group are men and women so locked into themselves, so trapped in secret lives of their own devising, that they have largely lost connection with an independent reality, with what positivism called the "true order" of the world around them. They represent for Dickens, in Miyoshi's phrase, "the romantic failure in self-discovery."

Many such characters are essentially comic, benign examples of our universal human tendency to live in the world as we would like it to be rather than as it is: Mr. Pickwick, for whom everything must be assigned its Pickwickian meaning, and Mr. Micawber, for whom sooner or later everything will "turn up"; Mrs. Gamp, whose world is peopled with her own inventions, and Mrs. Gamp's opposite number, Mrs. Billikin in *Edwin Drood,* who causes people to disappear simply by refusing to notice them; Mrs. Jellyby, for whom the present place and the present moment fade before a vision of distant and future benevolence; Mr. Podsnap, for whom anything un-English does not exist; and perhaps the most con-

summate solipsist in all the novels, Mr. Sapsea, whose "frantic and incon-
ceivable epitaph for Mrs. Sapsea,"[12] to use Chesterton's phrase, is the
very apotheosis of self-absorption.

Sometimes such characters, without entirely losing their comic appeal, acquire more sinister dimensions. There is, for example, Montague
Tigg, who creates himself anew and imposes himself on others by the simple expedient of changing his name to Tigg Montague; Harold Skimpole,
whose infantile egoism distorts not just his own private world but the
world of all those around him; and the Barnacle Clan, whose Circumlocution Office, for all of its appearance of connection with the running of the
state, is entirely self-referential, irrelevant to everything but its own existence. Then there are the true criminals, who, in Dickens's novels, are almost invariably trapped in nightmare worlds of their own creation, who
live the ultimate secret lives. One thinks of Fagin in his last hours, dying
over and over again in imagination; of Jonas Chuzzlewit, haunted by the
apparition of his murder victim; of John Jasper and his drug-induced visions which impose his own fantastic passions on the everyday world,
driving him to cry out, at one point, "The echoes of my own voice among
the arches seem to mock me . . . Must I take to carving demons out of my
heart?" And over all these novels broods the grand Dickensian metaphor
of the prison—from the Fleet to the Marshalsea to the Bastille to
Newgate—in part because of the writer's own personal associations with
the image, but more importantly because there could be no more fitting
symbol in the nineteenth century of the "failure of self-discovery," of in-
carceration in the "abyss of idealism." Not even Mr. Pickwick is spared,
for to seek to retreat into a world everywhere marked with one's own
name is already to be a kind of prisoner.

All of these elements appear with a peculiar intensity in *Great Expectations,* as though in this novel Dickens set out to make his closest examination of the social and metaphysical problems presented by the
romantic celebration of self. Self-reflexive characters and their imprisonment, actual or symbolic, crowd the story, from a minor but emblematic figure like Old Bill Barley, who never leaves his room and whose
primitive self-assertion takes the form of repeated announcements of
his own name, to Magwitch in the hulks, to the insufferable Mr.
Pumblechook, trapped in a lie he has told so often that it has wholly replaced reality, to the quintessential solipsist, Miss Havisham, who, by
sheer force of a perverse will, brings even time to a stop to commemo-
rate her private grief.

We realize that the road Pip must travel in his life will be a difficult
one when we note that there is a prison at each end. At home there is the
gothic Satis House, in which Miss Havisham has self-indulgently locked
herself away, and in London there is Newgate, representative of all the
greed and egotism and violence that comprise Little, rather than Great,
Britain. Indeed, we might perhaps see in this road, as in Pip's whole ca-

reer, Dickens's deliberate symbol of the journey of mid-century England away from the romantic prison of the secret life and toward the Victorian prison of materialism.

Pip's own journey along this road begins when, turned upside down by Magwitch, he finds that the whole world has turned upside down with him. His natural conclusion that the universe must therefore be coextensive with his own mind is precisely the Berkeleian idealism from which it takes him the rest of the novel to recover, an idealism Dickens slyly associates with the boy's regular imbibing of tar water, the popular nostrum originally concocted by (and still in the mid-nineteenth century credited to) Bishop Berkeley.[13] In the end, what Pip learns from his journey is that it is a capital mistake to have expectations—to suppose that the world will agree to shape itself to anyone's preconceptions and desires—a mistake which leaves him painfully unprepared for life's surprising and dangerous autonomy.

Of course, we must not be misled by the fact that Pip is himself the victim of other people's solipsism—of Miss Havisham's and Magwitch's and even Pumblechook's private fantasies—into missing this point about his own manipulation of reality. In the abyss of idealism, everyone is necessarily the figment of someone else's imagination, even while supposing himself to be the center of his own universe. H. M. Daleski suggests that the expectations of many of the characters in the novel "have their source in a desire for change, for the transformation of an existing situation; and the expectations are sustained in each case by the belief that such a transformation may be effected *through the agency of another*"[14] [italics mine]. But such expectations of change at the hands of another do not reflect genuine belief in a reality independent of self. Instead, because they are only further examples of wishful thinking—Miss Havisham's hope of achieving revenge through Estella, Magwitch's plan to escape the stigma of his past through Pip, and Pip's desire to change his own status with the aid of a patron—such expectations merely serve to confirm the unavoidability of solipsism, the ubiquitousness of self.

A second, contrasting category of characters in Dickens's novels consists of men and women who reject the secret life, with its treacherous subjectivity, in favor of a positivistic "objective world as in itself it really is," who seek to avoid the "abyss of idealism," the prison of self, by rigorously directing their energies outward, by heeding Carlyle's well-known exhortation to "Produce! Produce!" The most famous of these characters is undoubtedly Ebenezer Scrooge, ferociously dismissing every appeal to emotion as humbug and putting his faith instead in such palpable social institutions as stock exchanges, prisons, and workhouses. But Scrooge-like figures are everywhere in the novels: Mr. Merdle [*Little Dorrit*], "immensely rich," Dickens tell us, "a man of prodigious enterprise [whose] desire was to the utmost to satisfy Society, whatever that was"; Mr. Dombey [*Dombey and Son*], a wealthy merchant who ruthlessly suppresses all tender feelings and who, significantly, lives in a London whose interior is being torn out to make room for a railroad; Thomas Gradgrind [*Hard Times*], proprietor of a positivist educational theory whose chief objective is the stamping out of fancy; Edward Murdstone [*David Copperfield*], of whom Dickens writes "He had that kind of shallow black eyes—I want a better word to express an eye that has no depth in it to be looked into."

Characters like these clearly have in common a worldly success gained at the expense of their own interiority, share the Victorian commitment to surfaces which requires the severing of connections with an inner life in order to permit the establishment of corresponding connections with an outer one. At first glance, the logic of such procedure seems unimpeachable. In "The Palace of Art," for example, Tennyson's protagonist must renounce her at first complacent and later nightmarish secret life if she wishes to enter into useful relationships with others, and there is an easy moral symmetry in such an arrangement that must have appealed to early Victorian readers. But Dickens certainly means us to recognize, from our experience with his novels, the inadequacy of such a theory, means us to notice that such a procedure inevitably leads his characters not out of the prison of self but more and more irretrievably into it.

Why this should be so becomes clearer when we look at a few of the philanthropic figures in the stories. Especially in the earlier books, philanthropists are represented by such stock characters as Mr. Brownlow in *Oliver Twist* and the Cheeryble Brothers in *Nicholas Nickleby*, Dickens apparently unconcerned with motivation, with the psychology of metaphysics of charitable actions, and taking generosity at its face value. Elsewhere, however, the novelist is more analytic, more cynical, perhaps, and so we find such creations as Mrs. Pardiggle [*Bleak House*], a Visiting Lady of "rapacious benevolence" who bullies her reluctant children into participating in her charitable activities, and who likes nothing so much as lecturing to destitute slum-dwellers who have expressly asked her to stop. We have, as well, the Reverend Luke Honeythunder [*The Mystery of Edwin Drood*], a violent lover of humanity who demands strict compliance with his own moral vision and whose philanthropy is, Dickens informs us, "of that gunpowderous sort that the difference between it and animosity is hard to determine."

The treatment of philanthropy in Dickens's novels must be considered in the context of the prevailing Victorian attitude toward charity, an attitude which Alexander Welsh has described as "chiefly distinguished by its emphasis on the character of the recipient . . . an emphasis that inverts the long tradition of Christian charity as a practice contributing to the salvation of the charitable. The elevating influence of the gift on the giver is never denied, but the giver is asked to subordinate this (almost selfish) consideration to a concern for the effect of his gift on the recipient's character—an effect that is regarded as dubious at best."[15] Such a statement makes it clear why philanthropy must necessarily fail in its effort to achieve an escape from self into a genuine relationship with others. For if, on the one hand, philanthropists take pleasure in their own generosity, if beneficient characters like Mr. Brownlow and the Cheerybles have, as Humphry House puts it, "their full return in watching the happiness they distribute and in the enjoyment of gratitude and power,"[16] then they are guilty of a kind of selfishness; at the very least their openhandedness is tainted with vanity. Alex Zwerdling sums up this particular Victorian anxiety very well when, in discussing Esther Summerson in *Bleak House,* he explains that her reluctance to break with John Jarndyce and accept Allan Woodcourt results from her terror "not of hurting Jarndyce but of pleasing herself."[17] If, on the other hand, philanthropists should in fact succeed in suppressing all personal satisfaction, their act of charity must nevertheless compromise the autonomy, the otherness of the recipients, manipulate and impose on them even as Merdle and Dombey and Gradgrind, without any charitable intentions, manipulate and impose on the people with whom they live and the worlds in which they act. The stain of self in Dickens's fiction thus goes deep, indeed seems ineradicable, and the spectre of Carlyle's cannibalism is never far away; only not now saying "I can devour thee," but more chillingly, "Try as I will, I cannot *keep* from devouring thee."

Such cannibalism, such devouring is a key metaphor in *Great Expectations,* a story which, from the Christmas dinner at the forge to the grim, elegant suppers at Jaggers's house, is—as Angus Wilson reminds us[18]—full of unpleasant feasting. The book opens, of course, with Pip being forced to act under the literal threat of being eaten. The young man who is to roast and consume Pip's heart and liver, perhaps initially a Mrs. Harris-like figment of Magwitch's imagination, must inevitably be equated with the corrosive and manipulative Compeyson. His name meaning, literally, "co-countryman," Compeyson is everyone's secret companion, dark double, diabolical inner voice: like Magwitch, a prisoner; like Miss Havisham, a marriage partner; like Orlick, a criminal; like Pip, a gentleman. Ubiquitous and morbidly energetic, Compeyson is the representative inhabitant of a universe of isolation, despair, and death in which each person sees, endlessly duplicated, only his own likeness.

Miss Havisham too is an eater of hearts, first of her own and then of Estella's, consuming the girl and reconstituting her as the instrument of an alien vengeance, obliging her to be an eater of hearts as well. Even Magwitch's philanthropy, though it derives from genuine gratitude, is devouring, falling unavoidably into the two corruptions of charity identified by sceptical Victorians. First it is manipulative; Magwitch tries to shape Pip to his own perverse image of a gentleman, controlling even his choice of a name. Then it is self-serving; Magwitch returns to England so that he may himself enjoy the fruits of his philanthropy, that he may get a "full return in watching the happiness he has distributed and in the enjoyment of gratitude and power." Thus interpreted, generosity in the story is only another name for selfishness, charity another name for vanity, a vanity particularly subtle in its danger because it comes in the guise of self-abnegation: "the vanity of penitence," as Pip says to Miss Havisham, "the vanity of remorse, the vanity of unworthiness, and other monstrous vanities that have been curses in this world."[19]

What escape, then, is possible from the conflict between romantic solipsism and an equally self-serving Victorian materialism? If, on the one hand, romantic celebration of the inner life leads inexorably to isolation, to imprisonment in the self, to a Byronic stalking apart in joyless reverie, and if, on the other hand, Victorian renunciation of self in favor of work in the world not only fails to demolish that prison but makes it even sturdier and more secure, how can it ever be possible to cast off the oppressive burden of ego and enter into genuine relationship with others?

It is fair to say that this is always a key question in Dickens's novels. His characters, as has often been noted, are the great monologists of English fiction,[20] speaking much more often to assert themselves and their idiosyncratic views than to enter into real communication with the rest of humanity. Frequently orphans, they are, in Tocqueville's words, "ignorant of ancestors, uncertain of descendants, isolated from their contemporaries." They move at random through a concealing fog that represents the alienating influence of nineteenth-century materialism, and nothing seems more unlikely than that they should ever connect with others like themselves. Indeed, we might well ask whether, in the light of this analysis, it makes sense even to talk about such connection.

To this question at least, Dickens would certainly answer "yes," for what is clear from the novels is the strength of his belief in a universal ordering principle, what one critic has called the "tight web of cause and effect beneath the apparent chaos of daily affairs."[21] Another commentator identifies this order more precisely, observing that in Dickens's work as a whole, "the apparent randomness of existence conceals an underlying providence,"[22] a providence frequently taking the form of elaborate coincidence as a device for commenting on the complex connections which, in this view, always exist among people, even when they suppose themselves to be most imprisoned, most isolated from one another.[23] In *Great Expectations*, Dickens develops a network of connections, at a deep level of his plot, meant to be perceived only retrospectively by both readers and characters, meant to show, in Dickens's own words, "by a backward light, what everything has been working to—but only to *suggest*, until the fulfillment comes."[24] This is the real secret life of the novel, a force for wholeness and order awaiting its moment, one of which occurs at the death of Magwitch. At the bedside we find a settled calm, the bitterness and ignorance that have at one time or another separated Pip, Magwitch, and Estella are all suspended. Pip talks to the dying man about the mutual relationships—"You had a child once whom you loved and lost. She lived and found powerful friends. She is living now. She is a lady and very beautiful. And I love her!"—and for a moment we glimpse the secret life of the novel moving like a healing current, asserting connections that had always existed but had never till now been recognized. "It is in this way," writes Dorothy Van Ghent, "that the manifold organic relationships among men are revealed, and that the Dickens world—founded on fragmentariness and disintegration—is made whole."[25]

That it is only at this depth that the dilemma of self and other can be resolved, Dickens makes clear in the chapter immediately following, the scene of Pip's illness and recovery. A scene similar to this one occurs in *Martin Chuzzlewit* where young Martin, a prototypical Pip, riddled with the spiritual disease he calls, "Self, self, self," falls physically ill and is nursed back to health by his ever-cheerful friend Mark Tapley. In the earlier book, however, this incident is related entirely from the outside and we are left to guess at the actual process of the protagonist's regeneration. In *Great Expectations*, that process is what chiefly interests the author, the process of spiritual recovery from the disease of self.

What we learn is that the first step toward such recovery is *not* to reject the inner life and turn outward to the world, however logical such a process may seem. We have seen what that decision can lead to. Instead, we discover, paradoxically, but in the great mystical tradition, that recovery requires plunging deeper into that interiority, an act at first so unimaginable that for Pip it needs physical illness to initiate it. As his disease takes effect, Pip begins by falling deliriously into the painful isolation of personality which has always been his spiritual affliction, into the secret life that alienates and imprisons and from which he longs to escape. "I implored in my own person," he recounts one of his nightmares during this period, "to have the engine stopped and my part in it hammered off" (57:472).

In such dream work, itself a form of autobiographical story-telling like the book Pip will one day make of his life, elements that seem meaningless and absurd have in reality been constructed by a highly complicated activity of the mind which renders everything significant and which, moreover, obligates us to seek, by Dickens's "backward light," the providential and/or psychological order underlying apparently random experiences and coincidental events. For Pip, as identity begins to disintegrate under the influence of fever—is "broken by illness" as he puts it and for which he is afterwards grateful—he sinks deeper and deeper, past personality, in a silence beyond monologues, finding at last, at this depth, a second secret life, the true secret life that frees, connects, and heals, "our own only true, deep-buried self," as Matthew Arnold puts it in *Empedocles on Etna,* "being one with which we are one with the whole world." Significantly, it is at this depth that Pip is restored to Joe, with whom—and the phrase takes on special meaning in this *extremis*—he was "ever the best of friends." For it is permanence and continuity that is celebrated by the secret life at this level, greetings across gulfs, Joe and the young Pip raising their half-eaten bits of bread to one another in silent communion.

That word is suggestive of the elements of the Christian story that provide another deep pattern for the novel. The book opens at Christmas, Pip is present at the weird resurrection of Magwitch from behind the elder Pirrip's tombstone, on the horizon of the marshes are two gibbets and a beacon light, Jaggers washes his hands after each trial, Pip is rudely baptized in the Thames, when he is ready to leave England, he informs us, in Christ's words to the rich man, "I sold all I had," and so on (58:489). Not that Dickens intended a rigorous retelling of the Christian story in nineteenth-century terms, but as the premier Western myth of the fall into self and the recovery from it, the New Testament narrative inevitably offered useful points of reference.

Most striking, perhaps, of those points is the fact that in the Christian story, metaphors which, for the nineteenth century, were representative of alienation and despair, convey instead the ideas of connection and hope: Christ's imprisonment *gives* him to the world rather than sequestering him from it, his "premature burial" leads not to death but to life, the silence of God at the crucifixion is an invitation to, not an expulsion from, Paradise. Even more remarkable is the reversal of the metaphor of eating. Where, in Carlyle, that "I can devour *Thee*" is "the least blessed fact one knows of," a futile transaction in which the victim is diminished while the devourer gains only more self, during a communion ceremony, both eater and eaten are augmented. In *Great Expectations*, it is Joe's life that most clearly embodies these reversals of metaphor. Unlettered, silenced by his inadequate formal education, Joe is nevertheless spiritually eloquent. At the forge, a prison to Pip, Joe is entirely at home, and when he is nursing Pip, giving freely of his time, money, and substance in a way that ought rationally to deplete him, he in fact enlarges remarkably, becomes omnipresent, offers, to his hallucinating patient, "all kinds of extraordinary transformations of the human face" which sooner or later settle down "into the likeness of Joe" (57:472).

One of the elements of Christianity most attractive to Dickens, one critic comments, was the creed of "the fatherhood of God [which] allowed for a kind of ancestor worship."[26] Certainly, the many orphans or abandoned children in Dickens's fiction questing for reunion, either actual or symbolic, with lost parents, suggest how essential Dickens believed such reunion to be for the achievement of spiritual health. "Father is so much kinder that he used to be," Scrooge's sister happily reports, "that home's like heaven." To discover the lost father is to discover one's own place in the beneficent order of the generations, to escape from the prison of self into the amplitude of a universal community, to establish connections with ancestors, contemporaries, and descendants, connections whose disappearance from nineteenth-century society Tocqueville found so ominous. Certainly, from the moment Pip, in the depths of his illness, recognizes in Joe his spiritual father, a father he has been seeking since the first page of the novel, all traces of snobbish alienation from his own past vanish. Simultaneously, he becomes capable of a more generous judgment of his friend, Herbert Pocket, and later there is even a little Pip to carry on his name.

The darker fate of Estella only emphasizes the importance Dickens assigned to reunion with the father as a means of escape from the prison of self. Like Pip, Estella is brought up as an orphan, but unlike Pip, she has no Joe to represent the benign fatherhood of God. Magwitch, her natural father, she never knows, and the morally ambiguous Jaggers, who in fact "gives" her life, is himself a pathologically isolated figure, victim of a cold and alienating intellect gruesomely symbolized by the severed heads in his office. Cut off from connection with the world on this side, she is further isolated by the vengeful, witch-like Miss Havisham. For in the Victorian scheme, in which marriage is a woman's best hope of entering into the broad community of the father, the single woman is the ultimate metaphor for spiritual isolation, and to be left at the altar is to be condemned to a life sentence of solitary confinement, a sentence Miss Havisham ruthlessly executes upon herself in the name of a despised patriarchy and which she attempts, all too successfully, to impose on her ward.

The theme of the fatherhood of God is comically exploited in the Wemmick episodes. A character who, with his absurdly elaborate contrivances for isolating himself from the world, ought to symbolize solipsistic despair, Wemmick is, instead, shown to be spiritually healthy because he is the selfless preserver of a paternal community. Every one of Wemmick's actions is taken, very literally, in the name of the father, and indeed, the Aged Parent can be seen as Dickens's wry satire on gloomy Victorian pronouncements about the superannuation and silence of God. Like that Hardyesque God, the Aged P. cannot hear and is incapable of replying coherently to questions addressed to him. But there the comparison ends, for his is not the censorious silence of rejection and abandonment but rather the loving silence of a mutual understanding that requires nothing to be said.

Such a silent communion is for Dickens, as it was for Carlyle, a clear sign of spiritual health, the health of people secure in their own natures and participating so unself-consciously in the universal order that they have no need for words to influence or manipulate one another. Both writers seem to be echoing here Keat's famous contrast between the elector of Hanover, "who governs his petty state, and knows how many straws are swept daily from the causeways in all his dominions, and has a continual itching that all the housewives should have their coppers well scoured, and the ancient emperors of vast provinces, who had only heard of the remote ones and scarcely cared to visit them." Such negative capability as the ancient emperors displayed, such un-cannibalistic acquiescence in the uniqueness and sovereignty of others, has, we know, always been characteristic of Joe. From the start, exposed to the energetic cannibalism of Mrs. Joe, he seeks to protect Pip while unconditionally loving both. Later, he readily destroys Pip's apprenticeship papers, uncomplainingly relinquishing control over the boy while rejecting the worldly Jaggers's offers of compensation. His act is an authentically philanthropic one, asking nothing for itself and freeing rather than manipulating the recipient.

That by the end of the story Pip has become the true son of this spiritual father is perhaps clearest from the silence which he maintains about the money he had given to Herbert Pocket. Where Miss Havisham seeks credit for philanthropy she has not performed, and Magwitch taints his genuine philanthropy with a desire for gratitude, Pip finds his greatest happiness in self-abnegation, in a withholding of himself which, paradoxically, leads to the deepening of his relationship with his friend. Looking back, from this vantage point of the novel's end, on Pip's pilgrimage, we can see that Dickens has indeed been offering it as a paradigmatic nineteenth-century journey. Beginning where romanticism itself began, in the ultimate isolation of the graveyard, among graveyard poets and the tombstones of his prematurely buried siblings, and moving out into an encounter with frenetic Victorian materialism which only increases that isolation, Pip is shown undergoing a symbolic death of the self through which he is able to discover a place beyond personality where true community is possible.

It is natural for the reader of *Great Expectations* to wonder, however, whether such a resolution is a universal or an influential or even a convincing response to the nineteenth-century crisis of self, or for that matter to the situation presented in the novel. Certainly, it was not the only response available to Dickens's contemporaries. Just three years after the novelist's death, for example, Walter Pater was proposing, in his "Conclusion" to *Studies in the History of the Renaissance,* from which I have already quoted, that the effort to escape from the prison of self be abandoned in favor of an ecstatic cultivation of that imprisonment. And there can be no doubt that it was Pater's recommendation rather than Dickens's that more deeply influenced the last third of the nineteenth century. Indeed, an unsentimental reader may wonder if Dickens himself could seriously have believed that the tepid mysticism of a conventional—even an exhausted—Christianity was at all adequate to resolve the long-standing post-romantic problems of epistemological scepticism and the secret life.

Ironically, Pater's advice, which in the context of these problems as presented by Dickens is in fact a counsel of despair, seems to lead to more intense and more joyous experience than does the resigned, autumnal resolution of *Great Expectations,* a resolution which, for many readers, appears to reflect its author's own spiritual exhaustion at this stage of his career. "What is lacking in Dickens's magical solution," asks Edwin Eigner about the novel, "that it fails this time to bring off the conventional happy ending?"[27] The question clearly alludes to the absence of a cele-bratory marriage of hero and heroine at the end of the book, in either of the two final passages, but it also comments on the protagonist's long exile from his homeland, on the unexciting commercial career to which all his hopes for a dramatic life have led him, and in general on the low en-ergy level of the story's last pages.

It is particularly the absence of an intense, life-affirming energy, an energy we have come to expect from our reading of Dickens's earlier works, that we note in the resolution of *Great Expectations:* the absence of any equivalent, for example, of Scrooge's inspired declaration that, in his newly recovered innocence, he has become a baby again, or of the transfiguring fancy of Sairey Gamp, whose creativity, one commentator remarks, fills "the void in her life . . . casting the glow of imagination over the sordidness and solitude [of her world]."[28] The sober *dénoue-ment* of *Great Expectations* is hardly the place for Scrooge's magical re-turn to a pre-lapsarian state of grace. The warning message Pip had earlier received—"Don't go home!"—has become, by the end of the story, a more poignant "Can't go home," the young man's exile from En-gland representing, as well, an irrevocable exile from the Eden of child-hood. Nor will any Mrs. Gamp-like inventiveness serve this time to "cast a glow" over a sordid world. Pip's wildly fanciful story of his first visit to Satis House is by the end of the novel repudiated in favor of the sub-dued, serious-minded autobiographical account which we call *Great Expectations.* No wonder readers find unconvincing any suggestion that the book is about—in the words of one critic—"the Christian love and 'true fatherhood' by which [Pip], and not he alone, may be redeemed,"[29] It is precisely such redemptive energy that appears to be missing from the story's resolution, and the "lack" of which, as Edwin Eigner puts it, constitutes the work's "failure to bring off the conventional happy ending."

To speak of a "conventional" happy ending, however, is to speak of one's *expectations* for a story, and here we may begin to better under-stand the significance of the muted conclusion Dickens supplied for his novel. For in a book about the dangers of indulging in unreasonable ex-pectations, there could hardly be a wittier or more dramatic achievement for the author than to demonstrate to his readers that they are susceptible to the same solipsistic preconceptions as his protagonist, hardly a more effective device than to cause the audience to make the same mistake as the hero, the better to reveal the seductive nature of that mistake. Where, after all, have our disappointed expectations for the resolution of the novel come from if not, as Edwin Eigner suggests, from Dickens's own earlier fictions, from his many irresistible invitations to us to believe wholeheartedly in the ability of Scrooge to be a baby again and of Mrs. Gamp to "fill the void of her life" with tales of her own making; if not, in short, from his consistently and famously encouraging us in the romantic faith that a world created by the imagination is better and more appealing and ultimately truer than any positivistic universe "as in itself it really is?" And such an idea is exactly analogous to Pip's own romantic reliance on a magical rescue from "sordidness and solitude."

But in *Great Expectations*, the familiar Dickensian formula no longer applies. The passionate energy and creativity of Pip's fiction about Satis House, for example, a fiction appealing even to Joe, who, like the reader, knows it is a lie but wishes it were true, is presented here not as part of the resolution of the hero's difficulties but as itself the problem, an early instance of Pip imposing his own vision on the world. And to the extent that readers are delighted by the imaginative vitality of this fiction and feel disappointment at Pip's subsequent metamorphosis into sober autobiographer, they too are falling into what Dickens would have us understand is Pip's own self-indulgent error, into the familiar error of all readers everywhere who desire a favorite author to go on fulfilling their conventional expectations of him. "In the wilderness," lamented a reviewer of *Little Dorrit* in *Blackwood's Magazine*, "we sit down and weep when we remember thee, O *Pickwick!*"[30] But in *Great Expectations*, Dickens would have us recognize, the somber conclusion of the story constitutes not a loss of power and authority but a gain; the muted, autumnal tones of the book's last pages, he wants us to see, depict not the feebleness of disappointed desire but rather the tranquility of recollected emotion.

The Pip whose voice we hear narrating the story of *Great Expectations* is, we must not forget, a memoirist, a man quietly revisiting his own hectic past, and it is surely appropriate that Dickens, whose narratives tend often to circle back to their beginnings, should have found a Wordsworthian resolution for a story whose origins lie so deep in the Wordsworthian "abyss of idealism." Dickens's debt to Wordsworth, particularly to the latter's exploration of childhood innocence through the process of recollection, is great, his books owing much, Angus Wilson comments, "to the ethics of the *Lyrical Ballads*."[31] Other critics have noted this same indebtedness. Barry Westburg, for example, speaks of the importance of memory in Dickens's psychological scheme, commenting that "he dealt with it more fully than any other writer of his time (except possibly Wordsworth, whose *Prelude* was published the same year as *Copperfield*)."[32]

The theme of childhood revisited is a familiar one in early nineteenth-century literature, "often represented," M. H. Abrams points out, "as a circuitous journey back home. So represented, the protagonist is the collective mind or consciousness of men, and the story is that of its painful pilgrimage through difficulties, sufferings, and recurrent disasters in quest of a goal which, unwittingly, is the place it had left behind when it first set out and which, when reachieved, turns out to be better than it had been at the beginning."[33] The journey described by Abrams is a mystical one, most schematically depicted in the works of Dickens by Scrooge's astonishing recovery of his own youthfulness. But there is a danger inherent in such a mystical resolution, one apparent to even the most sympathetic readers of *A Christmas Carol*. For the fact that Scrooge's innocence is reachieved *in his own person* inevitably compromises its integrity, raising the possibility that the old man's revival may be just one more convolution of ego, a further solipsistic manipulation of reality rather than the genuine recovery from the disease of self it is supposed to represent.

Perhaps this is why a maturer Dickens found the Wordsworthian model of a return to the past *through another* so much more appropriate for a story like *Great Expectations*. The paradigm of this Wordsworthian strategy is, of course, "Tintern Abbey," an elegiac poem in which, after "a long absence" from an intensely experienced scene, the narrator is able to recover some of the power of that old emotion by empathically participating in his sister's experience of the same scene. Such recovery is necessarily at one remove from, and less passionate than, the original solitary moment, but it achieves a sweetness of its own through being shared, through its confirmation of the fact that beyond Pateresque self-reflexiveness there exists genuine otherness as an alternative to solipsistic isolation. "What we have loved," Wordsworth declares at the end of the *Prelude*, "others will love, and we will teach them how," such teaching or reporting further emphasizing the human obligation to, and connection with, others. The "Intimations Ode" makes the same point even more directly. Beginning with its famous concession that the ecstatic personal moment can never be recovered, it philosophically accepts as substitute the consolation of community inherent "in the primal sympathy / which having been must ever be."

Great Expectations, I am suggesting, derives in part from this Wordsworthian model. The well-known lines from "Tintern Abbey, for example:

> These beauteous forms,
> Through a long absence, have not been to me
> As is a landscape to a blind man's eye;
> But oft in lonely rooms, and 'mid the din
> Of towns and cities, I have owed to them,
> In hours of weariness, sensations sweet . . .

have their somewhat soberer counterpart in the opening passage of chapter 59 of the novel: "For eleven years I had not seen Joe nor Biddy with
my bodily eyes—though they had both been often before my fancy in the
East—when, upon an evening in December, an hour or two after dark, I
laid my hand softly on the latch of the old kitchen door" (489). After the
nearly fatal illness which purges him of ego, and after "many wanderings,
many years / Of absence," Pip revisits the scene of his early life. There he
finds his old place filled by a young child bearing his own name and recognizes the obligation which such an experience places on him to record
his history so that "what we have loved, / Others will love."[34] The tone of
such a history must necessarily be subdued and elegiac, not as a sign of its
author's spiritual exhaustion but as an indication of his newly acquired
"philosophic mind." The community beyond personality that Pip has discovered is also beyond the manic, self-advertising fables that provided a
specious vitality earlier in the book. Christian acquiescence in "the primal sympathy / Which having been must ever be"—here validated by its
Wordsworthian analog—always expresses itself most authoritatively,
Dickens suggests, through silence.

To talk of the silence of an autobiographer may at first seem paradox-
ical. Technically speaking, the only voice we ever hear in *Great Expectations* is Pip's, but what the young memoirist's story appears to tell us is
that representation in general, and language in particular—both spoken
and written—are all too frequently distorters of reality, concealing
rather than revealing truth. "Have you seen anything of London, yet?"
Joe is asked, and in some bewilderment he replies: "Why, yes Sir . . . me
and Wopsle went off straight to look at the Blacking Ware'us. But we
didn't find that it come up to its likeness in the red bills at the shop doors"
(27:244). Throughout the novel, words are shown to be deceptive and
imprisoning: susceptible to misunderstanding, as Pip misunderstands
"wife of the above," or to misspelling and misconstruction, as Pip's
"BlEve ME inFxN" may be misconstrued; capable of imposing one person on another, as indenture papers do, or of lying outright, as in Pip's
story about Satis House, or Pumblechook's self-congratulations, or
Jagger's collection of convict memoirs.

All these instances suggest that language is unavoidably an instrument for manipulating reality, for imposing one's own vision on others,
for promoting self-consciousness and irony and isolation. To speak or to
write, however scrupulously, is of necessity to deceive, to create a private, alternate universe and thus to destroy all possibility of that self-
abnegation and community which it is Pip's intention to urge in his
cautionary story. Certainly, the depiction of Joe in *Great Expectations*
supports this view. Unlettered and therefore "silent," Joe is the least manipulative character in the novel, the one who engages life most directly
and authentically, who grasps most unironically the self-evident proposi-

tion that "lies is lies" (9:100). Yet it would be a great mistake to suppose that the story means to resolve this dilemma of language by equating virtue with illiteracy or by celebrating Joe's naiveté over Pip's dearly bought sophistication as the more desirable human state.

One critic seeks to deal with the paradox of Pip's "silent" narration by distinguishing between "lies and fictions in general," through which Pip originally enters the fallen world of self, and "confession, that frees him from [that world]."[35] The distinction is a reasonable one, emphasizing the difference between language intended to impose solipsistically on others and language meant to facilitate surrender of self to a larger order. Pip's careful reportage, for example, never calling attention to itself as reportage, never inviting us to impugn its motives, clearly seems to belong in this latter category. In the end, however, we have no choice but to question the good faith of *any* linguistic reconstruction of reality, however well-intentioned. For as Frank Kermode argues in *The Sense of an Ending*, the chief objective of the novelist, autobiographical or otherwise, is to impose some personal structure on what appears to be the chaos of experience.

Kermode derives this view principally from his observation of fiction's need—a need not shared by life—to come to a satisfying or at least to a significant conclusion. But when we examine the ending of *Great Expectations* we find its writer remarkably—if unintentionally—withholding that final assertion of authority, of self, as if understanding, at least intuitively, how essential his own silence is to the credibility of the novel's resolution. Everyone knows how Dickens, having written the so-called "unhappy" ending of his story, the ending in which Pip and Estella meet briefly and then part, was then convinced by his fellow novelist Edward Bulwer-Lytton to write a second, "happy" ending in which the two meet and remain together. Consideration of this matter has tended to focus on two questions: which of the endings is better (critics take both sides), and what was Dickens's motive for making the change (did he do it simply to improve sales or for some other reason)?

We can pretty well dismiss the notion that Dickens acted out of crass commercialism. Bulwer-Lytton is on record elsewhere as stating that whether a book ends happily or not rarely affects sales, and as Edwin Eigner puts it, "from several letters to other writers we can reconstruct at least the nature of Bulwer's advice [to Dickens], and I believe we can conclude that it was based on esthetic principles which, however faulty they may be judged, should not be dismissed as either commercial or merely conventional."[36] Whatever we think of the quality of the emendation, however, and whatever we may conclude about Dickens's motives for making the change, there is one striking fact about which there can be no dispute. People who purchase modern editions of *Great Expectations* find themselves reading a novel with two endings. That Dickens never intended the endings to be printed together is beside the point. As far as our actual experience is concerned, *Great Expectations* presents its readers (and perhaps even its characters) with a choice of how the story should conclude.

At least one consequence of the alternative endings is to create the effect of an extraordinarily autonomous fictional world, one free even of authorial control and intention. Dickens's willingness to surrender some of his authority to Bulwer is itself an unusual instance of self-abnegation in a normally independent writer. Is it possible that, for the moment, Dickens was under the spell of his own story and its thesis, that he really perceived the prime value to be the withholding of self, an acquiescence in forces different from, and perhaps greater than his own? How, after all, could the ending of a story as rich and complex as this ever be limited to a single possibility? An author may all along have his secret intentions for the ending of his novel, but what of the novel's own, perhaps deeper intentions? If, as Murray Baumgarten suggests, writing has the capacity to "imprison the imagination . . . warp the world,"[37] what we may be seeing in the double conclusion of *Great Expectations*—and two endings imply, of course, an infinite number—is a chastened Dickens, struggling against the selfishness of language to allow for possibilities in the world that even this most imaginative of English novelists knew he could not imagine.

The striking authorial "silence" represented by Dickens's submission to Bulwer and his consequent creation of the two endings of *Great Expectations*, like the equally notable substitution in the book of a tone of settled melancholy for the usual Dickensian ebullience, are the key elements in this major Victorian response to the ubiquitous nineteenth-century dilemma of the secret life. I have already identified that dilemma as a conflict between healthy self-expression and solipsism, a conflict whose resolution appears to have presented more and more difficulties as the century advanced. Wordsworth, for example, aware as he was of the dangers of idealism, nevertheless found it unqualifiedly blissful to be young and self-absorbed, and his development of an empathic philosophy to take the place of potentially imprisoning youthful passions seems to have been accomplished cheerfully enough. By mid-century, however, such comparatively naive delight and maturation were hardly possible, and especially in Dickens's later novels as ineradicable self-consciousness and even self-parody intrude, often introducing a hectic note into their liveliest comic passages and darkening their moments of self-abnegation.

Readers today can trace, in this movement from the magisterial resignation of Wordsworth to the melancholy submission of Dickens, a line of development in nineteenth-century culture leading inexorably toward *fin-de-siècle* nihilism; toward, for instance, a naturalistic fiction in which human lives are not so much secret as— to use Hardy's term— obscure, in which men and women are abandoned by an unfatherly universe to an isolation from which there is not even the possibility of escape into a community beyond self. In this line of development, Dickens clearly occupies a middle position as the typical Victorian wanderer between two worlds, worlds represented by the two endings—one falteringly romantic, the other incipiently nihilistic—that he wrote for *Great Expectations*. Such a middle position has obvious advantages for the artist, discouraging simplistic formulations of problems, guarding against easy answers. Certainly, it is the delicate balance maintained among conflicting claims in *Great Expectations*, the aesthetically and philosophically rich texture of the story that has earned it its current status as the most respected of its author's novels. That balance can perhaps best be seen in the oxymoronic "silent" speech through which the story is told by its reticent narrator, in the willing relinquishment of will which is the essence of its ambivalent resolution. In the persistent nineteenth-century conflict between self-expression and solipsism, there could be no more complex or resonant figure than Pip, the passionate dreamer turned acquiescent realist who, choosing to renounce self, chooses also to tell the story of that choice.

Notes

[Ed. note: *DSA* is shorthand for the *Dickens Studies Annual*, *GE* for *Great Expectations*.]

1. The edition is dated 25 June 1844.

2. John Forster, *The Life of Charles Dickens*, 3 vols. (London, 1873), 2:24.

3. Paul Zweig, *The Heresy of Self-Love: A Study of Subversive Individualism* (New York: Basic Books, 1968), 37ff.

4. Alfred North Whitehead, quoted in Zweig, *The Heresy of Self-Love,* 122.

5. Ernest Bernbaum, ed. *Anthology of Romanticism* (New York: The Ronald Press, 1948), xxvi.

6. Quoted by Larry D. Nachman in "The Solitude of the Heart: Personality and Democratic Culture," *Salmagundi* (Fall 1979), 174.

7. Masao Miyoshi, *The Divided Self* (New York: New York University Press, 1969), 47.

8. Morris Kline, *Mathematics: The Loss of Certainty* (New York: Oxford University Press, 1980), 74.

9. Nachman, "The Solitude of the Heart," 175.

10. Miyoshi, *The Divided Self,* 107.

11. Peter Dale, "Symbolic Representation and the Means of Revolution in *Daniel Deronda,*" *Victorian Newsletter,* (Spring 1981), 25.

12. G. K. Chesterton, *Charles Dickens,* intro. by Steven Marcus (New York: Schocken Books, 1965), 239.

13. Pip's adulterating of the "authority" of brandy with the "scepticism" of tar water, as a consequence of the world turning upside down with him, clearly has implications for the rest of the novel.

14. H. M. Daleski, *Dickens and the Art of Analogy* (New York: Schocken Books, 1970), p. 238.

15. Alexander Welsh, *The City of Dickens* (Oxford: The Clarendon Press, 1971), 86.

16. Humphry House, *The Dickens World* (London: Oxford University Press, 1942), 111.

17. Alex Zwerdling, "Esther Summerson Rehabilitated," *PMLA*, 88(1973), 437.

18. See Wilson's "Afterword" in the Signet Classic edition of *Great Expectations* (New York: New American Library, 1963), 531.

19. *Great Expectations*, ed. Angus Calder (Harmondsworth: Penguin Books, 1965), 49:411. All subsequent citations from *Great Expectations* will be from this edition; chapter and page references will be included in parentheses in the text.

20. See, for example, V. S. Pritchett's comment that "the distinguishing quality of Dickens's people is that they are solitaries. They are people caught living in a world of their own. They soliloquize in it. They do not talk to one another; they talk to themselves." *The Living Novel* (New York: Reynal & Hitchcock, 1947), 88.

21. Lionel Stevenson, *The English Novel: A Panorama* (Boston: Houghton Mifflin, 1960), 298.

22. E. D. H. Johnson, *Charles Dickens: An Introduction to His Novels* (New York: Random House, 1969), 101.

23. Steven Marcus comments that "the coincidences in *Oliver Twist* are of too cosmic an order to belong in the category of the fortuitous." In *Dickens: From Pickwick to Dombey* (New York: Basic Books, 1965), 78.

24. The passage is quoted by Monroe Engel in *The Maturity of Dickens* (Cambridge, Mass.: Harvard University Press, 1959) from a letter of 6 October 1859 to Wilkie Collins.

25. Dorothy Van Ghent, "On *Great Expectations*," *The English Novel: Form and Function* (New York: Holt, Rinehart and Winston, 1953), p. 138.

26. House, *The Dickens World*, 111.

27. The phrase is drawn from the author's summary of the paper included in this collection.

28. Margaret Ganz, "The Vulnerable Ego: Dickens's Humor in Decline," *Dickens Studies Annual*, 1, ed. Robert B. Partlow, Jr. (Carbondale: Southern Illinois University Press, 1970), 31.

29. Robert Barnard, "Imagery and Theme in *Great Expectations*," Partlow, ed., *Dickens Studies Annual*, 1, 238.

30. The sentence is quoted in Ganz, "The Vulnerable Ego," 23.

31. Angus Wilson, *The World of Charles Dickens* (New York: Viking Press, 1970), 149.

32. Barry Westburg, *The Confessional Fictions of Charles Dickens* (Dekalb, Illinois: Northern Illinois University Press, 1977), 57.

33. M. H. Abrams, *Natural Supernaturalism: Tradition and Revolution in Nineteenth-Century Literature* (New York: Norton, 1971), 191.

34. In *The Metaphysical Novel in England and America* (Berkeley: University of California Press, 1978), Edwin Eigner paraphrases M. H. Abram's comment about works like *The Prelude* and "The Rime of the Ancient Mariner" which end with the poets' ability and compulsion to produce the poems we have just read" (213–14). Though for Dickens such a return from a circular journey was not necessarily an "end." Both Arthur Clenham, in *Little Dorrit*, and John Harmon, in *Our Mutual Friend*, are men who return from exile to *begin* their lives, and it would be a mistake to think of the still youthful Pip as someone whose own life is over.

35. Westburg, *The Confessional Fictions*, 132.

36. Edwin M. Eigner, "Bulwer-Lytton and the Changed Ending of *Great Expectations*," *Nineteenth-Century Fiction*, 25 (1970), 104–5.

37. [Ed. note: Murray Baumgarten, "Calligraphy and Code: Writing in *Great Expectations*" *Dickens Studies Annual: Essays in Victorian Fiction* 11 (1983): 61–72.]

Great Expiations: Dickens and the Betrayal of the Child*

Jack P. Rawlins

> As I walked along, the times when I was a little helpless creature, and my sister did not spare me, vividly returned.
>
> Pip, at Mrs. Joe's funeral[1]

Traditionally, Pip's progress in *Great Expectations* has been interpreted in one of two ways. Some critics have focused on Pip's personal moral failure, whereupon the novel becomes a myth of error, purgation, and salvation. Pip's ever-increasing tendency of self-blame is seen as the vehicle by which Dickens engineers his moral recovery from the sins of pride, snobbery, vanity, or fantasy (depending on the individual critic). Pip's sense of guilt is then awareness of his own sin, and moves him to reformation.[2] Other critics have focused on society's moral failure, whereupon the novel becomes a myth of original sin and scapegoat atonement. Pip's habitual guilt is seen as an awareness within himself of society's universal error—that there are good people and bad people, victims and oppressors, people of gentility and low-class people. Pip's guilt grows until he is ready to be beaten and burned into insight and to realize that we are all brothers in crime or in love.[3] In both interpretations Pip's guilt is a vehicle to growth and self-awareness; the myth of *Great Expectations* is curative.

I would like to suggest a third interpretation, in which the novel has its source in another myth. In this myth Pip has nothing to learn, his guilt does not lead him to health, and the two conventional interpretations, with which the societal Dickens would certainly agree, constitute a betrayal of the novel's original ego-centered impetus.

Writers are dreamers, and their work often serves the function of dreaming for them, allowing them to meet psychic needs that cannot be met in the conscious daytime. Dickens is apparently an unsuccessful dreamer; his literary dreams bring him no peace, and the longer he lives the more he resembles a man denied the release of dreaming. In his last years, the demons of his childhood tear at him with increasing violence; with increasing desperation he seeks escape in self-destructive behavior.

If we look at *Great Expectations* as Dickens's attempt to dream a healthy relationship with the child within him, we can see how the dream not only denies him peace, but actually turns on the dreamer and sides with the demons by reaffirming his guilt. The novel begins with Pip, Dickens's child, methodically wronged by the adult world around him, but ends with him doing penance; it begins with him as victim of society's corruption, and ends with him as the single unforgiven source of it. By the

*Reprinted by permission from *Studies in English Literature* 23 (1983): 667–83.

end of the novel Pip has internalized his tormentors—Jaggers, Orlick—and has become his own most vindictive prosecutor. And this revaluation of Pip's responsibilities is forced by Dickens at the expense of the novel's own evidence and dramatic logic.[4]

The psychological horrors of Dickens's childhood are well known and need not be detailed here. More significant for us than the pain itself—the horrors of the blacking factory and an imagined life trapped there, the apparent betrayal and abandonment by his parents, the torment at the hands of a whimsical Maria Beadnell—is Dickens's inability to share the pain with anyone else, and so accept it. Dickens knew that his parents were acting unnaturally—but no one else could see it. He knew his lover was inexplicably torturing him—but no one else could see it. Dickens learned so well that his experience of the world could not be shared that his immediate family learned about his days in the blacking factory by reading Forster's biography after his death,[5] and he was so unable to confront his past himself that his attempt at autobiography ended when the Beadnell episode proved unwritable.[6]

Every child learns that his world is not the world others see. Dickens's way of dealing with this ego/superego conflict is a common and unhappy one: "What's wrong with me, that I don't see things the way I should? I must be bad." That Dickens, given a choice between the two voices (one saying, "You hurt" and the other saying, "You shouldn't"), would feel compelled to choose the second is not surprising, since his age equates the first voice with vanity, anarchy, and madness; rather, it is the clarity with which that first voice is allowed to speak through the opening chapters of *Great Expectations*, before it is silenced, that amazes us.

One's shadow, the part of oneself one learns can't be looked at, insists on being seen. Fantasy has traditionally been a theater where the demands of the superego can be circumvented and one's shadow be allowed to triumph. *Great Expectations* seems to set out determined to provide Dickens with such absolution, but the novel changes its mind, and ends up arguing that Pip hurts only because he's a bad boy—that is, his feeling the pain at all is a measure of his corruption.

The novel begins with Pip caught in Dickens's own childhood nightmare: he looks at the world and sees everything out of joint, corrupt, and unfair, but the adult world assures him that everything's fine. Mrs. Joe seems "in [Pip's] young eyes" (to use Pip's habitual phrase) to be cruel, selfish, and mad; the world sees a devoted wife, guardian, and housekeeper. Miss Havisham and her household seem psychotic; the world sees only eccentricity. And so with Jaggers, Pumblechook, and the entire crew: Pip looks and sees what is—and sees that things are terribly wrong; the world looks and sees that all is well—but we know they see with lying eyes. One adult, Joe, might seem not to fit the pattern: he can't lie, and he can accept Pip's pain. But in fact he does fit it. He lies, but from a good heart. He insists against fact that his father was a good man and that Mrs.

Joe is a good woman, in fact that everyone is good and that in general the sun is shining brightly when Pip knows it's raining. Like the Aged P., he sees no evil, and thus is unable to validate Pip's vision of the world. Joe cannot rage, and so reinforces the lesson of the Pumblechookian perspective: a good person wouldn't feel what Pip is feeling.

Pip is tormented by the dissonance between his vision and society's and he habitually wonders if there is something wrong with him to account for the disparity, but we know surely where the fault lies. The first third of the novel rests on a bedrock of the child's congenital egocentric moral rightness. The child sees truly; adults have learned to see falsely. And, as is the way in wish-fulfilling fantasies, the voice of the serpent, the seducer who invites the dreamer to doubt and betray the self, is transparent and inept: society is spoken for by Mrs. Joe and Pumblechook, and we are not tempted to believe them.

Throughout the novel, "as if" similes represent the discord between Pip's view of things and the world's. The "as if" simile is a life-long stylistic device of Dickens, and many critics have offered interpretations of it,[7] but in *Great Expectations* similes multiply and take on a special emblematic significance. For Pip, the force of the simile is almost the opposite of its traditional function in poetry. Customarily, similes make connections between like things; the simile-maker fosters community by revealing likeness between things we saw as separate. Pip's similes do something like the reverse of this: they bring unlikes together, not because they have something in common, but because they don't, yet the world has perverted the tenor into something like the vehicle, and hence into something not itself. Pip witnesses an adult world where inauthenticity makes everything like something it is not like.

> 'Swine,' pursued Mr Wopsle, . . . pointing his fork at my blushes, as if he were mentioning my christian name. (58)

> A hackney-coachman . . . packed me up in his coach and hemmed me in with a folding and jingling barrier of steps, as if he were going to take me fifty miles. (187)

> The great numbers on [the convicts'] backs, as if they were street doors. (249)

To the objective eye, the world makes no sense. "Swine" isn't Pip's name—why does Wopsle act as if it is? Pip is riding a block or two to Jaggers's—why does the coachman seem to prepare for a long journey? Of course, as adults, we have answers: the coachman is trying to impress Pip with his labors and thus increase his tip, for instance. Generally, things look "as if" they were something they're not because the world is populated with posturing, dehumanized, compulsive confidence men. Pip finds the world incomprehensible to the extent to which he is innocent of its corruptions. Similes measure the extent to which the world has gone wrong, and so they flourish in scenes of extreme unnaturalness— the Hamlet performance, Mrs. Joe's funeral, and Joe's meeting with Miss Havisham, where Pip gives us the lesson of the simile directly by saying, "I could hardly have imagined dear old Joe looking so unlike himself or so like some extraordinary bird" (128).

Pip's vision is naturally true. It is also naturally just. Pip is not good; he is fair. In this novel, Joe is good, Biddy is good, the Aged P. is good— what we now call "nice." For Dickens, the essential act of goodness is Joe's dead wrong insistence that his father was a good man (77). The goodness is all in Joe, who imposes it on the world by the simple act of assuming it. Pip is immune to this kind of goodness in the beginning, as he makes clear in his response to Joe's judgment of his father—the man wasn't good, and nothing can make Pip overlook that. It is precisely this refusal to commit himself to Dickens's virtuous blindness that makes Pip Dickens's best hope for solving the puzzle of living in a world curiously good and bad at the same time. The dramatic question at this point in the book seems clear: can Pip continue to acknowledge the wrong he sees in the world, and still find a means to moral living without sealing himself off from the flawed human race in a private fantasy society of innocents, as Dickens's other heroes tend to do?

Pip's true judgment tells him he is victimized by exploitive adults who deny his humanity. "In the little world in which children have their existence . . . there is nothing so finely perceived and so finely felt, as injustice," he says in response to Estella's injustice to him; "Within myself, I had sustained, from my babyhood, a perpetual conflict with injustice. I had known, from the time when I could speak, that my sister . . . was unjust to me" (92). He unerringly spots the unfairness of a Pumblechook torturing Pip with sums "while he [sits] at his ease guessing nothing" (84). Who else but Dickens encourages a child to such a sense of self-worth? Who else would grant a child the right to feel violated by an adult rumpling his hair without his permission (125)? Indeed, Pip is not good. A good boy, reflecting upon his guardian's death, thinks of her virtues, however slight, his debt to her, however small, and the infinite mercy of God. Pip, meditating on Mrs. Joe's death, says, "the times when I was a little helpless creature, and my sister did not spare me, vividly returned" (298). In most literature, children are things for molding and shaping; in the opening chapters of *Great Expectations*, this child is a thing for defending—a thing that must battle with guts and spite against the adult forces that constantly demand a renunciation of the self.

Thus the novel begins less like a *bildungsroman* than like a quest, and Pip is more knight errant than vessel to be filled: Pip is perfectly, selfishly intact at the novel's beginning, and, as with Gawain or Parsifal, the question is, can he hold fast in a world of doubt? A series of sirens and dragons will bribe, torture, and argue in attempts to make him fail to persist. The world will offer only opportunities for straying.

Like all defenders of the right who aren't divine, Pip is racked by guilt. Sometimes he knows where the guilt comes from—Mrs. Joe and others drum it into him. "'Trouble?' echoed my sister; 'trouble?' And then entered on a fearful catalogue of all the illnesses I had been guilty of, and all the acts of sleeplessness I had committed, and . . . all the injuries I had done myself, and all the time she had wished me in my grave, and I had contumaciously refused to go there" (59). But righteous people, however clearly their integrity tells them the world is wrong, tremble at their audacity. A part of Pip knows that, "through all [his] . . . penitential performances" Mrs. Joe invents to teach him another answer (92), he's right and she's wrong, but another part of Pip fears that Mrs. Joe is right—he is guilty of being sick, of not going to his grave when asked to. The adult world encourages Pip to cultivate a sense of original sin; they know he's guilty, because he's a boy—they're just waiting for the crime to be manifested.

Pip learns to see himself through this adult perspective, and moments when he chooses without external reason to convict himself are frequent in the novel. When he hears George Barnwell's history, he feels somehow responsible for the murder (145). When Mrs. Joe is struck down, Pip assumes for a moment that he did it (147). When Mrs. Pocket rages at her children, Pip remarks without justification, "I felt quite abashed: as if I myself had done something to rouse" her anger (217). Pip's guilt complex is part of a larger picture, where guilt, crime, and violence are so confused in his mind that the sequence of act-consequence-reward breaks down. Pip doesn't strike Mrs. Joe down but he is guilty of the act, in that Orlick does it and Orlick acts out the life of Pip's bestial self. And others are as susceptible as Pip himself to sudden, violent retribution for noncrimes: Wopsle is executed, in Pip's imagination, for wet pants. He sits in the damp, and Pip concludes, "the circumstantial evidence on his trousers would have hanged him if it had been a capital offence" (72).

The novel's opening action, Pip's encounter with Magwitch, makes clear what the novel originally sees Pip as guilty of: he is tormented by fears that he will be caught in the act of charity.[8] And throughout the novel, Pip's natural humanity leads him to do what's right, only to sweat out nightmares in which he is shipped off to the Hulks for refusing to obey the adult world's corrupt commands. Pip feels guilty because his ego isn't strong enough for him to out-face the adult world and say, "I know you're all wrong." But to such a place we hope he will grow.

Thus far Dickens seems to have created in Pip a perfect vehicle for the exorcism of his childhood demons. Pip sees the truth of things; he is born with a rage for justice and a commitment to the preservation and nurture of the ego; he is racked with guilt, but we see that the guilt is the result of his attempt to integrate the dissonant voices of true ego and false superego. He is subjected to the horrors of the Dickensian childhood—he is stripped of his rights, found guilty of being himself, and rendered invisible—but he's not Oliver Twist this time, and he has the grit to decry his treatment and the determination to right his wrongs by his own hand. If the myth is played out, he will be tempted to forswear the self, but will hold fast; those in the adult world who are open to truth will be converted and will gather around him in a new community of authentic spirits, and those who are not will be expelled or destroyed. There are traces of this myth in the second half of the novel (most clearly with Miss Havisham, who is explicitly punished for her crimes to Pip, in front of Pip, and to whom alone Pip is allowed to express his pain and see it empathetically confirmed), but the novel principally abandons it for another. Pip discovers he really is at fault, that he is the bad boy the adults have been foretelling since his birth, and he ends up doing most of the expiating. From a focus on adults' injustice to him, we move to a focus on his injustice to Joe and Magwitch. Dickens works it out so that Pip's lifelong guilt is finally justified by his own apparent badness, and Pip is saved through cultivated self-loathing. Crying, "Strike me, Joe. Tell me of my ingratitude. Don't be so good to me" (472), he strips himself of money (i.e., worth and power) and dedicates himself to service—first to Magwitch, then to Herbert. Finally, after years spent breaking the spirit of fantasy at a clerk's desk, Pip can say with Estella, "I have been bent and broken, but—I hope—into a better shape" (493).

And it is more than Pip simply discovering his own imperfection. As the novel relocates the source of the problem, from a corrupt world to a vain and foolish Pip, it revalues many of the adult characters—Jaggers, Havisham, Magwitch, Joe—and excuses their former behavior. As Pip discovers the fault in himself, he discovers the relative faultlessness of others, so that the very fact that Pip originally saw wrongness in them becomes evidence at his own sentencing. This pattern is clearest in the treatment of Jaggers, because he seems so thoroughly beyond salvation. In the beginning, Jaggers is very nearly the Devil. He works from a desk chair like a coffin, "sets man-traps" for everyone (221), hires false witnesses, torments Molly for his own amusement in front of his dinner guests while boasting of his courtroom dishonesty, and generally in his dealings with the human race "has 'em, soul and body" (283). He is the archetypal adult in Pip's world: a puppet-master the world smiles on, who controls by inducing groundless guilt in others. Pip fears that the wine whispers to Jaggers things to Pip's disadvantage (264), but with Jaggers the world shares Pip's paranoia: Herbert, whose conscience is clear, meets Jaggers and concludes that Herbert himself "must have committed a felony and forgotten the details of it, he [feels] so dejected and guilty" (311), and Jaggers has a similar effect on Wopsle and everyone else at the Three Jolly Bargemen (163). Thus Jaggers personifies what Pip must learn to retain his integrity in the face of, and with Jaggers much of the rest of the world is ready to support Pip in his perception that the adult's relationship with the world is askew.

The lesson is told clearly in Joe's single encounter with Jaggers. Others accept Jaggers's poor opinion of them, but Joe knows who Joe is, and he knows just as plainly that Jaggers is trying to beat him up. He responds appropriately: "Which I meantersay . . . that if you come into my place bull-baiting and badgering me, come out!" (168–69). Something like this is what Pip needs: a confrontation with the hypercritical parent and an exorcising of the negative self-concept through a raging attack on the icon.

The confrontation takes place. Pip, armed with incriminating secret knowledge about Jaggers—that is, when the power balance between them seems finally to have tipped in Pip's favor—calls Jaggers to account. But the scene goes horribly wrong, and Pip is forced to exonerate Jaggers of all charges. Jaggers explains that his behavior in Estella's case has been humane; he "saved" her from the fate of the criminal's child, he "sheltered" Molly and "kept down the old wild violent nature," and so on (424–26). Finally Jaggers persuades Pip to keep Jaggers's secret, thus making him an accessory and winning from him tacit sanction for Jaggers's behavior. The oppressive parent has been discovered to be wise and loving—and what of Pip? He looked and saw the devil—there must be something wrong with him. Dickens saves Jaggers, but this salvation isn't Dickens's conventional rebirth through drowning, explosion, or whatever, and the psychological consequences for Pip are dire. Jaggers is not reborn; he is revealed *to have always been* benevolent—so apparently Pip saw falsely. Dickens has to cheat to bring this off—Jaggers cannot be benevolent, as the emotional truth of scenes like the brutalizing of Molly attests. Our grown-up tormenters know best, Dickens concludes, but he must lie to himself before he's convinced.[9]

As the novel continues, Dickens exonerates other characters, in each case forcing Pip to recant the supposed error of his original perception. Joe, who was a poor guardian, explains how his failure to protect Pip from Mrs. Joe was really wise and humane (478), and Pip again acknowledges the parental wisdom: Joe asks, "Is he right, that man?" (meaning himself), and Pip responds, "Dear Joe, he is always right."[10] Herbert, who has been benevolent but self-deceiving and ineffective throughout the novel, turns out to be "always right" too, and Pip takes all responsibility for his ever appearing otherwise: "I often wondered how I had conceived that old idea of his inaptitude, until I was one day enlightened by the reflection, that perhaps the inaptitude had never been in him at all, but had been in me" (489). Dickens's determination to find the world "always right" even embraces Trabb's boy, who is allowed to play hero at the sluice-house, after which Pip absolves him of all traces of "malignancy," discovers that he is merely a case of "spare vivacity," and expresses his regret at ever thinking ill of him (443).

And Pip is factually wrong in these cases. Just as Jaggers is a devil, so Herbert is a fool, and Joe was wrong—when he allowed Mrs. Joe to destroy Pip's ego, when he assured Pip that Pip was right to follow the money to London and forget the forge. Pip becomes his own Jaggers, his own prosecuting adult, convicting himself of imaginary crimes. He has now internalized his attackers so successfully that he can do to himself what they did to him, and his lectures to himself in the second half of the book are exactly the texts of Mrs. Joe's sermons: you're congenitally bad, you're always in the way, everything you do makes trouble for your betters. Now the lesson of the simile is reversed: the distance between the vehicle and the tenor is the measure of Pip's viciousness. The responsibility for wrong-doing lies with the person who creates the wrong by seeing it.[11]

Pip spends the last third of the novel visiting the adults he dared find at fault, exonerating each, and by implication accepting responsibility for their weakness or cruelty. He is a scapegoat, but Dickens seems to think the goat literally committed the sin in the first place. Thus Pip must do more than Christ; he must not only suffer for the sins of the world, he must believe he caused them. Christ is free of guilt, but Pip isn't, so, while Christ is willing to be crucified, Pip crucifies himself.

The conventional view of *Great Expectations* says in rebuttal to all this, No—Pip is guilty; he does indeed have much to expiate. This view, which accepts the older Pip's judgment of his young self, must now be examined. What does the young Pip do that is so bad? The elder Pip says, he fell victim to a vain dream of worldly glory. He wanted to be rich and grand, to impress the vacuous star Estella and win her love. This sin— call it vanity, egoism, fancy—led him to abandon his friends, devote his life to idleness, and deny his fundamental Christian brotherhood with Magwitch. When he is awakened to his error, he embraces Magwitch as his spiritual equal, acknowledges Joe's lack of striving, his acceptance of the world as it is, as a model for moral behavior, realizes that fancy is a betrayer, and puts himself to useful work. In this view, Pip's crimes begin with his love for Estella and are proven by his treatment of Magwitch. Yet the novel offers us the means to rebut Pip's interpretation of these actions.

In terms of the novel's original vision, Magwitch is the epitome of a basic adult perversion: the desire to create, own, and exploit human beings as property and extensions of the ego. When he and Pip meet in Pip's London apartments, Magwitch speaks in pure form the doctrine by which adults relate to children in Dickens's world: I made you; you exist only as an extension of me.[12] His view of the world is among the farthest from genuineness in the novel—he prizes books in foreign languages for his inability to read them, for instance (338). Pip has been intentionally prevented from learning a profession to satisfy Magwitch's twisted sense of what makes a gentleman (219–20), so Pip would be justified in seeing him as the head of a conspiracy, joined by every adult in the novel, to blind Pip, stuff his pockets with money, inflate his head, and send him off to London to run up debts, while assuring him he's thriving all the time. The older Pip often sounds as if young Pip defiantly embraced a life of vanity in the face of sound adult counsel to the contrary, but sometimes he knows better: "I acquiesced, of course, knowing nothing to the contrary" (220).

When Magwitch returns to England, the nature of the conspiracy is revealed to Pip. How does he react? We might expect one of two reactions. An ego-centered response would be to rage at his puppetmaster. A more mature reaction would be to acknowledge the puppet strings that manipulate the manipulator. Magwitch is of course not the source of the corruption that destroys Pip, any more than our parents invent the lies they teach us. Typically children move through their rage at the imperfect parent to sympathetic understanding. But Pip's response poisons his opportunity for either insight. He loathes Magwitch, but for reprehensible reasons. He does not respond to the moral horror of what Magwitch has done to him, or to what the world is doing to Magwitch and all of us, but is instead repulsed by the man's poor breeding and coarse manners. Thus he is able later to fault himself for being repulsed and do penance. Dickens avoids the ego-strengthening response to Magwitch and fixes on the rare one that facilitates Pip's self-loathing. Later, Pip is unable to see any but the single aspect of his relationship with Magwitch—that he was repulsed by him out of snobbishness. Pip is indeed guilty, but that sin treacherously prohibits Pip from dealing with the rest of the complex relationship—Pip can't be angry with Magwitch, because he now owes him. Again Pip has had the opportunity to confront one of the architects of his misery, and has been forced to accept responsibility for all evil and do penitential service.

This is a crucial loss for Pip, because Magwitch, more than Jaggers, is at the center of young Pip's complex and baffling relationship with the world. Pip's benevolence is first established by his helping Magwitch on the moors, his sense of guilt blossoms when he becomes a criminal for Magwitch's sake, and his sense of being ethically at odds with the world is focused by the world's indifference to the plight of convicts and Magwitch particularly. As the father of Estella, Magwitch is the physiological as well as financial maker of Pip's Expectations. He is Pip's symbolic father and child, benefactor and destroyer, supporter and exploiter, society's victim and a caricature of its vices. Given all this, the central moral question of the novel is, how should Pip feel toward Magwitch?

And how has Pip served him? He has fed him, stolen for him, risked his life attempting to effect his escape from England, sympathized with him and acknowledged his inherent human integrity from the beginning—and is shocked by his lowness in London. Out of all this, Pip finds a kernel with which to nourish a sense of his own error, and he takes it. And to perfect his own culpability, he does with Magwitch what he does with Herbert, Jaggers, and company: he redefines him free of blame. He says that Magwitch returned to England "for [Pip's] sake" (468), which is at best a gross oversimplification of some very questionable motives ("that there hunted dunghill dog . . . got his head so high that he could make a gentleman" (337)), and he sums up the lesson of the relationship by saying, "I only saw in him a much better man than I had been to Joe" (457).

The older Pip's perspective on his love for Estella is similarly narrow and oddly slanted to his own detriment. To him his love is simply proof of his folly, and is the constant target of his best mocking irony. He should love Biddy, he tells us. "It would be very good for [him]" to "get Estella out of [his] head," he says (157); when he sees things clearly, he knows that Biddy is "immeasurably better than Estella" and that the forge offers "sufficient means of self-respect and happiness" (159). His turning from Biddy and the forge is thus a rejection of goodness in favor of splendid surface. That his preference for Estella is a matter for the most severe contrition is made clear by the terms of his planned proposal to Biddy: "humbled and repentant," Pip hopes to be received "like a forgiven child" and allowed to submit to her guidance (481). Nothing could be more serious in the context of this novel than that Pip should seek a wife who will serve as authoritarian mother—that after a series of disastrous parent figures, Pip should abase himself before another parent, and this one someone he should, in Victorian terms, rule over—a wife. Perhaps we are never so aware of how much Dickens's late view of Pip differs from ours as when he denies Pip his Biddy and intends it as a bitter pill—and we gasp with relief.

We gasp because we know—the novel has let us know firmly—that, however much Pip should love Biddy, he doesn't, and for good reason: she, like the forge world, is good, but only good. She can't dream. The forge offers "simple faith and clear home-wisdom" (486), but Pip needs more in life, and we applaud his reaching out, however inadequately the world rewards the reaching out, however insistently the older Pip characterizes the reaching out as vanity. Biddy and Joe are archetypes of Christian passivity; they endure everything cheerfully, and it is precisely Pip's unwillingness to devote his life to such mere endurance that makes him great, and dangerous. Pip is here much like Clarissa. In the midst of his problems with Magwitch, Pip cries, "I would far far rather have worked at the forge all the days of my life than I would ever have come to this!" (358). Similarly Clarissa longs for her oppressive household when she is in Lovelace's grip. Both Pip and Clarissa momentarily see themselves as over-reachers who got justly burned and now regret their aspirations, but Clarissa probably returns to a more just estimate of things than Pip. Pip's words here acknowledge that life at the forge is a sentence—a death of the spirit. Both Clarissa and Pip think they have won a victory over pride when they own a fault they don't have.

The premise of the two novels is that Clarissa and Pip must hold out for a life that nurtures their spiritual greatness. Anna Howe and Biddy say, learn to want less—but we know they say this out of the sorry conventionality of their souls; they're satisfied with less because they can't dream. Clarissa says, "I'll never disobey my parents again"; Pip says, "I'll never dream again"—and we shake our heads as our heroes forsake exactly what has won our allegiance.

That Pip's love for Estella is an argument for his greatness shows when he learns of her plans to marry Drummle. She assures him that she will be out of his thoughts soon, and he replies with an outburst of which I will only quote the beginning. "Out of my thoughts! You are part of my existence, part of myself. You have been in every line I have ever read. . . . You have been in every prospect I have ever seen since. . . . You have been the embodiment of every graceful fancy that my mind has ever become acquainted with" (378). The rhetoric is thick, but the force is clear: here is what makes Pip glorious. And Estella, however unworthy of such feeling, is the nearest thing to a worthy object of aesthetic worship the world of the novel provides. Pip, like other artists, writes love sonnets to someone dwarfed by the poetry.[13] But, because Estella cannot bear the weight of Pip's sublime passion, he should marry Biddy, and forswear passion, and be merely good and happy? Never. Pip forgets why he knew he must leave home, but the convicts don't. One asks the other what Pip's country is like, and the other replies, "A most beastly place. Mudbank, mist, swamp, and work; work, swamp, mist and mudbank" (251). Pip need only add, "And no poetry."

In short, the older Pip, by thinking in terms of goodness, misses his own greatness. And what finally is his crime? To love grandly, despite the failure of women to deserve it; to aspire, despite society's failure to provide anything worth aspiring to; to dream, despite society's insistence that all dreams be in terms of money or social status. Pip is presented with a noble problem: can a poetic spirit fulfill himself and remain authentic in Dickensian society? Pip tries. He is wide open to the world, and the world fails to provide a woman worth adoring, a deed worth doing, an adult worth emulating.[14] Pip looks at the rubble that is his life and concludes, I should have been a Joe. But we know better. Pip is destined to be Dickens.

Why Dickens must find Pip to blame is made clearer by a modern analogy. Pip is like a great-souled woman in America in the 1950s. She is born to two options: stay at home and not really exist, or marry, and be a housewife. She will marry of course, and of course find it empty. When her soul cries out against the spiritual poverty, she will seek to escape to a life where her dreams can be lived, but society will offer her only one set of terms for such escape—sexual ones. She will have an affair. It won't work, because society lied when it assured her that sex is what she needed, but when her experiment at self-fulfillment fails she will blame herself. She was guilty, she will suppose, for dreaming at all; she should have been content with the housework. She will contritely return to make the marriage work. The boredom will now be seen as a measure of her depravity—good people don't feel bored. Why was I such a fool as to want more than what's right, she will ask herself, especially since when I got it I didn't really want it? If she is lucky, she will abase herself before her husband too late, only to discover that he has abandoned her for someone who knows her place enough not to dream.

This is exactly Pip's experience. His affair is with wealth and social position instead of sex, because he is of another age, but the real agent of the fiasco is the same: a society that says to the large-souled, this (money or sex) is what your dreams are really seeking. Pip and our imaginary housewife are both victims of "a certain spiritual grandeur ill-matched with the meanness of opportunity," as George Eliot says of her Victorian saint. Pip is much like Dorothea Brooke, but Dickens is not like George Eliot; his need to exonerate the parents is stronger. Finally, he saddles Pip with the same guilty message that therapists emasculated women with in the years before the women's movement: the fault is in you for feeling dissatisfied; feel less. Look at Joe: he's so "good" his wife can torture him, and he doesn't feel a thing.

In the Victorian period, Dickens's recantation must be expected. For him to maintain the validity of Pip's pain in the face of a unanimous adult assurance that he shouldn't hurt, Dickens would have to declare triumphant the subjective reality of the ego. But in a shared sense of what is lies society's last anchor in the winds of change. To presume the inherent validity of feelings is to make an idol of the self, as Tennyson's career reminds us again and again. Tennyson's protagonists risk loss of sanity through immersion in the self, and with luck find salvation in a commitment to externals. The object of devotion may be an illusion or (as in the case of the Crimean War) an atrocity, but it takes the protagonist out of himself, and thus the commitment is healthy—like Joe's devotion to a bad father and a bad wife.

So Dickens saves his community by silencing the seer of unpalatable truths and convincing him that he is somehow responsible for the evils by seeing them. Dickens plays Orlick, stringing Pip up for crimes like being "in the way" (436), seeing through masks, being genuine ("They writes fifty hands; they're not like sneaking you, as writes but one" (438)), and being responsible for what others have done. The poetic Pip dies then, survived by a clerk. But in his suffering he speaks more directly than Dickens ever was able to do of the agony of living in a society that demands a recantation of the self. Pip foresees his death, and considers the consequences: "Estella's father would believe I had deserted him, would be taken, would die accusing me; even Herbert would doubt me . . . ; Joe and Biddy would never know how sorry I had been that night; none would ever know what I had suffered, how true I had meant to be, what an agony I had passed through. The death close before me was terrible, but far more terrible than death was the dread of being misremembered after death. . . . I saw myself despised by unborn generations" (436).

"None would ever know what I had suffered." At the heart of Pip's regret is his sense that he, like Dickens, feels unknown to the world. I know of no more powerful expression in literature of the child's idea that his sense of himself clashes inexplicably, horribly with the adult world's image of him. And as is typical in cases of such self-contempt, Pip and Dickens grow to be admired, loved, and cherished by others, and remain misremembered and accused only by themselves.

Dickens takes his son upon the mountain, in what generations of critics have found a heroic sacrifice. For those who disagree, Dickens allows Pip a small ego victory. A man who has sacrificed his inner child the better to serve in society's militia often finds that child reborn in the body of his offspring. Pip has no children, but Joe and Biddy have one for him, a child taken for Pip's own by Estella (in the original ending). Thank God, Pip likes him. Perhaps this Pip will never have to cry, "Don't be so good to me."

Dickens is not so lucky. Unable to ask for recognition of his shadow self, unable to find service that is expiation enough, unable to infatuate enough women, sell enough copies, wow enough audiences to justify self-esteem, he finishes Orlick's task, and kills himself with overwork. None ever knew what he had suffered.

Notes

[Ed. note: *DSA* is shorthand for the *Dickens Studies Annual*, *GE* for *Great Expectations*.]

1. Charles Dickens, *Great Expectations*, ed. Angus Calder (Harmondsworth: Penguin English Library, 1965), 298. All subsequent quotations from the novel will be from this edition.

2. For interpretations of *Great Expectations* along these lines, see Barbara Hardy, "The Change of Heart in Dickens' Novels," *VS* 5 (September 1961), 49–67; Dorothy Van Ghent, *The English Novel: Form and Function* (New York: Holt, Rinehart and Winston, 1953); J. Hillis Miller, *Charles Dickens: The World of His Novels* (Cambridge, Mass.: Harvard University Press, 1958); and Harry Stone, *Dickens and the Invisible World* (Bloomington: Indiana University Press, 1979). That *Great Expectations* is an "implicit critique fantasy" is stated as a critical truism by Robert Ransom in a review of Stone, in *DSA* 9, ed. Michael Timko, Fred Kaplan, and Edward Giuliano (1981), 270. For a classic expression of the idea that *Great Expectations* is a morality play about a fantasist brought to reality's heel, see Paul Pickrel's classroom guide to *GE*, in *Dickens: A Collection of Critical Essays*, ed. Martin Price (Englewood Cliffs: Prentice-Hall, 1967), 158–68.

3. For interpretations along these lines, see Taylor Stoehr, *Dickens: The Dreamer's Stance* (Ithaca: Cornell Univ. Press, 1965), esp. 91–94; Van Ghent, *The English Novel*, and

Stone, *Dickens and the Invisible World*. Critics commonly observe both patterns simultaneously, and they need not be mutually exclusive.

4. It has been recognized by most critics that Pip is Dickens, in a way that's striking even in terms of Dickens's habitually autobiographical art. See Stone, *Dickens and the Invisible World*, 309, and E. Pearlman, "Inversion in *Great Expectations*," *DSA* 7 (1978), 190–202, on *Great Expectations* as inverted *Copperfield*. That *GE* is an attempt to redo the autobiographical business of *Copperfield*, but this time closer to the nub, is a critical commonplace, and Miller, *Charles Dickens* (252 ff.), argues that Pip is the archetypal Dickens hero. It is also frequently noted that *GE* is Dickens's first serious attempt to "get the good and bad together," in Edmund Wilson's famous phrase (in *The Wound and the Bow*)—that is, to deal with the notion that good and bad in the real world run complexly through the same plot lines, the same characters, and the same social milieux. Given this consensus view of *GE* as essential confrontation by Dickens with the issues of self and morality, it seems odd that Pip is so unliked—by himself, by his creator it appears, and by the novel's readers. And he is disliked for reasons opposite to the conventional dislike modern readers have for Dickens's good people: typically we find Dickensian heroes cloying in their niceness—they are too comfortably superego-dominated. Pip is ego-dominated, and generations of critics have been ready with Dickens to condemn him for not serving well enough. He is too proud (Miller, *Charles Dickens*, 274), and pride is exactly what we wish Esther and her ilk had more of.

5. Edgar Johnson, *Charles Dickens: His Tragedy and Triumph*, 2 vols. (New York: Simon and Schuster, 1952), 1:44. See also 1:132.

6. Johnson, *Charles Dickens*, 2:659–60. That Dickens could neither confront his past nor reveal it to anyone else is a major thesis of Johnson's biography and is developed in several passages beyond those cited here. The idea that Dickens uses his novels as dream vehicles for coming to terms with an intolerable, unfaceable past is a central theme of Stoehr, *Dickens*, esp. 91–94.

It can be argued that Dickens, at the time of writing *GE*, might be more preoccupied with the agonies of the present, most notably his affair with Ellen Ternan and the resultant potential destruction of his familial, social, and professional life, but his handling of the affair makes it clear that it is not a new problem—rather, it is a projection of lifelong demons, especially his search for a love that satisfies, and his belief that what he most centrally is is unfaceable and must therefore be hidden and hysterically denied. He is, in effect, acting out Pip's bad boy image.

7. See Stoehr, *Dickens*, 105, for a recent interpretation.

8. Critics are divided on the character of Pip's first service to Magwitch. Some see him motivated, as I do, by charity; others see him motivated by fear. It hardly matters, since fear equals self-preservation and charity is a recognition of the communal self one shares with others. Pip is acting rightly, either in terms of morality or in terms of the ego.

9. For another discussion of a manifestly malicious parent-figure whose benignity is insisted on for political reasons, see Harry Keyishian, "Griselda on the Elizabethan Stage: The *Patient Grissil* of Chettle, Dekker, and Haughton," *SEL* 16 (Spring 1976), 253–61. And for an alternative interpretation of Jaggers's apparent contradictions, see Anthony Winner, "Character and Knowledge in Dickens: The Enigma of Jaggers," *DSA* 3, ed. Robert B. Partlow, Jr. (1974), 100–21, where Winner argues that Pip grows by his ability to understand Jaggers's moral ambiguities. Winner argues that Dickens's heroes see things in moral blacks and whites, and Pip is morally superior to Dickens's other heroes because the lesson of Jaggers leads him out of a fantasy world of allegorical absolutes into the real world of moral greys, means vs. ends, and expediencies. Winner's argument is based on the common critical assumption, which I obviously do not share, that Dickens's characters are *supposed* to grow from the fantasy principle to the reality principle—that Pip's fancy is something to be fixed.

10. Pearlman, "Inversion" (195) discusses Dickens's dramatic difficulties in promoting Joe as worthy of emulation despite his failure as guardian, and offers a unique resolution of the difficulty.

11. Stone, *Dickens and the Invisible World* (337) and others note the basic unreason in Pip's "accepting responsibility for . . . his fellow's sins," but argue that in the unreason lies Dickens's message: that one must recognize the original sin shared by us all, expressed in a social sickness not of anyone's making, and awaiting a scapegoat expiation. Thus Van Ghent, *The English Novel*, argues that Dickens's enlightened characters purposely bow down before those who have trespassed against them, not before those they have trespassed against—Mrs. Joe bows down before Orlick, not Pip, for instance (138). This myth of Christian redemption is of course in the novel, and seems to have the societal Dickens's full support, but still seems a betrayal of the novel's original impetus. The central question is, is Pip's guilt, which all critics have recognized is the essence of his character, a congenital guiding light to wisdom, or is it something bred by the adult world and best unlearned?

12. *Great Expectations* apparently grew in Dickens's imagination from the seminal image of Magwitch as tragicomic puppetmaster of Pip's vain fortunes (Miller, *Charles Dickens*, 250). Of course Dickens may have shifted his focus later, and critics agree that if the world of the novel has a source of evil it is Compeyson, but Compeyson does not represent this particular childhood horror as well as Magwitch, because Compeyson's brand of manipulation is not so clearly a need to extend one's ego, to clone oneself, and so deny the separate existence of the manipulated party.

13. Criticism of *Great Expectations* traditionally tests itself by interpreting the novel's two endings in light of its thesis. I will attempt something of the sort. Estella cannot be a fit wife for Pip, because she cannot share his dreams. She is a symbol, and as such is more fit to pursue than Biddy, but she is fit only for pursuit. The first ending, though low-key, works because we can be convinced that Estella can be beaten into humble goodness and then married to a merely good man. But for her to marry Pip, we would need to know she had discovered more than goodness—she would need a firing of the poetic spirit, not a chastisement of the ego, and this we don't believe beating can produce. Dickens seems to realize, though faintly, what Pip really needs, because in both endings Estella suggests that at last she has suffered enough to empathize with Pip. She has learned "to understand what [Pip's] heart used to be," and this phrase is almost the only thing the two endings share. To this point in the novel, no character could claim to share Pip's vision of the world beyond bits and pieces. With that benediction, the novel can end. If we thought that Estella meant it in any profound way, perhaps they could wed, but we don't.

14. Miller, *Charles Dickens*, (254) to my knowledge is alone in acknowledging that Pip's path to Great Expectations is the most sensible choice among the alternatives society provides for him.

Prison-Bound: Dickens and Foucault*

Jeremy Tambling

Great Expectations has been called an analysis of "Newgate London,"[1] suggesting that the prison is everywhere implicitly dominant in the book, and it has been a commonplace of Dickens criticism, since Edmund Wilson's essay in *The Wound and the Bow* and Lionel Trilling's

*Reprinted with permission from *Essays in Criticism* 37 (1986):11–31.

introduction to *Little Dorrit*, to see the prison as a metaphor throughout the novels. Not just a metaphor, of course: the interest that Dickens has in prisons themselves was real and lasting, and the one kind of concern leads to the other, the literal to the metaphorical. Some earlier Dickens criticism, particularly that associated with the 1960s, and Trilling's "liberal imagination," stressed the second at the expense of the first, and Dickens became the novelist of the "mind forg'd manacles" of Blake, where Mrs. Clennam can stand in the Marshalsea "looking down into this prison as it were out of her own different prison" (*Little Dorrit*, par. 2 chapter 31). this romantic criticism became a way of attacking the historical critics who emphasised the reformist Dickens, interested in specific social questions: Humphry House and Phillip Collins, the last in *Dickens and Crime* and *Dickens and Education*, (1962 and 1964). With Foucault's work on the "birth of the prison"—the subtitle of his book *Discipline and Punish*, (1976)—it may be possible to see how the physical growth of the modern prison is also the beginning of its entering into discourse and forming structures of thought, so that the literal and the metaphorical do indeed combine, and produce the Dickens whose interest is so clearly in both ways of thinking about the prison.

Discipline and Punish is the first of Foucault's books about modes of power operating in western societies, and it succeeds his inaugural address at the Collège de France in 1970, the "Discourse on Language," where his interest is in showing the way that knowledge is a form of manipulation, and must be thought of in the same breath as the word "power." Power in the absolutist state takes its bearings on the body, illustrated in the first part of the book, but the "gentle way in punishment," associated with late 18th century enlightenment thought, leads to a change in the way power is exercised—from "a right to take life or let live to a form of power that fosters life, the latter being described as a power over life, in contrast to the former sovereign power, which has been described as a power over death."[2] At the end of the 18th century, penal codes were drawn up which addressed themselves to the mind of the criminal, not defined as such, nor as an offender, but as a "delinquent" (251).[3] A personality type is thus created: the change Foucault marks is one towards the creation of an entity: a mind to be characterised in certain ways, (whereas earlier the body was directly marked), to produce the "docile body"—"one that may be subjected, used, transformed and improved"—and thus fitted for new modes of industrial production. A "technology of subjection" comes into use: Foucault refers to Marx's discussion of the division of labour in this context (221). The arrangement of the bodies of individuals for productive and training purposes is facilitated by the renewed attention given to the mind, to the prisoner as personality.

Foucault's subject is thus the "disciplinary technology" engineered in western societies, but perhaps the most compelling image in the book is the very utopist idea of the Panopticon—that which would have been the appearance of the superego in time, if it had been realised, not merely been left on paper by Bentham. The Panopticon, with its central tower where the unseen warders may or may not be looking at the several storeys of individually divided-off prisoners, who can see neither their controlling agency, nor the others in the cells, but are arranged in a circle around this surveillance tower, presents the possibility of total and complete control being exercised over the prison's inmates. Philip Collins discusses it in *Dickens and Crime*—a book still useful for its donkey work, though very undertheorised, and not able to question the role of the prison in western society—and Collins stresses that the Panopticon, while it was itself not to be recognised as a project, was to provide the model for all other types of institution: the birth of the prison means the birth of all kinds of normalising procedures, carried out in buildings still very familiar today, that all look exactly like the exterior of the 19th century prison. Collins quotes Bentham: "Morals reformed, health preserved, industry invigorated, instruction diffused, public burdens lightened, economy seated, as it were, upon a rock, the Gordian knot of the Poor Laws not cut but untied—all by a simple idea of Architecture!" Something of the Panoptical method is at work in *Hard Times* too: the idea being thought suitable for schools and factories. In Gradgrind's school, the pupils are so raked that each can be seen at a glance, and each are individuated, though with a number, not a name. Leavis's influential account of this book stresses how Benthamism in Coketown stifles individuality, and life and emotions, but Foucault's argument implies that the Panopticon idea stressed individuality, though not in the idealist manner that the romantic poets, themselves contemporary with this "birth of the prison," saw that concept of the individual. The Panopticon's rationale was the sense that each subject of care was to be seen as an individual mind. Alongside this creation of separate sentiences, goes a discourse to sustain it—in the formation of the "sciences of man . . . these sciences which have so delighted our 'humanity' for over a century . . . (which) have their technical matrix in the petty, malicious minutiae of the discipline and their investigations" (226). The social sciences emerge out of what Foucault calls the "constitution" of this individual with an individual mind, as "a describable, analysable object," (190), the origins of the sciences of man may have their origin, Foucault suggests, in the files of prisons and institutions, "these ignoble archives, where the modern play of coercion over bodies, gestures and behaviour has its beginnings" (191). This new carceral framework "constituted one of the armatures of power-knowledge that has made the human sciences historically possible. Knowable man (soul, individuality, consciousness, conduct, whatever it is called) is the object-effect of this analytical investment, of this domination-observation" (305). It is a retreat from this positivist conception that stresses "man's unconquerable mind"—the conclusion to a poem significantly written to a man in prison—and that invests the mind with unknowable, unfathomable qualities—as both Dickens and Leavis-like criticism do. The two stresses run together.

Bentham, more than just the inspirer of Mr. Gradgrind, is a voice behind a whole new "disciplinary technology," then, and the Panopticon becomes a metaphor, or, to quote Foucault,

> the diagram of a mechanism of power reduced to its ideal form; its functioning, abstracted from any obstacle, resistance or friction, must be represented as a pure architectural and optical system: it is, in fact, a figure of political technology that may and must be detached from any specific use. It is polyvalent in its applications; it serves to reform prisoners, but also to treat patients, to instruct school children, to confine the insane, to supervise workers, to put beggars and idlers to work. It is a type of location of bodies in space, of distribution of individuals in relation to one another, of hierarchical organisation, of disposition of centres and channels of power, which can be implemented in hospitals, workshops, schools, prisons. (205)

As a metaphor, what is implied is that the prison will enter, as both reality and as a "type" that will form the discourse of society. Trilling's discussion of the prevalence of the prison motif in 19th century literature finds its explanation here: the sense that metaphysically the prison is inescapable—reaching even to a person's whole mode of discourse and creating even Nietzsche's "prison-house of language," so that nothing escapes the limitations of the carceral—is objectively true in the domination of the prison in other 19th century forms of discourse.

What is in question is normalising delinquent mentalities and preserving them as abnormal, for Foucault makes it clear that normalising powers succeed best when they are only partially successful, when there can be a marginalisation of certain types of personality, and the creation of a stubborn mentality that resists educative and disciplinary processes. "The prison, and no doubt punishment in general, is not intended to eliminate offences, but rather to distinguish them, to distribute them, to use them . . ." (272). On such bases, the vocabulary of power is sited, where, for additional prop, not the law, but the norm is the standard, and where not acts, but identities are named. The law was however involved as well: police surveillance grew especially in the 1850s, with as a result the nearly inevitable criminalising of so many sections of the population, due to the growth of number of penal laws.[4] In the Panopticon, that "mill grinding rogues honest and idle men industrious,"[5] identity is created and named: while the model prison (i.e., solitary confinement, either partial, and belonging merely to the prisoner's leisure time, or total, as in Philadelphia) is discussed by Foucault in terms of the way isolation becomes a means of bringing prisoners to a state where they will carry on the reform work of the prison in their own person, where the language of the dominating discourse is accepted and internalised.

To come with these insights of Foucault to *Great Expectations* is to discover two things. It is to see how far a 19th century text is aware of this creation of power and of oppression that Foucault has charted so interestingly: to examine the text's relation to this dominant ideology as Foucault has described it. It is also to read the book, as having itself to do with "the power of normalisation and the formation of knowledge in modern society," which is how Foucault describes what *Discipline and Punish* is concerned with (308). The issue of seeing the prison as an essential condition of Victorian society, as also of the generation that was pre-Victorian, turns on the libertarian notion of the prison as inherently oppressive; that much is clear in the novel, with its Hulks, Newgate, and transportation, and prisonous houses, such as Satis House and even Wemmick's castle. It also has to do with Dickens's registering of the prison being bound up with questions of language and the control of language—which, of course, entails ways of thinking, a whole discourse. In other words, the book shows an awareness of the fact that to learn a language is connected with the control of knowledge. In the Panopticon, the knowledge of a person is both coloured and colouring, and to acquire knowledge, by entering into the dominant discourse, is to learn the language of oppression.

In Dickens there is a move from literal treatment of the prison from *Sketches by Boz* onwards, including the visits to the isolation penitentiaries in the United States in 1842, where he saw the "Auburn system" at work—based on the prison at Gloucester (which Foucault refers to, p. 123) at both Boston and Connecticut;[6] his accounts of both appear in *American Notes,* chapters 3 and 5. The "silent association" system there—partial solitary confinement only—he preferred to the Eastern Penitentiary at Philadelphia. It is not hard to see both systems as relations of the Panopticon dream.[7] Dickens found what he saw distasteful. He questioned, in a letter to Forster, whether the controllers "were sufficiently acquainted with the human mind to know what it is they are doing": while *American Notes* finds "this slow and daily tampering with the mysteries of the brain to be immeasurably worse than any torture of the body." The person must be returned from this state "morally unhealthy and diseased." It is halfway to Foucault's gathering of criticisms of the prison that were made in France between 1820 and 1845: indeed, Dickens's comments are sited within those criticisms, commented on in *Discipline and Punish* (265–8).

But, as criticism, it isn't free from the point that the thinking about the nature of the prison has not gone far enough to question its rationale, as a social fact, as the product of a type of thinking. The point may be made from *Great Expectations,* at a moment where Pip (the moment is almost gratuitous—Dickens is moving away from treatment of literal prisons) is invited by Wemmick to visit Newgate: "At that time, jails were much neglected, and the period of exaggerated reaction consequent on all public wrongdoing—and which is always its heaviest and longest punishment—was still far off. So, felons were not lodged and fed better than the soldiers (to say nothing of paupers) and seldom set fire to their prisons with the excusable object of improving the flavour of their soup."[8]

Collins links this observation to the riots that took place at Chatham Convict prison early in 1861,[9] and makes it clear that Chatham represented a heavily reactionary kind of discipline, certainly no "better" than the Newgate Pip is describing. I put "better" in quotation-marks to suggest that the concept of progress in prison discipline and order cannot be assumed: in Foucault's terms, the more enlightened the prison, the more subtle its means of control, that is all. Can much be said in favour of this passage? Many readers of Dickens will assume it to be part of the dominant mode to be noted in Dickens's speeches and letters: the voice of the liberal consensus, wanting prisons as simply neither too hard nor too easy. But the quotation also gives the register of Pip, who is historically at the moment when he is furthest away from his knowledge about the criminal basis of society; most alienated from his own associations with criminality—hence, of course, the irony that the chapter closes with the facial resemblance that Estella has to Molly. In terms of writing, he is looking back ("at that time") and seems to have learned nothing: at least he still wishes to place prisoners as below soldiers and paupers, not seeing that both these groups endure the same oppression that makes people prisoners—a conclusion that the novel often comes to, not least in giving Magwitch the significant name of Abel and so making him the original innocent and hunted down figure. Pip's language, then, is still part of that of a "brought-up London gentleman" (339): it belongs to a Victorian dominant discourse. (And "brought-up" also suggests "bought-up" and goes along with the equations of property and personality that go on throughout; compare Havisham—Have-is-sham, even Have-is-am; the last the latest development of the Cartesian cogito. The dominators, no less than the dominated, receive their individuality from their position in the carceral network.)

Those who identify Pip's attitude with Dickens's assume there is nothing in the text to qualify what is said here, or else that a plurality in the text allows Dickens to engage in a journalistic point in the middle of Pip's narration. Either may be right, but I would rather regard the utterance as being ironic rather than sincere—a disavowal, in this most confessional and disavowing of books, of a way of thinking once held. Pip's mode is autobiographical and confessional almost in the Catholic sense of that last word: the book reveals Dickens's autobiography and self-revelation of disgust in the same way. The reader of *Great Expectations* is able to reject the opinions expressed at the start of chapter 32 in the light of the reading of the rest of the book. Behind the narrator, the author asks for a similar dismissal. Behind Pip's confession, lies Dickens's own: or Dickens's as the representative of a precisely positioned class, of the liberal petit-bourgeoisie. The novel distances itself from Pip's confessions perhaps in order to listen to Dickens's. But then that one—Dickens's—may itself be refused, be shown to be as relative as the one that it shadows.

What is clear is the prevailing confessional note of *Great Expectations*. TO BE READ IN MY CELL (132) is apt metalinguistically. That is to say, it comments on the text's sense of the way it should be read, and what Pip thinks it is about. This is not the fictional Augustinian mode of confession, though a "cell" would well suit the Catholic form of confession: it is rather that the mode of autobiography fits with Protestant thought. Trilling comments on the late 18th century "impulse to write autobiography" and says that "the new kind of personality which emerges . . . is what we call an individual: at a certain point in history men become individuals."[10] The ability to confess in autobiography is constitutive of the subject for him-herself—but as Foucault would add, it would be "subject 'in both senses of the word,'"[11] for confession would be the means whereby the dominant discourse is internalised. Foucault continues: "The obligation to confess is now relayed through so many different points, is so deeply ingrained in us, that we no longer perceive it as the effect of a power which constrains us; on the contrary, it seems to us that truth, lodged in our most secret nature, 'demands' only to surface." *The History of Sexuality* is the continuation of that theme of power as constitutive of knowledge that runs through *Discipline and Punish* and it is a keypoint of the novel that Pip is ready always to confess: such is his autobiography, a disavowal. The interest in the prison and the interest in autobiographical confession: these two things converge.

For *Great Expectations* certainly recognises itself to be about the creation of identities, imposed from higher to lower, from oppressor to oppressed. From the first page there is the "first most vivid and broad impression of the identity of things," where a considerable amount of naming goes on—"I called myself Pip and came to be called Pip"; where the 7-year-old child names "this bleak place overgrown with nettles" as "the churchyard" and similarly characterises the marshes, the river, the sea, and himself as "that small bundle of shivers growing afraid of it all and beginning to cry" who "was Pip." The phrasing of the last part suggests that the act of naming the self and nature is a rationalisation, an incomplete and unsatisfactory way of labelling what resists formulation. It fits with that pejorative way of describing the self just quoted: that too fits the confessional position. The self is mis-named from the beginning, minimised; and gross acts of naming take place thenceforth, from Mrs. Hubble's belief that the young are never grateful, not to say "naterally wicious" (57) to Jaggers saying that boys are "a bad set of fellows" (111). Wopsle and company identify an accused with the criminal (chapter 18),

Pip sees himself as George Barnwell, and receives a number of descriptions and names—Pip, Handel, "the prowling boy" (199), "you young dog" (36), "my boy" (50), "you boy" (91), "you visionary boy" (377). Anonymity, though not the absence of naming, hangs over Mrs. Joe (defined, absurdly, through the husband), Orlick, whose name Dolge is "a clear impossibility" (139), Magwitch—Provis at all times to Jaggers, Trabb's boy, Dummle—the Spider—the Aged P. and Mr. Waldengarver. The power of naming confers identity: Q. D. Leavis's analysis sees the power as one that implants guilt.[12] That guilt-fixing belongs to Foucault's Panopticon society, and indeed the sense of being looked at is pervasive—whether by the young man who hears the words Pip and Magwitch speak, by the hare hanging up in the larder—an early execution image—or by the cow that watches Pip takes the wittles on Christmas Day. Pip expects a constable to be waiting for him on his return; has the sensation of being watched by relatives at Satis House, has his house watched on the night of Magwitch's return, has Compeyson sit behind him in the theatre (where he himself is watching), and is watched by the coastguard and the river police in the attempt to take off Magwitch (none of the friendship here with the police implied in the 1853 article "Down with the Tide": The Dickensian hero is shown here as in flight from the agents of law). Where such spying is an integral part of the book, the sense of being someone constituted as having a secret to hide is not far away. Pip feels himself a criminal, early and late; and Orlick tells him he is: "It was you as did for your shrew sister" (437)—this coming from the man who has tracked Pip constantly, and shadowed Biddy, too. Reflecting the first chapter's growth of self-awareness—where the child is crying over his parents' grave, as though not just feeling himself inadequate, but as already guilty, already needing to make some form of reparation— Magwitch says that he "first became aware of himself down in Essex a thieving turnips for his living" (360). Jaggers identifies Drummle as criminal—"the true sport" (239)—and encourages him in his boorishness and readiness to brain Startop. His method of cross-examination is to criminalise everyone, himself resisting classification, no language being appropriate for one as "deep" as he. "You know what I am, don't you?" is the last comment he makes after the dinner party where he has hinted that Molly (whom he seems to own) is a criminal type. The question is to be answered negatively, for he is like the unseen watcher in the central tower of the Panopticon, naming others, but not named himself (his centrality is implied in the address of his office), in the position, as criminal lawyer, of power, conferring identities, controlling destinies—not for nothing are those criminals in Newgate compared to plants in the greenhouse, and regarded with the scientific detachment that for Foucault is part of the "discourse of truth" of 19th century positivism.

Identities all become a matter of social control and naming: Estella might have turned out one way as one of the "fish" to come to Jaggers's net, yet she is constituted differently (though almost as nihilistically) by the identity she receives from Miss Havisham's hands. Pip remains the passive victim whose reaction is to blame himself for every action he is in: his willingness to see himself as his sister's murderer (chapter 16) is of a piece with his final ability to see himself as characteristically unjust to Joe. Q. D. Leavis's account works against those which see the book as "a snob's progress"; her emphases are useful in suggesting that it is *Pip* who sees himself thus; and that now he is "telling us dispassionately how he came to be the man who can now write thus about his former self."[13] The "us," by eliding the 1860s readers of the text with these who come a century later, implies that there is a central, ahistorical way of taking the text: a strong liberal-humanist ideology underwrites this assumption which also implies that there is some decent norm Pip could approximate to, which would untie all his problems. It thus assimilates all historical differences, at the least, to the notion of the free subject, who is at all times accessible to decent human feelings—and capable of reaching a central normality.

If what Q. D. Leavis said were the case, it would mean Pip had reached some degree of "normality" by the end of what has happened to him, before he starts narrating. He is not a central human presence, but a writer whose text needs inspection for its weakness of self-analysis; for he never dissociates himself from the accusations he piles on himself at the time of the events happening, and afterwards. In Wemmick's and Jaggers's character-formulations of people as either "beaters or cringers" he remains a cringer, and unable to recognise himself in Herbert's genial view—"a good fellow, with impetuosity and hesitation, boldness and diffidence, action and dreaming, curiously mixed in him" (269). That positive evaluation, binary nonetheless in its terms, in the same way as the Panopticon system lends itself to an extreme form of binary division, is beyond him: his self-perception makes him oppressor, while, more accurately, he is victim. Foucault stresses how the healthy individual is defined in relation to that which has been labelled as delinquent, degenerate or perverse; and his studies of madness, of the birth of the clinic and of the prison all meet in this: "when one wants to individualise the healthy normal and law-abiding adult, it is always by asking him how much of the child he has in him, what secret madness lies within him, what fundamental crime he has dreamed of committing" (*Discipline and Punish*, 193). On this basis, Pip might be said to be the creation of three discourses that intersect: he remains something of the child—his name, a diminutive, establishes that; he is never in a position, he feels, of equality with anyone else; his dreams of the file, of Miss Havisham hanging from the beam, of playing Hamlet without knowing more than five words of the play, his nightmarish sense of phantasmagoric shapes perceived in the rushlight in the Hummuns, and his sense of being a brick in a house-wall, or part of a machine, "wanting to have the engine stopped, and my part in it hammered off" (472)—all proclaim his "secret madness." His sense of criminality is fed by virtually each act and its consequences that he undertakes.

A victim of the language system, only on one or two occasions does he reverse the role and become implicitly the accuser; one is where he prays over the head of the dead Magwitch: "Lord be merciful to him a sinner" (470) where commentators such as Moynahan have found something false. It is inappropriate, but it seems to belong to the Pip whose sense of himself is not free enough to allow himself to deconstruct the language system he is in. The odd thing is not that he fails to see himself as the sinner, as in the parable (*Luke* chapter 18), but that he should want to name Magwitch as such. But that act of naming is a reflection of the way the dominated have no choice but to take over the language of their domination—to continue to beat, as they have been beaten, to continue to name disparagingly, as they have been named. That act in itself continues to name Pip—implicitly, as the Pharisee, of course. The question the novel asks is what else he might do: he seems caught. The self can only retreat from that dominant discourse through schizoid behavior, as happens with Wemmick and his dual lifestyles, yet does not the "Castle's" existence betray the prison's presence still in Wemmick's thinking? He, too, has not got away.

A second time when the language of Pip's oppression becomes one to oppress another is at the end of the book where he meets the younger Pip and suggests to Biddy that she should "give Pip to him, one of these days, or lend him, at all events" (490). To this Biddy responds "gently" "no," but her answer might well have been a horrified one in the light of what surrogate parents do to their children in the book: Pip is offering to play Magwitch to Biddy's child. He has learned nothing: is indeed a recidivist, unaware of how much he has been made himself a subject of other people's power and knowledge. Magwitch, similarly "owns" Pip (339) as he says with pride: it is well-meaning as a statement, but with Foucault's aid it may be seen that Magwitch as a member of the class marginalised and set apart by the Panopticon society, has had to take on those dominant oppressive values, and talks the same language of property. His attitude is not inherently selfish, but it is a mark of his social formation which conditions him to speak as he does. In this most sociologically interactionist of novels, it is recognised that the self can use no other language than that given to it. What liberty there is is suggested by Orlick, who cringes after Joe beats him, beats Mrs. Joe and secures her cringing—which, indeed, as "a child towards a hard master" (151) she seems to enjoy, as she continues to draw the sign of his power over her: such is the token of her self-oppression. (The contrast with Rosa Dartle, also the victim of a hammer-blow, is worth attention: Rosa's whole position as poor relation is self-oppressive.) Orlick, through a certain upward mobility, derived from his association with Compeyson, changes from the cringer himself (paid off by Jaggers from service at Satis House) to the accuser of Pip in the sluice-house. He perceives he has been marginalised, in some ways defined as delinquent, but it is an insight that could not be the source of social action or improvement, for it never extends beyond himself: as he says to Pip, "you was favoured and he [Orlick] was bullied and beat" (437). Out of that crazed imperception, he lashes out at Pip: the reverse action to Magwitch's, who almost equally arbitrarily identifies Pip with himself. (The novel wishes to close the gap between the convict and Pip, so Herbert says that Pip reminded Magwitch of the daughter he had lost.) Orlick and Magwitch go in opposite directions: what unites them (as it links them with Pip) is their sense that they are the watched, the ones under surveillance. Orlick's reactions to Pip look like Nietzsche's *ressentiment*,[14] that quality that Foucault has made much use of in discussing the origins of the impulse towards power. Dickens's "cringer" is like Nietzsche's "reactive personality": for Nietzsche, it is characteristically this type that, fired by resentment, tries to move into the legislative position. Orlick's rancour is born out of the inability that those watched in the Panopticon society have (since they have been put in individual cells, they cannot see each other) to read their situation as akin to that of other marginalised figures.

Thus the production, and reproduction, of oppression is what the book charts. Orlick attempts to move over to the other side in the Panopticon, and from the attempted assumption of that position, turns against Pip. Magwitch's acquisition of money is his attempt to move to the other side, to create a Pip, whom he surveys. In fact, he remains the criminal in the way he is named. Nor can Orlick change, and though he is in the county jail at the end, the replication of the book's past events seems safe with him when he is released: he really has no alternative, and as such he remains an apt commentary on the course an oppressed class must follow. Pip, in terms of status, moves over to the other side, in Panopticon terms, but his social formation is already firm, and basically he cannot change either: the events in the second part of his "expectations" are an aberration from what he is in the first and third parts. Ironically, since he is cast there as guilty, what he is at those points is preferable to what he becomes in the second part.

As the recidivist, he wishes to be given Biddy's child, which would start again the whole cycle of oppression; and self-oppressive to the end, he writes out his autobiography—one that remains remarkably terse as to its intentions and its status as writing and which rolls out as though automatically, the product of a consciousness that remains fixed. Comparisons with the modes of David Copperfield's, or Esther Summerson's, or George Silverman's narratives would bear out this frozen, and at times almost perfunctory, manner. Miss Wade begins her account of herself sharply with the statement that she is "not a fool." Pip says nothing about himself as he is at the time of writing. He remains as someone who seems not to have gone beyond the emotional state documented in the writing, so that there is nothing cathartic about the confession, and no release is gained, just as Dickens's revised ending remains as ambivalent as the former, much more telegraphic one. For "I saw no shadow of another parting from her" (493) allows the ambiguity that they did or did not separate, and the narrator shows how his mind is closed now: what follows is not known. Writing about himself and his childhood experience, Dickens said "I know how all these things have worked together to make me what I am"[15] in a confidence belonging to the *Copperfield* period and akin to that expressed so often in Wordsworth's *Prelude* of 1850. The distance from *Great Expectations* is pronounced: the very dryness of the narrative is an ironic comment on the book's title. The more buoyant, earlier statement may have its optimism unfounded as far as its belief in development goes, but the mode of writing in Pip's case may be seen as carceral: it belongs to the prison in its sense of giving an automatic, unstopping confession, which pauses not at all in its recounting of events and its self-accusation.

Foucault's "birth of the prison," the concept of the individual, the privileging of the autobiographical mode—these related ideas are intrinsic to the novel, and while there is the creation of the human subject through a relaying of oppression and through a dominant discourse that he/she is within, there is also, in *Great Expectations*, implicit commentary about the mode of autobiography. Autobiography defines the subject confessionally; it puts upon it the onus of "explanation," makes it prison-bound: a state that proves naturally acceptable to so much romantic writing, where the tragic intensity of those who have to inhabit alienating spaces or constrictions can be defined as the source and inspiration of their reality. "We think of the prison"—Eliot's reading of F. H. Bradley in *The Waste Land* proves comforting as it suggests that the essence of humanity is that it is confined, this is its common condition. In contrast, Foucault's analysis is precisely useful in its stress on the prison as the mode that gives the person the sense of uniqueness, the sense of difference from the others. In that sense, autobiography becomes a mode that assists in the reproduction of the discourse that the Panopticon society promotes. And in Pip's case, subjugated as he is by these discourses, the mode becomes a vehicle for "self-reflection"—and for nothing else. Not, that is, the self thinking and moving from there into an area of thought where it can question the terms of its language, but the self continuing to reify its own status, to see it as an isolated thing. It continues a divisive trend. Not only is Pip's autobiography one that is markedly end-stopped in the sense that there is no feeling for a future, no way in which there can be a further development of the self, so that experience seems to avail nothing; but that cut-offness exists too in Pip's relations with others, in his inability to see others' complicity in the events surrounding him, save perhaps with Pumblechook, and there it is hardly difficult to see. It is appropriate that Miss Havisham should say to him "You made your own snares. *I* never made them" (374). It is manifestly untrue as a statement; and especially as far as the second sentence goes, as Miss Havisham's own confession suggests, finishing as it does with her self-condemnatory immolation and her entreaty, "take the pencil and write under my name, I forgive her" (414)—Miss Havisham is the "cringer" here, as so often. What is interesting is that Pip seems to receive this analysis and can't see that to individualise the issue in this way won't do. *Great Expectations* comes close to suggesting that in an understanding of a society, the concept of the individual is unhelpful, that what is important are the total manipulations of power and language by whatever group has the power of definition and control. Autobiography provides an inadequate paradigm.

Is that the final irony of *Great Expectations*, that it displays the bankruptcy of Pip's efforts to understand what has happened to him? That he speaks throughout in a language that has been given to him, and that includes the language of his perception of himself as a particular kind of being? If that is so, discussion might move at this point from what Pip might do with regard to his own inarticulateness in face of the dominant discourse, to what the text might do. The post-structuralist in Foucault displaces human consciousness for larger historical processes: Dickens as a 19th century novelist is marked by more confidence in individual sentience. It might be possible to find in *Great Expectations* a modernity of attitude which means that its parabolic kind of narrative is open-ended; that the title hints at the space within it for the reader to construct his/her own sense of how to take it; that, unlike the warder at the heart of the Panopticon, the author is not felt to be directing and encouraging a labelling; that the text resists single meaning. The ambiguity of the ending, already discussed, is relevant here, and so too is the sense that the reader has only Pip's text to work upon, and that this is certainly not final or necessarily authoritative. At the same time, however, the bourgeois Dickens has been located often enough within the book: for example, what do we make of Herbert's reporting of his father's principle of belief that "no man who ever was a true gentleman at heart ever was, since the world began, a true gentleman in manner . . . no varnish can hide the grain of the wood, and . . . the more varnish you put on, the more the grain will express itself" (204)? Is not this like the voice of the conscious novelist, and if so does it not express a different, more essentialist view of humanity than the very relative one formed throughout the whole pattern of the book with its insistence on the social construction of identities? Herbert's decent liberalism of attitude, which is intended to cut through class distinctions, both in relation to the upwardly mobile and the aristrocratic-snobbish, is tactfully put, but it represents a transhistoricalism, in its view of human nature "since the world began," an "essentialist" view of humanity.

I give this example as one of the many that might be cited to suggest that the novel resists the irony of its form—which, in its radicalness, is where Raymond Williams finds "Dickens's morality, his social criticism";[16] and that it might allow for a basic human nature, which would stand against Foucault's account, since for the latter there can be no cutting through a statement which is not framed within the limits of a particular discourse. The passage quoted from the opening of chapter 32 has been similarly seen—as the authorial voice, as part of the classic realist text, as that where "bourgeois norms are experienced as the evident laws of a natural order."[17] But in response to this view that the novel does invest time and space in a "decent" common-sense attitude, several points might be urged. The first would be that it was no more necessary to take the comment in chapter 32 as authorial than to assume that Herbert's views are purely normative. And even if they were, and Mr. Pocket's views about what constituted a gentleman coincided with Dickens's, the statement might still be situation-specific, having to do with what a gentleman might be in a society that laid so much stress on this bourgeois title. But in any case, Mr. Pocket's views themselves are not beyond criticism: chapter 23 where he appears presents him wittily as the liberal whose "decent" attitudes are themselves subverted by his wife's tyrannies—he is nearly as helpless as Joe, and that ineffectuality itself invites criticism, is indeed even part of a self-oppression. Moreover, although the concept of a true gentleman may be a mirage pursued through the book (cp., Pip's uttering "penitently" at the end about Joe—often seen as the ideal—"God bless this gentle Christian man" (472), as though here at last disinterested, decent qualities were being displayed), as a term it is itself not allowed to stand by the novel.

Joe drops out again of the London scene after Pip has recuperated: Pip's terms for him are part of the vocabulary he has learned to deploy from Satis House—and from exposure to Estella's power, which makes him tell Biddy that he wants to be a gentleman (154). The term—even in Mr. Pocket's oppositional formulation about it—is not one that fits Joe, even in Pip's modified way of putting it. Joe needs to be seen in another set of relations, and what Pip says about him is inappropriate because it bears more on Pip's sense of his own deficiency; Joe is what *he* is not; he has not succeeded in living up to the terms of his cultural formation that have been dictated to him, so he believes. What Joe is in rescuing Pip requires a set of terms that do not involve assimilation of him into the power relations and language of middle-class society, from which he is nearly totally excluded, save when he has to wear holiday clothes, and which are supremely irrelevant to him.

It is the cruellest irony for Pip that he must disparage himself and praise Joe so constantly in his narration. Joe does not require any setting down, but Pip has no means of assessing the forge and the village life independent of his own given language: under the influence of Satis House and its language he feels ashamed of home (134). Nothing more is given of the forge in the novel apart from Pip's perception of it, and the absence of such a thing makes the torture for Pip, the prisoner in the Panopticon societal prison, the more refined. For it remains as a deceptive escape for him, although one that he cannot endorse (so that his intention to go back and marry Biddy has something masochistic and self-oppressive within it), and any step that he takes, either of accepting or rejoicing it, remains a compromise. The split is caught finely in the scenes leading to his going to London in the first instance, and a compromise is dictated to him by the dividing nature of the society as prison. For Foucault argues that there is no "knowledge that does not presuppose and constitute at the same time power relations" (*Discipline and Punish*, 27). That is, the birth of the prison—that most divisive of institutions—is an instrument not only to create Man as individual, to be known thus, but also ensures that there is no common language—no means of making a value-judgment which is outside the terms of a particular set of power-relations. Foucault is opposed to totalising interpretations of society precisely because of the way they ignore the endless replication of modes of oppression, of imposition of languages. The methods of deployment of power are various, as are the social groupings; indeed *Great Expectations* displays something of that variousness. What Pip finds to be true of himself is the result of the way he has been set up; at the same time, he does not possess a set of terms to think about a different way of life—the forge—that are not themselves instrumental for control over that way of thinking. Difference is not allowed for. Pip is bought up completely. The illusion he is given is of seeing things whole, but to the very end he cannot see the forge way of life as something different from his, and one that his own language formation cannot accommodate, from the moment he got to Satis House.

The modernity of the novel lies in this area: Dickens commits himself to no view about Joe or Biddy, or Pip, but writes rather a *bildungsroman* where the expectation that the hero will learn through experience is belied, and not only by the title. Readerly assumptions generated through the lure of the narrative are set aside, for the central figure can only proceed on the language assumptions given to him. *David Copperfield* was the standard kind of *éducation sentimentale*; *Great Expectations* questions the ideological assumptions inherent in the earlier book, by presenting (with the earlier novel consciously in mind, re-read just before embarking on it) a development that can be no development. If the hero learns at all, it is only within his terms of reference, so there is no breaking out from the obsession with the self. The mode of the novel is ironic (it is noticeable how Dickens emphasises what is "comic" about it to Forster, as Forster relates in the *Life*, 9.3): "Comic," in spite of the comedy within it, seems inappropriate, but perhaps it may draw attention to what is subversive about the book. And Dickens's absence of explanation about it only emphasises the extent to which he as author has receded: the novel stands alone, open-ended, marked out by the lack of "closure" within it supplied by the moralist Dickens.

Whatever liberalism affects the book—as in the "poor dreams" that nearly save Mr. Jaggers in spite of himself, or in the way that Pip seems to enjoy a reasonable bourgeois existence in the Eastern Branch of Herbert's firm, or in its casualness about dates and historical positioning—is not central: the book has little faith in human nature considered as a romantic, spontaneous and creative thing; no sense that the issues it addresses may be met by the middle-class values that commonly sustain the 19th century novel. The interest in character here—which still so often forms the basis of Dickensian criticism—does not sanction belief in the individual as ultimately irrepressible. Rather, the idea of the Panopticon as the chief model for the formation of any individuality in 19th century Britain makes for something much more complex and gives rise to the sense that the formation of individuality is itself delusory as a hope. It is itself the problem it seeks to solve—through its way of dividing a society and separating it. The prison is not the "human condition" in a trans-historical sense, as Denmark was also a prison for Hamlet, but is the apt symbol for enforcing models of helplessness: the more aware the self is of its position, the more it confirms the prison, and thus cuts itself off further. To that diagnosis, which demands a consideration of power structures in society such as Foucault gives, and which draws attention to language as a way of making the person prison-bound, the autobiographical mode of *Great Expectations* bears witness. In itself the mode works to keep the narrator in the prison. Just as Wemmick's father and his pleasant and playful ways, and the possibility that Jaggers himself might one day want a pleasant home, also ensure that the prison's durability is not in question: these individual escapes, simply by staying within the limits of the individual idea, address, effectively, no problem at all.

Notes

1. F. R. and Q. D. Leavis, *Dickens the Novelist* (1970), 331.

2. Barry Smart, *Foucault, Marxism and Critique* (1983), 90.

3. Michel Foucault, *Discipline and Punish*, trans. Alan Sheridan, (Harmondsworth, 1979). All textual references are to this edition.

4. The theme is dealt with in Michael Ignatieff, *A Just Measure of Pain: the Penitentiary in the Industrial Revolution, 1750–1850* (1978).

5. Jeremy Bentham, quoted in Collins, *Dickens and Crime* (1962), 18.

6. See the *Letters of Charles Dickens*, vol. 3, 1842–43, ed. Madeline House and Graham Storey (Oxford, 1974), 105, 436, 110, for details on these prisons.

7. See *Michel Foucault* by Mark Cousins and Athar Hussain (1984), 183, 192, for further details about these prisons.

8. Quotations from *Great Expectations* are from the Penguin edition, ed. Angus Calder.

9. Collins, *Dickens and Crime*, 20–21.

10. Lionel Trilling, *Sincerity and Authenticity* (1972), 24.

11. Michel Foucault, *The History of Sexuality* vol. 1 (Harmondsworth, 1981), 60.

12. Leavis, *Dickens the Novelist*, 288. Apart from this account of the novel, I am greatly in debt to Julian Moynahan, "The Hero's Guilt: the Case of *Great Expectations*," *E in C*, 10 (1960), 60–79; and A. L. French, "Beating and Cringing: *Great Expectations*," *E in C*, 24 (1974), 147–168.

13. Leavis, *Dickens the Novelist*, 291.

14. "*Ressentiment*" is translated as "rancour" and discussed in detail in the first essay of *The Genealogy of Morals*, trans. Francis Golffing, (New York, 1956); see especially p. 170.

15. John Forster, *Life of Charles Dickens 1*, chapter 2.

16. Raymond Williams, *The English Novel from Dickens to Lawrence* (1970), 48.

17. Roland Barthes, *Mythologies*, trans. Annette Lavers (1982), 140.

Stories Present and Absent in *Great Expectations**   By Eiichi Hara

In the plethora of criticism on *Great Expectations* one central issue, although it has been recognized and referred to implicitly by many critics, has not yet been discussed substantially: the problem of authorship. By author I mean not the actual writer of the novel but the one "implied" in the text, an entity quite different from the real author.[1] For Pip, as for David Copperfield, the novel is a kind of autobiography or memoir. But when the peculiar narrative situation in *Great Expectations* is considered the other way round, from the side of the narrated story, it seems to present Pip's "authorship" as something hollow and void. If one takes the enigma of Pip's secret benefactor to be the central axis of the novel, as it indeed is, it is clear that the author of the story is not Pip but Magwitch, who has been devising, plotting, and writing Pip's story. Magwitch is a character representing the double meaning of "author": the writer and the father.[2] He is both the author of Pip's story and the father who has secretly adopted him as his son, begetter of the text and its hero at the same time. Thus the central axis of the novel poses the problem of authorship, providing a clue to other layers of the novel where story and its authors stand in ambiguous and sometimes quite incompatible relationships with each other. When Pip, urged by some inner compulsion, strives to write the story of his own life, just as David had done before him, his pen constantly fails him; for, as he writes, the written text slips out of his hand and is instantly transformed into stories written by strange authors. The problem of authorship is in fact the problem of writing or the failure of writing.[3] Pip fails to write his life story; the novel is never to be written by this "author." As Magwitch's writing of Pip's story suggests, Pip can

*Reprinted from *ELH* 53 (1986): 593–614, by permission of the journal.

never be the writer nor the independent hero of his own story; rather, the novel is structured around the central story of Pip as written by Magwitch, with other stories, also of Pip, encircling this central axis. Just as the Magwitch story destroys all Pip's false hopes, decomposes itself, the structure of these stories in the novel is to be seen as a self-destroying process, an unwriting, a structure that is nonstructure. Because the stories of Pip are always written by other authors, they collapse by their alienation from the hero. Pip, always a passive object to be written, fails to be the "hero of my own life": unlike David Copperfield, he fails to be the novelist, the writer of his own life story. But when presence of stories gives way to absence of stories, a story that is absent in *Great Expectations* emerges whose absence will guide us to the innermost depth of Pip's failed narrative. It is this structure of presence and absence, of author and story, that I would like to elucidate in the following argument.

2

Poetics of narrative fiction is perhaps the facet of literary studies that has profited most from the structuralist enterprise. Although such rigorously structuralist systems as Genette's *Narrative Discourse* or Todorov's *Poetics of Prose* will come to be seen with some misgivings in the wake of deconstruction, there is no doubt that they have clarified the workings of a fictional text and supplied useful terms and concepts for the discussions of narrative fiction. Among the most fundamental and useful of concepts is the distinction between "story" and "plot" bequeathed by the Russian Formalists. Here story means "the story in its most neutral, objective, chronological form—the story as it might have been enacted in real time and space, a seamless continuum of innumerable contiguous events" and plot is "the actual text in which this story is imitated, with all its inevitable (but motivated) gaps, elisions, emphases and distortions."[4] As this definition indicates, story is the hypothetical construct that could be reassembled and arranged in chronological order from the often confused texture of actual narrative, with a beginning, a middle and an end neatly arranged as a completed whole. It is an assumed primal text or metatext that the reading process recovers and reconstructs, though the paradox is that it is to be recuperated a posteriori, only after the plot is worked out in narrative fiction. Of the two aspects that comprise narrative it is plot that has generally been the object of aesthetic studies since plot is what a novelist actually writes and is primarily present to the reader. Thus studies of the basic structure of *Great Expectations* have been concerned mainly with its plot.[5] In a recent and important essay, for example, Peter Brooks describes the novel as "concerned with finding a plot and losing it, with the precipitation of plottedness around its hero, and his eventual 'cure' from plot" (Brooks uses the word "plot" in a somewhat different sense from the one defined above as he considers it "not only design but intentionality as well").[6] Without questioning the validity of studies of plot, however, I would like to call attention to the presence—indeed the predominance—of *story* in the novel. Story, normally reconstructed almost as an afterthought from the actual narrative text, is in *Great Expectations* a presence a priori. It is already there, written by some writer other than the hero-narrator Pip, with its beginning, middle and end all complete even before the plot begins. My description of the novel would be that Pip does not find any plot but that story finds and traps him, plot as intentionality remaining always outside him. He is not "cured" from plot; story or stories collapse and become absent, leaving him in the vacuum created by this absence.

That intentionality is outside Pip, that he is not the writer of his own story, is indicated in the novel's opening scene, in which he is a being poised in the space of ontogenetic ambiguity with an insignificant monosyllable for a name. His actual name is given in the text only as an appellation designated his by some alien agency: "I give Pirrip as my father's family name on the authority of his tombstone. . . ,"[7] Here the double meaning of author as father and writer as well as the pure textuality of Pip's existence come to the fore. Pip's father is dead, he has become a text, the inscription on the tombstone that locates Pip in a fixed space-time; and the contours of Pip's being begin to flesh out only after this textual location. He takes his being from the text of his absent father, whose authority is symbolically represented by Magwitch who starts up, like an apparition of the real father, "from among the graves at the side of the church porch" (2). Magwitch establishes complete control over the terrified child immediately; he turns him upside down, threatens him with cannibalism (" . . . what fat cheeks you ha' got. . . . Darn Me if I couldn't eat em"), orders him to bring a file and "wittles," and extracts a pledge of strict silence. Thus, from the very beginning, Pip becomes involved in the world of criminality where crime, guilt and bad faith torment him. Though this criminality is to be the primal text in which he is caught, we would be mistaken to regard Pip as a guilty being who carries the burden of some transcendental original sin. The guilt here does not belong to him; it is something that is imposed upon him by outside authority. The helpless orphan boy is placed in an atmosphere of criminality by a force over which he has no control.

The otherness of the taint of criminality in Pip, the alienation of essence from being, is manifest in the fact that he is always regarded as a boy with criminal propensities by the adults around him who, like Magwitch, have incontestable authority over him. These adults are possessed with the idea that the young are "naterally wicious," Pip especially so. With this preconception they treat him as if his life were already written and finished as a story, the plot of which Pip is going to follow as a predestined, assigned path. As authors of the story of Pip's criminal career, Wopsle and Pumblechook are more adept in writing stories than Mrs.

Joe, who uses only her hand and occasional applications of the Tickler. For example, at the Christmas dinner at Joe's house, they are quite aware of the nature of the novel's semiotic universe, in which one can write a story even in a word:

> Mr. Pumblechook added, after a short interval of reflection, "Look at the Pork alone. There's a subject! If you want a subject, look at Pork!"
>
> "True, sir. Many a moral for the young," returned Mr. Wopsle; and I knew he was going to lug me in, before he said it; "might be deduced from that text."
>
> ("You listen to this," said my sister to me, in a severe parenthesis.)
>
> Joe gave me some more gravy.
>
> "Swine," pursued Mr. Wopsle, in his deepest voice, and pointing his fork at my blushes, as if he were mentioning my christian name; "Swine were the companions of the prodigal. The gluttony of Swine is put before us, as an example to the young." (I thought this pretty well in him who had been praising up the pork for being so plump and juicy.) "What is detestable in a pig, is more detestable in a boy." (57–58)

Here a seemingly innocent word "pork" undergoes radical transformations with an ever increasing semantic density. What is merely a thing to be eaten becomes a "text" and the biblical reference brings forth "swine," with its connotations of gluttony and sensuality, and "prodigal," inevitably associated with the story of the Prodigal Son.[8] Thus a sign, a word, is transformed into a story, a finished tale with a beginning, a middle and an end, which becomes a story of Pip as Pumblechook immediately transforms Pip into Swine with his pompous authority: "If you'd been born a Squeaker . . . would you have been here now? Not you. . . . You would have been disposed of for so many shillings according to the market price of the article, and Dunstable the butcher would have come up to you as you lay in your straw, and he would have whipped you under his left arm, and with his right he would have tucked up his frock to get a penknife from out of his waistcoat pocket, and he would have shed your blood and had your life" (58). The story of Pip the Prodigal Son is thus present, written by these authors, even before any plot development could be introduced.

The story written by Wopsle and Pumblechook may seem an incomplete realization of the story of Pip the Criminal since the story of the Prodigal Son does not include any criminal act, though, of course, the son is guilty of a moral crime against his father. Pumblechook's reference to the butchering of Pip the Swine, however, recalls the gallows and the execution of criminals. In the popular tradition, a story depicting the life of a criminal ends in his execution or suicide. Dickens, who had an avowed interest in crime and criminals, faithfully follows this tradition. Bill Sykes, Ralph Nickleby, Jonas Chuzzlewit and Mr. Merdle all meet violent deaths at the end of their careers in crime. Pip's story as written by Pumblechook and Wopsle must also include the hero's death in total misery and wretchedness as the morally plausible outcome of a criminal life. The story will become complete when a plot that will realize it in a particular circumstantial context is established. For Wopsle and Pumblechook, there is no need to work out the story in all its squalid details since they have only to choose a text that fits into the prescribed pattern from the stock-in-trade of the popular criminal literature. Wopsle discovers a pertinent text in a bookshop: "the affecting tragedy of George Barnwell," Lillo's *The London Merchant*. As it is his inevitable fate to come across authoritarian figures, Pip is seized by Wopsle in the street and made to listen to the recitation of the drama in the Pumblechookian parlor. The story of George Barnwell who, seduced by a harlot called Millwood, robbed his master and murdered his uncle, so alien to the innocent child, is turned into the story of Pip the Criminal. The transformation is so complete that Pip speaks of Barnwell as himself:

> What stung me, was the identification of the whole affair with my unoffending self. When Barnwell began to go wrong, I declare that I felt positively apologetic, Pumblechook's indignant stare so taxed me with it. Wopsle, too, took pains to present me in the worst light. At once ferocious and maudlin, I was made to murder my uncle with no extenuating circumstances whatever; Millwood put me down in argument, on every occasion; it became sheer monomania in my master's daughter to care a button for me; and all I can say for my gasping and procrastinating conduct on the fatal morning, is, that it was worthy of the general feebleness of my character. Even after I was happily hanged and Wopsle had closed the book, Pumblechook sat staring at me, and shaking his head, and saying, "Take warning, boy, take warning!" as if it were a well-known fact that I contemplated murdering a near relation, provided I could only induce one to have the weakness to become my benefactor. (145)

Identified with Barnwell, it is only natural that Pip believes he "must have had some hand in the attack upon my sister" that happened just at the time. Orlick is wrong, however, to see Pip's guiltiness here as metaphysical ("It was you as did for your shrew sister"),[9] because the Pip who feels guilt is the Pip defined by Pumblechook and Wopsle and written into the story of Pip the criminal, not the actual Pip who is perfectly innocent. As he is not the author of the story of Barnwell, begetter of the criminal Pip, he has no authority even over the feelings he has or the narrator says that he has. He feels guilt only because subjectivity, the "I," has become unstable, because the story of Barnwell, which actually can never be the story of Pip, envelops him.

3

But George Barnwell, for all his difference from Pip, shares a significant factor with him. When criminality is removed from the story of Barnwell, it comes nearer to Pip's story: they are both apprentices torn by agonizing desire for a worthless woman. Here again, as in the case of "pork," the word "apprentice" contains in it a complete story (or stories) that is present *a priori*, before plot is conceived and actualized. Moreover, the Barnwell story is only one aspect of a dualistic structure. There is another side, a positive story paired with the dark, negative story of the criminal apprentice. The duality of the apprentice story is best exemplified in William Hogarth's series of engravings *Industry and Idleness*, by which Dickens was no doubt greatly influenced.[10] Hogarth presents two apprentices whose contrasting careers have almost exact parallels in the apprentice stories in *Great Expectations*. The story of the Industrious Apprentice, modeled on the legend of Dick Whittington, presents Francis Goodchild, who gains his master's confidence through his industry and honesty. He becomes partner in his master's business, marries his master's daughter, and finally attains the highest rung of the middle-class social ladder by becoming the Lord Mayor of London. The Idle Apprentice, Tom Idle, modeled apparently on George Barnwell (who had been a subject of popular ballads as early as the second half of the seventeenth century[11]) goes astray through his idleness and association with bad companions. Committing one crime after another, he is betrayed by his whore, arrested and brought before Goodchild who as magistrate must condemn him. Tom Idle is finally executed at Tyburn. For Dickens the dual story of the apprentice was the source of many characters and stories. The good apprentice appears as such heroes as Oliver Twist, Walter Gay, and in the references to Dick Whittington in *Dombey and Son* and *Barnaby Rudge* that indicate their origin.[12] The idle apprentice is presented in those villains who obstruct the hero's progress in life; Noah Claypole in *Oliver Twist*, Simon Tappertit in *Barnaby Rudge*, Uriah Heep in *David Copperfield* and Dolge Orlick in *Great Expectations* are typical examples. Again the explicit references to George Barnwell in *Barnaby Rudge* and *Great Expectations* reveal the origin of this recurring type.[13] For Dickens, to be an apprentice is to choose between the two poles of a story, each of which will lead to a course of life fundamentally incompatible with the other. But the uniqueness of *Great Expectations* among Dickens's novels consists in the fact that these two poles have been combined into one. For, if we follow the argument of critics like Julian Moynahan, the bad apprentice, Orlick, might be a psychological double, an alter ego, of Pip the good apprentice.[14] But, in Orlick's view at least, the disparity between the two is very marked because, as he tells Pip in the lime-kiln, Pip was the favored, petted one who was always in Orlick's way; Pip, according to him, even came between him and "a young woman" he liked (435). Pip will succeed Joe some day in his profession and marry Biddy, frustrating all the expectations of the other apprentice. While the story of the criminal apprentice has been written by other authors, the story of the good apprentice Orlick describes might be the one that Pip can virtually be author and hero of. However much he deviates from the path of honesty, no one can deny his innate goodness, and as a Dickens hero he has qualifications enough to be another Francis Goodchild.

In fact, to pursue the course of the Industrious Apprentice, to live the story of Goodchild, is undoubtedly the life most natural to Pip. He is accustomed to the life at the forge and to his master Joe, who is both a father and best friend to him. With his unfailing goodness and kindness Joe will be an ideal master and companion to the orphan boy. Joe himself looks forward with genuine delight and expectation to the day when Pip will be his apprentice; he tells Pip that when Pip is apprentice to him, "regularly bound," they will "have such Larks! . . ." (48). For Pip, however, this natural state of life, the life of an apprentice to Joe, is suddenly transformed into something strange and unnatural, a story written by an alien hand, in Satis House.

The encounter with Miss Havisham is of great importance in Pip's life because she is expected to be the donor of both wealth and the beautiful maiden. But the encounter with Estella carries far greater weight, not only for the hero but for the overall structure of the novel. Estella is not only—and melodramatically—Magwitch's daughter, but she also plays a role essentially identical with her father's, the role of an author with dictatorial authority over his subject. Magwitch, as we know, is the anonymous author of Pip's fortunes; Estella also drastically changes the meaning of life for Pip when, with queenly disdain and cruelty, she ridicules his low birth and commonness. Pip, who has lived (albeit not very happily) with serenity and modest hopes, is compelled by Estella to look at his existence from an entirely new angle. Playing "beggar my neighbour" with her, he is called "a common labouring-boy"; his language, his limbs and his attire all become the objects of her spiteful attacks:

> "He calls the knaves, Jacks, this boy!" said Estella with disdain, before our first game was out. "And what coarse hands he has! And what thick boots!"
>
> I had never thought of being ashamed of my hands before; but I began to consider them a very indifferent pair. Her contempt for me was so strong, that it became infectious, and I caught it.
>
> She won the game, and I dealt. I misdealt, as was only natural, when I knew she was lying in wait for me to do wrong; and she denounced me for a stupid, clumsy, labouring-boy. (90)

As Pip cannot be anything other than a future blacksmith, Estella's ridicule is directed against that state of existence which is most natural to him. A blacksmith's hands are coarse and black from work, the thickness of his boots is proper in the forge, and his language, as Joe demonstrates, is often capable of sustained dignity. There is no need for Pip to be ashamed of himself in front of this spoilt and proud girl. But he smarts, smarts terribly, because Estella, who is the erotic symbol of the great expectations, is not only proud but very beautiful; by virtue of her beauty she has power, irresistible authority over him. Pip is caught less in the magic web of Miss Havisham than in the text of an apprentice story that becomes thralldom not because of the class system but because Estella has rewritten the natural state of Pip's existence into a story alienated from himself. Suddenly his hands and boots, which have "never troubled" him before, do trouble him; now he is "much more ignorant than" he has considered himself so far and is "in a low-lived bad way" (94). Thus, Estella becomes the author of the story of Pip the Apprentice which, though a presence from the beginning of the novel, becomes a hollowness, an absence when Pip, trapped in Estella's authority, becomes aware of his alienation from it. It is a story written and imposed upon him by others, by the social system or by Estella, a story he himself can never be the author of. But Pip has been caught in this story from the beginning. There is no way out; he is tightly "bound" there by society and its institutions. Here the contrasting stories of Tom Idle and Francis Goodchild are synthesized through the catalyst of the hero's alienation; he is alienated from both aspects of the dualism. When the time comes for Pip to be apprenticed to Joe, it is no longer the moment of fulfillment, the moment of "larks," but the moment of execution in which to be bound apprentice is tantamount to being bound in the halter:

> The Justices were sitting in the Town Hall near at hand, and we at once went over to have me bound apprentice to Joe in the Magisterial presence. I say, we went over, but I was pushed over by Pumblechook, exactly as if I had that moment picked a pocket or fired a rick; indeed, it was the general impression in Court that I had been taken red-handed, for, as Pumblechook shoved me before him through the crowd, I heard some people say, "What's he done?" and others, "He's a young 'un, too, but looks bad, don't he?" One person of mild and benevolent aspect even gave me a tract ornamented with a woodcut of a malevolent young man fitted up with a perfect sausage-shop of fetters, and entitled, TO BE READ IN MY CELL.
>
> The Hall was a queer place, I thought, with higher pews in it than a church. . . . Here, in a corner, my indentures were duly signed and attested, and I was "bound"; Mr. Pumblechook holding me all the while as if we had looked in on our way to the scaffold, to have those little preliminaries disposed of. (132–33)

It is quite fitting that Pumblechook, the prime author of the story of Pip the Criminal, is present as custodian in the scene where Pip is "bound" in the story of Pip the Apprentice, a story now no more his own than the story of George Barnwell. Pip reflects, "I . . . had a strong conviction on me that I should never like Joe's trade. I had liked it once, but once was not now" (134).

4

After three years of apprenticeship to Joe, during which Pip works at the forge with forced industry much "against the grain," nursing deep dissatisfaction, anguish and burning passion for Estella in his bosom, Jaggers, the dark lawyer, comes to him with the "great expectations," the gift from an anonymous benefactor. The gift lifts Pip out of the apprentice story and, this time with his willing acceptance, places him in another story, the story of Great Expectations. Harry Stone and Shirley Grob, among others, have pointed out the strong presence of the fairy tale in *Great Expectations*. Viewed as a structuring principle, the fairy tale provides the basic materials of this new story in which Pip is henceforth to live.[15] Miss Havisham may be regarded as the fairy godmother, Estella as the beautiful princess, and Jaggers as the wizard who looks sinister at first but will prove, perhaps, benevolent in the end. The hero is Pip, of course, the knight errant who will rescue the princess caught in the magic castle, Satis House. As this arrangement of basic elements suggests, the story of Great Expectations has its origin in and follows, or seems to follow, the pivotal plot of a fairy tale that could be identified with one from the stock of traditional tales. Shirley Grob mentions "The Golden Goose" as the typical example of the primitive form of fairy tale that Dickens uses with pointed irony. However, with regard to Satis House and its inhabitants, "Sleeping Beauty," as Harry Stone suggests, is the fundamental text for the story of Great Expectations. Because of some fatal incident that occurred long ago Satis House set itself outside the flow of time and, making barriers to protect itself from the intrusion of outside forces, has slumbered in a timeless world. As Pip noticed when he first visited this strange place, the house "had a great many iron bars to it"; windows were walled up or rustily barred, and even the courtyard was barred (84–85). There in the darkness Miss Havisham lives in the wedding dress she has worn since the fatal wedding day, stopping all the clocks at twenty minutes to nine, forever living in that moment when her heart was broken, but also perhaps sleeping forever in full outfit to receive the bridegroom who will never come. Time, with cruel disregard for her determination, has ravaged her body and dress but the decayed Sleeping Beauty is now replaced by a budding new one, Estella, whose coldness and remoteness suggest to Pip that she also is in a state of slumber, from which he as her knight hopes one day to arouse her. Pip imagines himself to be the hero of this romance of expectations—a significant departure from the apprentice stories. George Barnwell and Dick Whittington were roles Pip was made to play;

their stories were grounded in a void that was to bring about their own undoing. In the fairy tale, however, Pip feels comfortably at home because the tale not only offers salvation from alien stories but also promises to fill the void engendered in Satis House, to satisfy the want, the horrible sense of deprivation he experienced at Estella's taunts. It is a story that he constructs for himself, building his groundless dreams about Miss Havisham and Estella. Circumstances, full of "attractive mystery," have eloquently contributed to this false construction. But even in this fairy tale world, can Pip actually be the hero? Is his construction of this story wholly independent of those outside forces that have kept him, "bound" him in the written text from the start?

The author of a story, the author in the sense we have been using it, is someone who maintains definitive authority over his creation, who determines and directs the course of action or plot of the story. The author of the fairy tale "Sleeping Beauty" can be identified with a character who, though no hero nor heroine, is in complete possession of the destinies of heroes and heroines: the witch or fairy godmother. The fairy godmother is decisively important in the construction of the hero's or heroine's story, as is evident in "Sleeping Beauty." She is a prophetess, a visionary who foresees and determines the future. The hero or heroine, perfectly under her control, has virtually no freedom in choosing his course of action in the story. Despite all the precautions taken to keep her away from any spindle, the princess wounds herself on one, falling into a sleep of a hundred years and her sleep, however long and profound it may be, is instantly broken by a kiss from the prince. In Pip's version of "Sleeping Beauty," Miss Havisham, the fairy godmother, has decided and prescribed the destiny of the hero Pip in a way that is absolute and unchangeable. Neither wealth nor beauty is in Pip's power to achieve; they are things given, bestowed by the fairy godmother whose will functions as the inevitable logic in the fairy tale structure. Thus Pip is deluded; since he has no power to create his life story, he can never be its real hero, the hero as author. Although he believes that in this dream world he has finally found a place congenial to his needs, he is still caught in a text written by a hand other than his. Pip remains a reader of texts. Max Byrd identifies "reading" as the crucial, pervading theme in the novel and points out that Pip, through his unreasonable, incorrect reading of texts, creates a fiction that tends to enclose him, "to transform him into a monomaniac: he begins to believe the fiction to be truth, indeed, the whole truth."[16] The story of Great Expectations is the most inclusive of those fictions Pip has built by reading others' texts and in which he finds himself enclosed.

However, this fiction proves to be fictional in a double sense: it is, as we know, a fiction that Pip constructs with the aid of a heavy reliance on circumstances rather than on concrete evidence, and it is a fiction whose author turns out to be the wrong one. The abnormality, timelessness and madness associated with Miss Havisham has made Pip believe that the fairy godmother cannot possibly be any other person in his book of fairies. Yet Mr. Jaggers's initial announcement to him that the name of his "liberal benefactor remains a profound secret, until the person chooses to reveal it" (165), indicates that the "expectations" of this unfinished story are pointed expressly toward the future revelation of authorship. In the awaited denouement the fairy godmother reveals herself to be not Miss Havisham, not even a female, but the convict Abel Magwitch, who declares himself to be Pip's "second father" (337). The unmasking of the author/father instantly undoes the fairy tale, destroys its mirage, and transforms it into a hollowness, an absence. "Miss Havisham's intentions towards me, all a mere dream; Estella not designed for me; I only suffered in Satis House as a convenience, a sting for the greedy relations, a model with a mechanical heart to practice on when no other practice was at hand" (341). After the destruction of his dream Pip cannot attain wealth and gentleman's status with Magwitch's money, though it has been honestly earned by the transported convict, because the book Magwitch has written is utterly incompatible with his inner needs and desires, and also, because in the world of sober realities Pip regains his natural goodness of heart.

5

When the novel's central axis breaks down and the pivotal story of Great Expectations becomes absent, what are we left with? Is it only "the impression of a life that has outlived plot, renounced plot, been cured of it"[17] that we have here? But neither plot nor stories have yet been exhausted. Before arriving at the sense of a life "that is left over" we have to consider the moral framework in which Pip seems to remain even after the breakdown of the central story.

If the final meaning of the novel, the sum total of all its processes and plot workings, is the moral theme and the wisdom gained by the hero in his life story, Great Expectations manifests the moral orientation of the "great tradition" rather starkly, as a simple moral of the sort appended to fables and "moral tales." For the novel might be taken to be, as Edgar Rosenberg suggests, "a cautionary tale about an engaging, slightly contaminated young man whose head has been turned by his unwarranted expectations, who, confronted by the actualities of his situation, experiences a change of heart, and in the end gets more or less what he deserves."[18] Rosenberg's summary seems an exact description of the kind of moral tale the novel is, an amalgamation of the dual story of Hogarth's apprentices. Pip discards the simple life of apprenticeship because of his infatuation with a foolish dream and, becoming morally degenerate as a result, finally loses everything. Bewitched by a worthless woman, he throws away his true friend Joe and his sweetheart Biddy, and incurs just punishment. When he goes back to Joe's forge to propose to Biddy, having finally recognized his own folly after the deaths of Miss Havisham and Magwitch, he finds that Joe has just married her. Thus Pip, the penitent Idle Apprentice, exiles himself from England to work as an industrious clerk at Clarriker and Co. for eleven years.

If we were to take this moral fable, the cautionary tale, as it is, Pip's return to the forge and his marriage to Biddy would be his return to and recovery of the story in which he can truly be the hero, the story to be reinstated after the breakdown of all the other, false, stories. Surely the moral framework of the novel seems to call for this as the norm from which Pip has deviated. Accepting the moral theme unreservedly, Forster and Bernard Shaw, and many critics following their lead, have voiced objections to the altered ending of the novel.[19] The hero who has gone astray from the path of honesty should be justly punished, whereas the happy (if equally sad) ending allows him to be united with Estella, the evil and worthless *femme fatale*. The critics claim that the revision is a falsification of the moral meaning of the story that does less than justice to the total moral framework that has been so carefully and expertly constructed. But is the cautionary tale really Pip's true story if he withdraws from it with a feeling not of despair but of relief and gratitude? Upon recovering from the first shock of the news of Biddy's marriage to Joe, Pip feels "great thankfulness that" he has "never breathed this last baffled hope to Joe." Thanking his good fortune in not disclosing his intention, thanking Joe and Biddy for all they have done for him and all he has "so ill repaid," asking forgiveness of both, he leaves them to go abroad (487–88). Why is the feeling of relief and gratitude predominant in the final crisis of Pip's life? It may be explained, as Milton Millhauser suggests, in terms of the insurmountable disparity between the state of the village blacksmith and that of the urban gentleman Pip has now become; for Pip, it is both impossible and actually impracticable to return again to Joe's class after his experiences in the upper sphere.[20] However, his feeling of relief and gratitude may also be explained in terms of the fundamental structure of the novel we have been discussing, the structure of stories constructed and destroyed, of presence made into absence. Pip feels relief because, the place of hero being justly occupied by Joe, he does not have to go back again to a story that is not his own. The story of Pip the Apprentice is alien to him, written by a hand other than his; it is quite unnatural for him to return to it. Or to put it otherwise, it is only too natural for an apprentice gone astray to go back with a penitent heart, after wandering and hardship, to the place where he naturally belongs. This would be to follow the moral pattern too neatly, to conform to the logical sequence of artificial moral fables. Instead, the final moral meaning that the novel offers suggests its own hollowness and falsity by being too neat and logical a construction. Moreover, according to the other forces at work in the novel, it is quite likely to be destroyed by its own artificiality. Why is this so? Why are natural outcome and logical sequence denied here?

When even the moral fable that seemed to be the ultimate story present in *Great Expectations* is undone by the hero's withdrawal from it at the last moment, we are directed to the novel's deepest stratum.

6

If Pip had been a character who acts and behaves according to the dictates of reason, the ending neatly and logically ordered would have been naturally his. But it is precisely at this point that logic fails because if he had been such a character, he would not have deviated from the path of the Industrious Apprentice in the first place; it would have been simply impossible for him to err so flagrantly in his choices. Actually Pip has always been a character motivated and compelled by a force to which reason, logic and morality are utter strangers. Because of this, the logical and moral outcome finally eludes him; the teleological drive in the text rejects him at the last moment. The character who symbolizes this demonic impulse in Pip is Estella. It is a strange neglect among the criticism and commentary on the novel that Estella has not received the critical attention she deserves as a character who controls Pip's life in a more profound way than even Miss Havisham or Magwitch. It is true that Estella is the novel's least realized character: her frigidity and remoteness throughout give an impression of unreality and when her heart melts at the last meeting with Pip, it is unconvincing. She appears infrequently, providing the reader with few chances of penetrating into her inner self even to find the void there. However, Estella's influence on Pip is inordinately great compared with the scarcity of her characterization. As I indicated earlier, Estella transforms Pip's natural state of existence into a story alienated from him. Because of her strong sexual attraction a "poor dream," the desire of becoming a gentleman, is engendered in him. If apprenticeship is the norm, the moral standard, to which Pip should finally return, Estella must be regarded as the character of decisive importance because she first disrupts that standard.

While the critical censure of Pip's infatuation with Estella is valid, before making judgments too facile to be worth making, we must notice that Pip himself has been quite aware of the madness and foolishness of his passion for Estella from the start. He has already passed a forcible verdict on his own conduct when, as a young boy, he confesses to Biddy his desperate passion for another girl. Biddy asks him who it was that told him he was coarse and common and Pip, compelled by uncontrollable impulse, replies:

> "The beautiful young lady at Miss Havisham's, and she's more beautiful than anybody ever was, and I admire her dreadfully, and I want to be a gentleman on her account." Having made this lunatic confession, I

began to throw my torn-up grass into the river, as if I had some thoughts of following it.

"Do you want to be a gentleman, to spite her or to gain her over?" Biddy quietly asked me, after a pause.

"I don't know," I moodily answered.

"Because, if it is to spite her," Biddy pursued, "I should think—but you know best—that might be better and more independently done by caring nothing for her words. And if it is to gain her over, I should think—but you know best—she was not worth gaining over."

Exactly what I myself had thought, many times. Exactly what was perfectly manifest to me at the moment. But how could I, a poor dazed village lad, avoid that wonderful inconsistency into which the best and wisest of men fall every day?"

"It may be all quite true," said I to Biddy, "but I admire her dreadfully."

In short, I turned over on my face when I came to that, and got a good grasp on the hair on each side of my head, and wrenched it well. All the while knowing the madness of my heart to be so very mad and misplaced, that I was quite conscious it would have served my face right, if I had lifted it up by my hair, and knocked it against the pebbles as a punishment for belonging to such an idiot. (156)

Here Biddy's is the voice of the moral guide, the teacher she has always been to Pip, the voice of reason and common sense. Her judgment of Estella is absolutely and impeccably right. Pip cannot by any means contradict her since he himself has seen the truth already. But what we hear as the truth transcending the truth of reason and common sense is Pip's, or rather the narrator's voice remembering that hopeless passion which seized the boy, "that wonderful inconsistency into which the best and wisest of men fall every day." What reason and common sense tell him "may be all quite true," it is "exactly what was perfectly manifest" to him at the moment; yet, all these manifest truths notwithstanding, he loves her "dreadfully." Moreover, in the desolation of his heart, Pip is quite aware of his folly, of how "mad and misplaced" his passion for Estella is. Yet he loves her simply because he "found her irresistible." He knew he "loved her against reason, against promise, against peace, against hope, against happiness, against all discouragement that could be" even when he was misled into believing that Miss Havisham had reserved Estella for him (253–54). In spite of the voice of reason, which is also his inner voice, in spite of Estella's warnings to him, in spite of Herbert's friendly admonition, he goes on loving her. His passion has already gone beyond the pale of rationality; Biddy admits, while teaching him, that Pip has "got beyond her" and her lesson is "of no use now" (157). When passion has taken such complete hold, it is no longer possible for either outside or inside voices to have any influence, since the passion has already become a part of the essential being. Pip's mad passion is his life: "it was impossible for me to separate her, in the past or in the present, from the innermost life of my life" (257). He declares to her, not in a high-flown romantic confession of love but in a painful farewell: "You are part of my existence, part of myself. . . . Estella, to the last hour of my life, you cannot choose but remain part of my character, part of the little good in me, part of the evil" (378). For better or worse, Estella has been, in a sense, Pip himself. Thus the rational outcome, the logical ending of the moral fable, eludes him simply because of its rationality, naturalness and morality. The system of the fable as a completed whole entailing ordered chronology and an overriding logos or reason is alien to Pip because his true identity lies where such systems or stories are disrupted by impulses springing from the innermost depth of his psyche. After the destruction of all the stories, Pip's unquenchable passion remains impermeable to that dissociating force at work in the novel.

Pip fails, however, to write his own story, the one faithfully following his irrational love for Estella. He fails because Pip and Estella have been enclosed in the texts and stories written by others. Pip has been a subject to be written by Pumblechook, Magwitch and others, Estella a subject in Miss Havisham's writing of the story of revenge upon men in general. Or to advance our argument a step further, they have been enclosed in the text of *Great Expectations*, in Dickens's novels, which are enclosed again in the context of the nineteenth-century English novel. It was imperative for Dickens's novels to conform to the traditional framework, a plot structure dependent on moral teleology and the closed system of the novel. The disturbing, irrational depths of human beings had to be tamed and explained away in the unfolding of the moral plot so that the reading public and the dominant social order would not be offended. Yet the self-destroying structure of *Great Expectations* finally reveals the centrality of Pip's irrational passion for Estella, an instance of the irrationality, of the nonconformity to any systematizing, persistently felt in Dickens's novels. Dickens often presented irrational passion, madness and violence capable of breaking through the closure of the novel system, beginning with some of the interpolated tales in *The Pickwick Papers* and pursued in the murderous impulses of Sykes and Jonas Chuzzlewit in *Oliver Twist* and *Martin Chuzzlewit*, in the perverted sensuality of Quilp in *The Old Curiosity Shop*, in the lunacy and wild violence of *Barnaby Rudge* and *The Tale of Two Cities*. Though these passions are treated always in the melodramatic mode, they often go beyond the merely sensational as is evident in the mob violence in the two historical novels and in the psychological agony of Bill Sykes that was Dickens's own nemesis. This irrationality is profoundly dangerous as it tends to destroy the traditional story on which Dickens's plot is always modeled and, at the same time, puts the concepts of fiction and its closure into doubt. Writing can be a dangerous act when it is influenced by this subversive force. The writing of *Great Expectations* accomplishes just that dangerous act, an act of unwriting in which the stories present at all levels in the novel are continuously vacated by the very act of writing.

Thus Dickens's novels are fundamentally different from other multiplot novels of the Victorian era. In Dickens the multiplicity of plots may be replaced by multiplicity of stories, yet this multistoried structure is always threatened with disintegration. The formula of the polyphonic novel, which Mikhail Bakhtin presents as the fundamental principle in Dostoevsky's poetics, can be applied with little modification to describe the basic structure of Dickens's novels. A Dostoevsky novel is "dialogic," "constructed not as the whole of a single consciousness, absorbing other consciousnesses as objects into itself, but as a whole formed by the interaction of several consciousnesses, none of which entirely becomes an object for the other."[21] This dialogical principle is at work in Dickens's novels: the stories of the Idle Apprentice and the Industrious Apprentice are vying with each other to dominate the novel, each failing to absorb the other to create a single unified consciousness or story. Yet submerged under this dialogue is another dialogue that is not the dialogue between two stories, between two different kinds of logic (*dialogos*), but the more radical struggle between story as logical and moral system and the suppressed yet primordial force of subversion. This force, which continually undermines the system of the novel, should be identified with Bakhtin's carnival. During carnival the "laws, prohibitions, and restrictions that determine the structure and order of ordinary, that is noncarnival, life are suspended. . . . what is suspended first of all is hierarchical structure and all the forms of terror, reverence, piety, and etiquette connected with it."[22] Carnivalistic life is "life drawn out of its *usual* rut, it is to some extent 'life turned inside out,' 'the reverse side of the world.'"[23] Dickens's early novels are brimming with carnivalistic life linked essentially with the irrational, the comic and the non-serious. *Pickwick, Nickleby* and *The Old Curiosity Shop* are typical carnival literature full of animal vitality and disorder where the most fundamental rite of carnival, of decrowning (of Mr. Pickwick, Squeers and Quilp, who are all to some extent Lords of Misrule), is repeatedly staged. But Dickens, being a novelist, had to curb his wild imagination to bring his work to a more or less orderly conclusion. Because carnivalistic life is essentially incompatible with closure (the public square is the center of carnival), it has to be suppressed in a final working-out of the plot; otherwise it would be simply impossible to complete a novel. As Dickens "matured" into a prestigious novelist this repression of carnival is more and more successfully undertaken in his writing. But in his most "serious" and "mature" novel the system of stories is shattered and now the absent, subversive force of carnival finally succeeds in making its irrepressible presence felt. The ending of the novel is actually the beginning of the absent story, the beginning of the greater dialogue between logos and passion, between story and carnival.

Though Pip has failed to write the true story of his life, failed to live his madness, his irrational passion, rooted in the core of his nature, asserts itself even in the final hour of the story's ordered chronology. Right after his declaration to Biddy that his poor dream "has all gone by" he visits the site of the old Satis House, the ruins of texts and stories, to meet Estella, a being whose potential for a passion as warm as Pip's has failed to be actualized. Dickens has been very careful in suggesting this potential: when her identity is revealed Estella is found to be the daughter of a woman who "had some gipsy blood in her" (405). This woman had not only acted according to the traditional ideas of gipsy women in literature by murdering another for jealousy, but proves to be a descendant of the fiery witch of Colchis, Medea, who killed her own child by Jason in revenge for his betrayal; Estella's mother "was under strong suspicion of having, at about the time of the murder, frantically destroyed her child by this man—some three years old—to revenge herself upon him" (406). When we are faced with the essential similarity between Pip and Magwitch—they are orphans manipulated by authoritarian figures—it is hard not to see that the story of Magwitch and Molly might easily have been one in which Pip and Estella figure as hero and heroine. Yet this story of two passionate human beings capable of ignoring morality and hierarchy or any interdiction society might impose upon them is absent in *Great Expectations*.[24] Pip's story as written by others has already come to an end; the system of the novel has closed itself. Yet Dickens had to write again the ending that is really a beginning; Pip and Estella, the two with more fundamental characteristics in common than they are aware of, must meet again to begin to write the story of their love just as Pip and Magwitch had encountered each other at the beginning to begin their entirely different love story. In a final paradox, however, this absent story has already been written. If the ultimate message of the novel may be seen as the disclosure and destruction of alienating stories and the revelation of irrationality that transcends textuality, the story Pip will write cannot be anything other than the text that has been *Great Expectations*.

Notes

1. Wayne C. Booth, *The Rhetoric of Fiction* (Chicago: Univ. of Chicago Press, 1961), 71–73. See also Seymour Chatman, *Story and Discourse: Narrative Structure in Fiction and Film* (Ithaca: Cornell Univ. Press 1978), 148–49.

2. For the discussion of various meanings of author and authority, see Edward Said's influential book, *Beginnings: Intention and Method* (New York: Basic Books, 1975). The problem of the father figure in *Great Expectations* has been given attention by many critics; the fullest consideration so far is: Lawrence Jay Dessner, "*Great Expectations*: 'the Ghost of a Man's Own Father,'" PMLA 91 (1976), 436–49. See also Dianne F. Sadoff, "Storytelling and the Figure of the Father in *Little Dorrit*," PMLA 95 (1980), 234–45.

3. The problem of writing in *Great Expectations* has been discussed recently by Robert Tracy and Murray Baumgarten. Tracy is concerned with the tension between writing and speaking in the novel, the former, according to him, being constantly put into doubt;

and Baumgarten's focus is on calligraphy as "writing that bridges hieroglyphic and phonetic systems." See Robert Tracy, "Reading Dickens's Writing," and Murray Baumgarten, "Calligraphy and Code: Writing in *Great Expectations*," *Dickens Studies Annual* 11 (1983), 37–72.

4. David Lodge, *Working with Structuralism: Essays and Reviews on Nineteenth- and Twentieth-Century Literature* (London: Routledge, 1981), 20. This, I find, is the fullest and most succinct definition of *fabula* and *sjuzet* of the Russian Formalists. See also Tzvetan Todorov, *The Poetics of Prose*, trans. Richard Howard (Ithaca: Cornell Univ. Press, 1977), 45–46.

5. See, for example, Dorothy Van Ghent, *The English Novel: Form and Function* (New York: Harper, 1967), 154–70; John H. Hagan Jr., "Structural Patterns in Dickens's *Great Expectations*," *ELH* 21 (1954), 54–66; and E. Pearlman, "Inversion in *Great Expectations*" *Dickens Studies Annual* 7 (1978), 190–202.

6. Peter Brooks, "Repetition, Repression, and Return: The Plotting of *Great Expectations*," in *Reading for the Plot: Design and Intention in Narrative* (Oxford: Clarendon Press, 1984), 113–42. Brooks's essay was originally published as "Repetition, Repression, and Return: *Great Expectations* and the Study of Plot," *New Literary History* 11 (1980), 503–26.

7. All references are to *Great Expectations*, ed. Angus Calder (Harmondsworth: Penguin Books, 1965) and will be included in the text hereafter.

8. See Brooks, "Repetition," 131–32. Brooks asserts that "all texts eventually speak of Pip himself as an unjustified presence, a presence demanding interpretations." Yet the point of this scene is that interpretation is always a priori, already completed when Wopsle and Pumblechook trap Pip in an established story which does not allow any further designing or plotting.

9. Some critics have followed suit, notably Van Ghent, *The English Novel*. See 168.

10. See Ronald Paulson, *Emblem and Expression: Meaning in English Art of the Eighteenth Century* (Cambridge: Harvard Univ. Press, 1975), 58–78, for a detailed discussion of Hogarth's work. Paul B. Davis points out that perhaps Dickens "had the series in mind as he wrote *Great Expectations*; the account of Pip's apprenticeship seems to be one point where Dickens's general indebtedness to Hogarth becomes specific." "Dickens, Hogarth, and the Illustrated *Great Expectations*," *The Dickensian* 80 (1984), 131–43.

11. See *The London Merchant*, ed. William H. McBurney (London: Edward Arnold, 1965), xv.

12. See *Dombey and Son*, ed. Peter Fairclough (Harmondsworth: Penguin Books, 1970), 98–99; and *Barnaby Rudge*, ed. Gordon Spence (Harmondsworth: Penguin Books, 1973), 302.

13. See Spence, ed., *Barnaby Rudge*, 80.

14. Julian Moynahan, "The Hero's Guilt: the Case of *Great Expectations*," *Essays in Criticism* 10 (1960), 69–70.

15. Shirley Grob, "Dickens and Some Motifs of the Fairy Tale," *Texas Studies in Literature and Language*, 5 (1964), 567–79; Harry Stone, "*Great Expectations*: The Fairy-Tale Transformation," *Dickens and the Invisible World: Fairy Tales, Fantasy, and Novel-Making* (London: Macmillan, 1980), 298–339.

16. Max Byrd, "'Reading' in *Great Expectations*," *PMLA* 91 (1976), 259–65.

17. Brooks, "Repetition," 138.

18. Edgar Rosenberg, "A Preface to *Great Expectations*," *Dickens Studies Annual* 2 (1972), 333. Rosenberg borrowed the term "cautionary tale" from the German scholar Ludwig Borinski.

19. John Forster, *The Life of Charles Dickens*, ed. A. J. Hoppé (London: Dent, 1966), 2:289; George Bernard Shaw, "Foreword to the Edinburgh limited edition of *Great Expectations* 1937," rpt. in Stephen Wall, ed., *Charles Dickens: A Critical Anthology*

(Harmondsworth: Penguin Books, 1970), 294. For the problem of the novel's ending see, among numerous others: Marshall W. Gregory, "Values and Meaning in *Great Expectations*: The Two Endings Revisited," *Essays in Criticism* 19 (1969), 402–9; Martin Meisel, "The Ending of *Great Expectations*," *Essays in Criticism* 15 (1965), 326–31; Milton Millhauser, "*Great Expectations*: The Three Endings," *Dickens Studies Annual* 2 (1972): 267–77; Edgar Rosenberg, "Last Words on *Great Expectations:* A Textual Brief on the Six Endings," *Dickens Studies Annual* 9 (1981) 87–115.

20. Millhauser, "The Three Endings," 271.

21. Mikhail Bakhtin, *Problems of Dostoevsky's Poetics*, trans. Caryl Emerson (Minneapolis: Univ. of Minnesota Press, 1984), 18. Dickens's influence on Dostoevsky has been studied by Donald Fanger, *Dostoevsky and Romantic Realism: A Study of Dostoevsky in Relation to Balzac, Dickens, and Gogol* (Chicago: Univ. of Chicago Press 1967); N. M. Lary, *Dostoevsky and Dickens: A Study of Literary Influence* (London Routledge, 1973); and Loralee MacPike, *Dostoevsky's Dickens: A Study of Literary Influence* (London: George Prior, 1981).

Peter K. Garrett has found it feasible to consider the multi-plot baggy monsters of the Victorian age from the new point of view offered by Bakhtin. *The Victorian Multiplot Novel: Studies in Dialogical Form* (New Haven: Yale Univ. Press, 1980), 8.

22. Bakhtin, *Problems*, 122–23.

23. Bakhtin, *Problems*, 122. Ronald Paulson in his study of eighteenth-century subculture revealed the ambiguities involved in Hogarth's *Industry and Idleness*. Ronald Paulson, *Popular and Polite Art in the Age of Hogarth and Fielding* (Notre Dame: Univ. of Notre Dame Press, 1979), 21–22.

24. The absence may be explained also in terms of the paramount interdiction imposed upon their relationship. As Magwitch is Estella's real father and also Pip's "second father," their love could not be anything but incestuous. The possible perversity in Pip's love for Estella was pointed out by A. L. French, "Beating and Cringing *Great Expectations*," *Essays in Criticism* 24 (1974): 151–58. See also Pearlman (note 5), 201; and Brooks, 128, for similar points.

INDEX